POLAND

POLAND

THE LAST DECADE

ADAM BROMKE

MOSAIC PRESS
"Publishers for Canadian Communities"

Canadian Cataloguing in Publication Data

Bromke, Adam, 1928-
  Poland: the last decade

ISBN 0-88962-144-6 (bound)
ISBN 0-88962-143-8 (pbk.)

1. Poland — Politics and government — 1945 —
— Addresses, essays, lectures. 2. Poland —
History — 1945 — Addresses, essays, lectures.
I. Title: Poland: the last decade

DK4440.B76   943.8'055   C81-094880-X

Published by Mosaic Press
P.O. Box 1032, Oakville, Ontario, Canada L6J 5E9

Published with the assistance of the Canada Council and the Ontario Arts Council.

ISBN 0-88962-144-6 cloth
ISBN 0-88962-143-8 paper

Typeset by Erin Graphics
Cover design by Doug Frank & Laurie Genoe
Printed by Les Editions Marquis

Acknowledgements

I should like to express my gratitude for permission to reprint my articles originally appearing in the following publications (as noted in the text): *Canadian Slavonic Papers, East European Quarterly, Foreign Affairs, Foreign Policy, International Journal, Polityka, Problems of Communism,*the *Toronto Sunday Star* and *The World Today.*

I should also like to thank Professor Harald von Riekhoff for co-authoring Chapters IX and X with me.

Table of Contents

Introduction

This volume is a collection of articles covering the developments in Poland from the late 1960s to the early 1980s. It is a continuous story dealing with the major events, internal as well as external, from the collapse of the Gomulka regime, through the ups and downs of the Gierek government, to the Polish workers' upheaval in 1980.

As such the book is largely a supplement to my *Poland's Politics, Idealism vs. Realism* (Harvard University Press, 1967) which covered the first twenty years of the Communist rule in some detail. I am using here and, in a way, testing against the passage of time, the model of Polish politics which I presented in that previous volume. Chapter I explicitly addresses itself to this question and, thus, perhaps provides an overall thematic unity.

The remainder of the book is divided into three main parts. Chapters II-VII explore chiefly the internal developments in the country. They deal with the political junctures in 1968 and 1970, with the hopes of the early years of the Gierek regime, and with their subsequent decline, which culminated in the acute new crisis at the close of the decade.

The second part, composed of Chapters VIII-XII, primarily reviews Poland's position in the international sphere, and particularly in the Soviet orbit. The crises in Poland are compared to those in Hungary in 1956 and Czechoslovakia in the 1968; the role of the improvement in Polish-West German relations is assessed; and, finally, the influence of East-West détente, and especially the CSCE process, upon Eastern Europe is discussed.

The third part deals with the most recent dramatic events in Poland. Chapter XIII describes the situation in the country on the eve of the workers' strikes. Chapters XIV-XVII cover the popular revolt in Poland and from July 1980 until May 1981 which, as of the moment of writing, is still going strong.

The book, thus, is a chronicle of the political developments in Poland in the last fifteen years. It is written by an outside observer but a close one, of the Polish scene. During that period I visited Poland fifteen times, sometimes for a fairly prolonged period. I have travelled quite extensively throughout the country and I also have had the opportunity to meet many of the *dramatis personae*, both on the side of the government and in the opposition.

In my writings about Poland I have tried to be as detached as I possible can. The bulk of the book therefore, is purely factual and analytical. I have not concealed, however, that my sympathies, although tempered by awareness of the realities of the country's geopolitical position, have always been on the side of the Polish nation in its legitimate aspirations towards greater freedom.

The three largely normative pieces arise from occasions when I was explicitly asked to offer advice either to the western governments or to the

Polish people. These are: the article in *The World Today* published on the eve of the Helsinki Conference, the piece in *Foreign Policy* written after the outburst in Poland in 1980; and an interview granted to *Polityka* late in the winter of 1981. Their different styles, incidentally, fit the different audiences to which I was addressing myself.

Except for minor cuts to eliminate at least some repetitiveness, all of the articles are published in their original form. As such they reflect the hopes and the fears of the different periods when they were written. It is up to the readers to judge how they have withstood the test of time.

A.B.

I.
Poland's Idealism and Realism in Retrospect*

When I received the invitation to give the Adam Mickiewicz Memorial Lecture, naturally I decided to select a topic which was a part of my own intellectual experience at Carleton. It was during my early years at this university that my first writings on Poland's politics — seen as a dichotomy between idealism and realism — were published.[1] They were the fruits of my research conducted at Harvard in 1960-62, but in a way they reflected even deeper layers of my own past, and in particular the two episodes in Polish history in which I was personally involved: the Warsaw uprising of 1944[2] and the "peaceful revolution" of 1956 which, albeit from afar, I had the opportunity to follow closely.[3] I became fascinated by the question of how it was possible for the same people, within the span of twelve years, to assume such diametrically different postures and to follow such sharply contrasting policies.

On the one hand, the Warsaw uprising confirmed the traditional western stereotypes of the Poles as foolhardy idealists who, despite all odds, were ready to fight, and if necessary to die, for their freedom. On the other hand, in 1956 (especially when contrasted with the Hungarians' revolution) the Poles startled the West with their thoroughgoing realism. On that occasion they displayed a remarkable degree of circumspection and a considerable talent for political compromise. In attempting to trace the connection between these two events, I had to go back to developments in Polish history and, in turn, I tried to project my findings into the future. In short, as one reviewer of *Poland's Politics* observed, I strove to explain to the western reader why there are both white and red in the Polish national colours.[4]

In constructing the model of Poland's politics as a continuum between the two extremes of foolhardy idealism and thoroughgoing realism, I derived inspiration, of course, from many sources, both Polish and western. Among Polish writings of the past, the early political thought of Roman Dmowski impressed me. Among contemporary thinkers I owe an intellectual debt to two persons: Stanislaw Stomma, whose program of neo-positivism, formulated in his articles in *Tygodnik Powszechny*, from the late 1950s, indicated the changes in the Poles' political attitudes after World War II,[5] and Jan Szczepanski who, in his lectures to the Club of the Crooked Circle in 1957, amplified the goals of Polish "peaceful revolution."[6]

From western political thought I borrowed many concepts, adapting them to the Polish circumstances. I was influenced by the realist school in the study of international relations, notably by the writings of Edward H. Carr, John H. Herz, Hans Morgenthau and George F. Kennan. In order to explain the intricacies of Polish politics to Anglo-American readers, I deliberately adopted western rather than Polish terminology. The concepts of "idealism" and "realism" in the context of my writings, however, correspond quite closely to the Polish terms of "romanticism" and "positivism" respectively.

The division between idealists and realists is not, of course, unique to Poland; to a lesser or greater extent it is present in the political life of all nations. What is exceptional about Poland, however, is the significance which this split has acquired in that country. This is a result of the fact that for the past two centuries Polish politics has been characterized by *Primat der Aussenpolitik* — the primacy of foreign over internal politics. Since the country's decline as a great power in the eighteenth century, the Pole's major preoccupation has been the preservation of their independence from foreign rule. Generally, they have not been successful in their endeavours. From the final partition in 1795 until today, a fully sovereign Polish state existed for only twenty years, i.e., from 1918 to 1939; for the rest of the time the Poles at best have enjoyed some form of national autonomy, and at worst have been threatened with national extinction.

Under these circumstances it is only natural that the split between the idealists and the realists became central to Poland's politics. The division came into prominence toward the end of the eighteenth century and persisted throughout the entire era of the partitions. The idealist, or "romantic," school of political thought gave first priority to the restoration of Poland's independence. The idealists advocated a relentless struggle against the occupying powers, especially Russia, and looked to France for assistance. To advance their goals they were prepared to undergo great sacrifices. In contrast, the realist, or "positivist," school became reconciled with the necessity of a limited national autonomy. The realists did not abandon the ultimate goal of Poland's freedom from foreign rule, but they repudiated the striving for it at any costs. Their first concern was to protect the nation from repeated and futile losses and, instead, to secure for it as normal an internal development as possible.

At various stages of history the two programs underwent substantial modifications to fit the changing external, as well as internal, circumstances. Yet, over the last two hundred years they have also retained a basic continuity in their respective assumptions. Indeed, in recent Polish history a cycle can easily be discerned in which one school and then the other is clearly in the ascendancy. From the Napoleonic wars until the ill-fated Polish uprising against Russia in 1863 the idealist school was dominant, while from then until World War I the realist school prevailed. From 1918 to 1945 the Poles once again followed the idealist program. During World War II they waged a desperate struggle for independence and in those efforts they hoped for assistance from the West.

At the end of the war, and especially after the shattering defeat of the Warsaw uprising, the Poles shifted once more from idealism to realism. Three major factors contributed to this development. First, there was a spontaneous revulsion against the continuation of a futile military struggle.

The Poles became painfully aware of the tremendous losses they had suffered during World War II and of the urgent need to protect the nation from any further bloodshed. Second, the shift of Polish territory at the end of World War II to the west, which led to a bitter and prolonged border dispute with Germany, made the Poles look to Russia for protection. Finally, there was the reality of the preponderant Soviet power in East-Central Europe and the inability of the West to do anything about it. The ambivalent attitude of the western powers over the Polish-German territorial dispute only increased the Poles' disillusionment with the West and pushed them toward alignment with the U.S.S.R.[7]

As a result of those combined experiences, the Poles — communists and non-communists alike — moved away from political idealism. They accepted the fact that at least for the time being restoration of Poland's independence, such as had existed in 1918-39, was not possible and they strove to achieve a *modus vivendi* with the Soviet Union. "Since World War II," as Stanislaw Stomma put it in 1960, "a significant change in the opinions of the Poles has taken place. This change is the victory of political realism."[8]

The model of Polish politics as a dichotomy between idealism and realism is by no means novel. It has been expounded by many political and historical writers in the past.[9] I should like to think, however, that I managed to introduce into this traditional Polish controversy (if only by injecting into it some contemporary western concepts) somewhat greater rigour. My ideas, thus, have evoked considerable interest and considerable controversy too. Both the descriptive and the prescriptive aspects of my model have been submitted to severe criticism.

The descriptive part has been censured mostly by the western academics. Several were dissatisfied with my analytical framework. They argue that the concepts of "realism and romanticism belong properly to literature: positivism and idealism to philosophy," and are of little help in explaining political phenomena.[10] Moreover, even when they agree that the dichotomy is useful in interpreting Poland's political history, they believe that the schema is less satisfactory when applied to contemporary events. In particular, critics have charged that it cannot adequately explain changes stemming from domestic roots, including, significantly, the socio-economic transformations under communism in Poland.

There is a good deal of truth in these criticisms. Admittedly, my model of Polish politics is more applicable over the long run, although I think it does provide a useful tool for evaluating contemporary developments as well. Also, it is a one-dimensional model — it focusses primarily on the linkage between external and internal affairs. As such it does not do justice to all the domestic changes and should properly be supplemented by other types of political, as well as sociological and economic, analyses. Yet, as long as *Primat der Aussenpolitik* remains valid, the dichotomy between idealism and realism will continue to be an extremely important, if not a crucial, aspect of Polish politics. And, unfortunately, I see little evidence that in this respect the situation of Poland has undergone major change.

It is, however, not the descriptive, but the prescriptive, part of my writings which has provoked the most dispute. Western political scientists and historians may have been critical of my theoretical framework but, nevertheless, they have generally agreed with my assessment of the situation in post-war Poland. In contrast, while most Polish writers both at home and abroad have accepted my presentation of the dichotomy between idealism and realism,[11] they have taken strong exception to the political conclusions for present-day Poland that I have drawn from this model. Those attacks only intensified as I elaborated my ideas further, especially in Polish-language publications.[12] Obviously, I must have touched upon a very sensitive nerve in the modern Polish national consciousness.

I have been denounced simultaneously from two sides. On the one hand, those writers from Poland who support the present political system think that I have not moved far enough in the direction of realism. They argue that the communist system is not only inevitable, from the point of view of international politics, but also desirable because it has accomplished positive domestic changes, and they have criticized me for not adopting a similarly "realist" position.[13] On the other hand, anti-communist émigré writers believe that I have leaned too far toward realism. They interpret my conclusion, that for the time being the communist system cannot be abolished, as evidence that I approve of it, and some have even accused me of abandoning the ultimate goal of Polish independence.[14] Coming under attack from both the militant realist and idealist positions in fact vindicates my stand, as presented in the concluding chapter of *Poland's Polticis*, that a synthesis is needed between these two extremes.

Neither idealism nor realism is an end in itself. They are merely alternative means to advance Poland's national interests. Depending on the circumstances, either one or the other should be followed. In their moderate forms both are useful. As Edward Carr aptly observed, idealism without realism is naïve, and realism without idealism is sterile.[15] In their extreme forms, however, both are harmful. Idealism, which, in the name of national independence, exposes the nation to the peril of national extinction, and realism, which, in order to preserve the biological survival of the people, exposes them to the danger of losing their own identity, are both self-contradictory. The avoidance of both of these extremes and the choice of a proper synthesis of idealism and realism — aimed at attaining an optimum of the national interests available at any given time — represents the essence of good statesmanship.

The art of politics — moving on a continuum between idealism and realism, at times embracing one and at times the other — was aptly practised by the Poles during the era of the partitions. After the Congress of Vienna the Polish generals who had served under Napoleon joined the Polish army under the command of the Russian tsar. Following the uprising of 1830

Poland's Idealism and Realism in Retrospect

Prince Adam Czartoryski, a former Foreign Minister under Alexander I, became a leader of the Polish émigrés in France. Margrave Aleksander Wielopolski, who in 1830 was an emissary seeking assistance from France and Britain to the Polish insurrection, in the early 1860s emerged as a leading proponent of cooperation with Russia. Adam Asnyk, who played a major role in the uprising of 1863, later assumed the role of an ardent advocate of positivism. And Roman Dmowski, a former chairman of the Polish faction in the Russian Duma, during World War I formed Polish units in France. Political idealism, of course, reigned once more in Poland from that time until World War II.

The search for a new synthesis between idealism and realism was revived in post-war Poland. It periodically came into the open — usually in order to by-pass communist censorship — under the guise of historical controversy. In fact, as Andrzej Kijowski observed recently, such debates have raged regularly every ten years.[16] The idealists and realists clashed in the immediate post-war years and again after 1956.[17] In the mid-1960s their discussions took the form of heated polemics over the books of Zbigniew Zaluski and over Andrzej Wajda's film, *Popioly*.[18] In 1977 the two programs were once again reassessed on the pages of the Catholic *Tygodnik Powszechny* and the communist *Polityka*.[19]

In the post-war years the clearest exposition of the realist position — confined strictly to geopolitics and devoid of any ideological overtones — was the program of "neo-positivism" formulated chiefly by Stanislaw Stomma. It served as a platform for participation in the Polish parliament of a small group of Catholic deputies — the so-called "Znak Circle" — which Stomma chaired for almost twenty years.[20] In 1976, however, the "Znak" group split and Stomma, after ostentatiously abstaining in a vote over a new Polish constitution, did not enter the next *Sejm*. Later in the same year he published, significantly, in the West, an article entitled "The Tragedies of Polish Realism." In it, although veiling his message in the Aesopian language of historical analogies, the Polish Catholic leader admitted to frustration with his past political activities and argued that there are limits beyond which realists cannot go. When their repeated efforts at a compromise find no response, there is no other way but resistance.[21] Stomma's statement clearly heralded a new shift on the continuum of Polish politics from realism toward idealism.

What is it that has triggered Polish political leaders to move from one position to another — at times to embrace idealism and at times to shift back toward realism and vice versa? Is it a simple biological cycle, the fact, as John Herz put it, that "even if the older generation should sometime, as a consequence of its disappointing experience, turn to political realism, the young would always be there to unfold anew the flag of idealism"?[22] Or is it a matter of rational choice between the two alternatives — a conscious search for their synthesis, taking into account both internal and external political circumstances?[23]

In the final analysis an equilibrium betwen idealism and realism is preserved in a largely self-regulating manner. As an American physiologist observed, in a nation, as in a human body, "hardly any strong tendency . . . continues to the stage of disaster; before the extreme is reached corrective forces arise which check the tendency and they commonly prevail on themselves to cause a reaction."[24] The shifts from idealism to realism fall into this category. They are largely uncontrollable — there comes a moment when the people cannot take it any more and, regardless of the views of their political leaders, they spontaneously abandon the struggle. This was precisely the reaction which prompted Poles to foresake idealism and turn to realism after national catastrophies in 1863 and again in 1944. Should such an unfortunate situation develop once again in the future, it would most likely evoke a similar response.

In contrast, the shifts from realism to idealism are, or at least should be, more amenable to rational control. Basically, there are three situations in which this may happen. First, oppression may be intensified to the point that the people can no longer endure it and a spontaneous popular revolt occurs. To a degree this element was present in all the Polish uprisings. The fact that they were mostly unsuccessful, and often led to even stronger repressions, mattered little. This type of situation is least subject to reason, although it is still the duty of political leaders to calculate its potential consequences and, if these appear adverse, to try to forestall an upheaval.[25] In contrast, a situation may develop in which the oppressors are weakened considerably. To seize such an opportunity for expanding the scope of freedom — if necessary by resorting to an armed struggle — is a mark of good statesmanship. This is, of course, precisely what happened in Poland during World War I.

Finally, even if the relationship between the oppressors and the oppressed remains basically unchanged, a shift from realism to idealism may simply occur as a result of a change-over of generations. As Herz rightly observed, a father's defeatist memories cannot be passed on to his sons. As a result, younger people are usually more confident and less inclined to accept restrictions on their freedoms. Such a situation arose on two occasions in Polish history. In 1830 young cadet officers, ignoring the better advice of the Napoleonic generals, started on their own an uprising against Russia. It ended in defeat and even further curtailment of Polish autonomy; this, in turn, prompted another disastrous insurrection in 1863. A similar situation developed in the 1890s. When the younger generation, free from the defeatist memories of 1863, turned once again to idealism. In 1893 student demonstrations against Russian oppression took place in Warsaw. They were quickly suppressed, but political ferment in the country continued. There was a marked revival of political thought and activity. It was at that time that the main modern Polish political movements — the Socialist Party, the Peasant Party, and the National Democratic Party — came into existence. All three repudiated the positivist program of reconciliation with the occupying powers and strove to advance Poland's national interests through political action. This time, however, as a result of astute political leadership, a catastrophy was averted.

A split between younger political leaders soon ensued, however. The Polish Socialist Party, and especially its militant wing, led by Jozef Pilsudski, turned back to the idealist insurrectionists tradition. On two occasions, in 1905 and again in 1914, they strove to instigate Polish uprisings against Russia. At both times they were successfully countered by the National Democratic Party, led by Roman Dmowski. The leader of National Democracy was acutely aware of the principle of *Primat der Aussenpolitik*, and of the urgent need to synchronize internal and external developments. He opposed Pilsudski's insurrectionist plans because, in his opinion, they did not fit into the prevailing situation in the international sphere. Yet, Dmowski never abandoned the ultimate goal of Poland's independence (though he was accused of so doing by some of his critics), nor was he necesarily opposed to promoting it through military struggle. In fact, during World War I, when he felt the situation was ripe, he embraced both of these positions.

Dmowski consciously strove to arrive at a synthesis between idealism and realism. In the opinion of some people, he wrote in 1908, "our political thought is doomed to shift from one extreme to the other. Either revolution, conspiracy and the seeking of independence through military uprising . . . or the abandonment of all aspirations to independent existence, the complete acceptance of fate, the unconditional surrender. There is thesis and antithesis, but there is no attempt to seek a synthesis."[26] In the place of either extreme, Dmowski recommended "political struggle carried out every day and everywhere; a struggle which, even if it does not secure gradual successes, at least protects the nation from constant losses."[27]

My early writings on idealism and realism in Poland dealt primarily with the events in the late 1940s and the 1950s. A generation has passed since then. How has this model withstood the test of time? In what way does it apply to the situation existing in Poland in the late 1970s? To what extent do the three factors responsible for the rise of realism in the post-war years remain valid?

Several significant changes have occurred in the last decade that have taken the Poles away from idealism and brought them toward idealism. First, the younger generation, free from the defeatist memories of World War II, has come of age. The young Poles are more restive under the restrictions on their freedoms, and are bolder in articulating their demands for democratic reforms, than were their fathers. In this respect the new political atmosphere in the country was signalled as early as the student demonstrations in 1968. Today these former student leaders are in the forefront of the democratic opposition.

Since the mid-1970s the activities of various opposition groups in Poland have been greatly intensified. When, late in 1975, the communist government proposed amendments to the Polish constitution, bringing it closer to the Soviet document, there were massive protests from the intellectuals, so much so that at least the most objectionable charges were modified. When, following the workers' riots in Radom and Ursus in June 1976, many participants were arrested, the Committee for the Defence of the Workers came into existence and ultimately won the release of all the prisoners. In 1977 other opposition groups — such as the Movement for the Defence of Human and Civil Rights, the National Self-Defence and the Students Solidarity Committee — were openly founded; while clandestine groups, notably the Polish Coalition for Independence, also made their presence known. *Samizdat* publications have proliferated — some twenty of them appear regularly at present. In the fall of 1977 the "Flying University," offering courses on a wide variety of subjects free from communist influence, was established.

The position of the Catholic church has also stiffened. As a precondition for its cooperation with the communist government, the church has adamantly insisted on official recognition of its special status. It has demanded that discrimination against Catholics holding public office be ended, and that the church have access to the public media. No doubt the elevation of Karol Cardinal Wojtyla to the Throne of St. Peter has given a tremendous moral boost to the Polish Catholics. Clearly, in the second half of the 1970s a new mood of confidence, if not of buoyance, has emerged among the Polish opposition.

There have been important changes in the international sphere affecting Poland's external position as well. Above all, the intensity of the Polish-German territorial dispute has diminished considerably. The 1970 treaty between Warsaw and Bonn, although it still does not provide for a *de jure* recognition of the present boundary, represents a milestone in this direction.[28] The normalization of diplomatic relations between Poland and the Federal Republic of Germany has paved the way for extensive economic and cultural contacts between the two countries. Visits to Poland by Chancellor Brandt (with his moving gestures of sorrow for the harm done during World War II) and by Chancellor Schmidt, have taken the sting out of the communist exhortations against the danger of German revisionism.

In the spring of 1978 the Polish Coalition for Independence issued a document proposing even more far-reaching improvements in Polish-German relations. It acknowledged the positive changes which have taken place in West Germany since World War II, and observed with satisfaction the growing integration of that country within the western European community. Should this trend continue and, above all, should the Federal Republic of Germany unconditionally accept the present frontier with Poland, the main reason for Polish-Russian alliance would disappear. This, the document concluded, could pave the way for eventual re-unification of the two parts of Germany and for Poland's freedom from Russian domination.[29]

Poland's Idealism and Realism in Retrospect

There is no question that the overall climate of East-West détente has contributed to the improvement of Poland's external position. In the new international atmosphere the danger of a Soviet invasion of Poland, similar to that of Czechoslovakia in 1968, has been reduced. Such a step would be regarded by the West as a major violation of the Helsinki accords, and it would have very adverse repercussions in East-West relations. Détente also provided a useful protective umbrella for the expansion of Poland's diplomatic, as well as economic and cultural, relations with various western countries including, significantly, the United States. Warsaw's growing influence in various western capitals, in turn, has strengthened the Gierek régime's hand in its dealings with Moscow.[30]

The expansion of economic contacts between Poland and the West has been of special importance. Poland's heavy dependence on western trade and credits has given the western powers broader access to that country and a restricted, but nevertheless real, political leverage. In order to keep its good standing in the West, the communist régime must continue to steer a moderate course at home. Resorting to widespread repressions internally would hurt its prestige and, no doubt, adversely affect its economic relations with the western democracies.

Finally, some changes, both external and internal, have taken place in the U.S.S.R. The Sino-Soviet conflict has seriously weakened the Soviet position in Asia and has thrown the international communist movement into disarray, greatly reducing its ideological appeal.[31] The rise of democratic Euro-communism, like East-West détente, has diminished the danger of the eastern European régimes resorting to outright repression. The emergence of the dissident movement in the U.S.S.R. has also been helpful. Although the influence of the Soviet dissidents is incomparably smaller than that of the Polish democratic opposition, their very presence has to some extent legitimized such activities in the communist orbit.[32]

It must not be lost sight of, however, that all of these developments in the international sphere have not advanced far enough to affect the crucial element of Poland's external position. The U.S.S.R. has remained an expansionist power, determined to retain its paramount influence in East-Central Europe. Conflict with China and divisions in the international communist ranks have in no major way impaired the Soviet ability to do so. In the era of détente the Western role in eastern Europe has been somewhat expanded, but it is still subject to serious restraints. In the conditions of nuclear parity the Western powers cannot challenge the Soviet Union there without invoking the danger of World War III. The basic reality of Poland's position — namely, that in the event of an open Polish uprising against Russia's suzerainity, the Poles could not count on effective assistance from outside — has not changed.

The hopes voiced in the document issued by the Polish Coalition for Independence, anticipating cooperation between Poland and Germany against Russia are, to say the least, premature. The improvement of Polish-

German relations is undoubtedly a constructive international development and represents an important contribution to East-West détente. It must be approached, however, primarily in this context. For some twenty years after World War II, West Germany, supported not only by western Europe but also by the United States, tried and failed to achieve reunification through policies openly antagonistic toward the Soviet Union. In the late 1960s the Federal Republic of Germany came to the conclusion that the best chance to advance its goal was through East-West accomodation and since that time it has consistently been one of the leading practitioners of the policy of détente with the U.S.S.R. Under those circumstances a reversal of Poland's alliances between its two neighbours is unrealistic, not only because the Russians would not permit it, but also because the Germans would not accept it.

The changes in Poland, thus, have taken place primarily in the domestic sphere. In the last ten years the younger generation, free from their fathers' disappointing experiences, have come of age and have unfolded anew the flag of idealism. The younger people are no longer satisfied with the *status quo* and have started to search for new ways to improve their country's position. At the same time, moreover, there have been several important developments in world politics. Above all, the rise of East-West détente has widened the scope for Poland's manoeuvring in the international sphere. The basic reality of Poland's external situation, however, has not yet changed. The principle of *Primat der Aussenpolitik* is still binding.

There are no two historical situations which are identical in every aspect. Thus, in drawing historical parallels one must also take into account existing differences. Viewed in this fashion Poland's present position is, naturally, unique. Yet, one analogy suggests itself. The situation in contemporary Poland is in many respects similar to that which existed in the country near the end of the nineteenth century. Today, as in the 1890s, an internal transformation has already brought about a substantial shift from realism toward idealism, but the external changes, although they are in the making, have not kept pace with it.

There is an awareness of this historical analogy among the Poles themselves. As one writer put it, considering "on the one hand the present attitudes of the Polish people and on the other hand the international developments . . . we find ourselves in a situation similar to that [which existed] around 1900. . . . It is virtually certain that the international changes will continue. Meanwhile, our task is to re-learn as quickly as possible how to will, to think and to act."[33] And another writer argued that the contemporary situation is similar to "the point of departure" near the end of the nineteenth century, when there was a re-awakening of political thought and all the modern Polish "political movements — national democratic, peasant and socialist parties — came into existence."[34] Indeed, among the people searching for new ways of political action there is a growing division between those who come close to militant idealist programs and those who temper them with a healthy dose of realism.

An organ of the Movement for the Defence of Human and Civil Rights, *Opinia*, has occasionally expressed quite extreme views. In an editorial in March 1978 it excluded any possibility of a compromise between the communist government and the democratic opposition, and declared that either one stands for subordination of Poland to the U.S.S.R. or for the country's independence. "There is no third way," it concluded.[35] At times the students' paper, *Bratniak*, has prepared similarly militant opinions. An article commemorating the fifty-ninth anniversary of the restoration of Poland's independence in 1918 praised the people who contributed to that achievement through clandestine activities and uprisings.[36] And in the spring of 1977 the Polish Coalition for Independence came out with a statement defending the anti-Russian insurrectionist tradition. It admitted that the uprisings were often futile and costly, but it argued that during the era of the partitions they were indispensable to preserve Polish national consciousness. "It is owing to the conspiracies, insurrections and resistance movements," it exclaimed, "that today we are a nation."[37]

More sober views, however, have also been expressed in the *samizdat* press; indeed, at present they seem to represent the dominant trend. These have been best articulated by a writer using the *nomme de plume* of Marek Turbacz. His assessment of Poland's present position vis-à-vis the U.S.S.R. is characterized by cold realism. "We are not able to free ourselves from Russian domination," he wrote. "The restoration of Poland's sovereignty ... would be possible only if preceded by a fundamental change in Russia itself, or by a drastic shift in the constellation of forces in the world at large. For this we may have to wait as long as a quarter of a century."[38]

The renunciation by the young opposition leaders of insurrectionist means does not imply, of course, that they have abandoned the ultimate goal of Poland's independence. Nor are they ready to wait passively for it. On the contrary, they aim at bringing it closer through continuous and ardent political struggle. As the National Democrats did at the turn of the century, the leaders of the democratic opposition today reject both extreme idealism and extreme realism and search for the best attainable synthesis between the two. "There is an essential difference," Turbacz wrote, "between compromise and blind submission, as there is a distinction between the realist policy and collaboration." The opposition, he asserted, should not incite "revolutionary upheavals, but rather promote everyday demonstrations of civil courage."[39] Another prominent opposition leader, Antoni Macierewicz, carried the debate to its logical conclusion when he pointed to Dmowski's repudiation both of military uprisings and of reconciliation with the occupying powers, and drew a parallel with the middle course which the contemporary democratic opposition has been following.[40]

If the analogy with the 1890s is correct, then Poland today is at a turning point in its history. Neo-positivism, as the evolution of Stanislaw

Stomma demonstrated, is defunct. The younger generation will certainly not go back to it. The only way the clock of history could be turned back would be by exposing the Poles to a bloodbath similar in intensity to those of 1863 and 1944. In the present international situation such a development is unlikely. The costs of suppressing Poland by brute force — in terms of its prestige on the world scene — would be extremely high for the Soviet Union. And no half-repressive measures would do — in fact, they could only aggravate the Poles' resentment against Russia and push them in the direction of extreme idealism.

At the same time the Poles must not lose sight of the fact that the USSR has at its disposal enough force to throw them to their knees and, in the final analysis, no one could stop Moscow from taking such an action. The Polish opposition, thus, had best not try Soviet patience by pushing its idealist goals too far or too fast. If it does, it could bring about the very result which it wants to avoid. Through provoking brutal Soviet repressions the Polish opposition would not only fail to advance its idealist ends, but it might throw the country back to extreme realism.

The present situation in Poland carries with it both grave peril and considerable promise. In order to minimize the former, and to maximize the latter, a new synthesis between idealism and realism — fitting the country's present historical stage — should be found. The Poles, as Jan Szczepanski warned, must avoid being "carried away by the emotional traditions which have worked with such regularity in [their] history."[41] Instead, as in the 1890s, they must at all times opt for reason. They should not dissipate their strength in another premature uprising but, while waiting for improvement in the international situation, they should carry on a relentless political struggle. If the Poles manage to stay on this middle course, there is every prospect that by the end of this century they will succeed in their endeavours.[42]

* Originally published in *Canadian Slavonic Papers* March, 1979. This is a revised version of a paper originally presented at the tenth annual Adam Mickiewicz Memorial Lecture at Carleton University on 17 November 1978.

Footnotes

1   "Political Realism in Poland," *Survey*, no. 51 (April 1964), pp. 111-17; "Communism and Political Realism in Poland," *Journal of International Affairs*, XX (1966), no. 1, 137-50; *Poland's Politics: Idealism vs. Realism* (Cambridge, Mass., 1967).

2   For the impact of the Warsaw uprisings on my thinking about Polish politics, see O. Budrewicz. "Bromke — 'opinion maker'," *Panorama Polska* (Warsaw), December 1977, pp. 8 and 13; see also A. Bromke, "Kronika Zastepu 'Debow'," *Zeszyty Historyczne*, XVIII (Paris, 1972), 108-29.

3   In 1955-56 I was in charge of the Polish Overseas Project in the Free Europe Committee, which consisted of distributing leaflets in Poland by balloons sent from the West. In these two years well over 14 million leaflets were distributed; the operation was suspended on 20 October 1956 and never resumed.

4   Z. Lasinski, "O idealizmie i realizmie w polityce polskiej," *Horyzonty* (Paris), XII, no. 129 (February 1967), 12-16.

5   These articles subsequently appeared as a book: S. Stomma, *Mysli o polityce i kulturze* (Cracow, 1960).

6   J. Szczepanski, "Proba diagnozy," *Pzeglad Kulturalny*, 22 August 1957; and "Proba diagnozy — uzupelnienie," *ibid.*, 31 October 1957.

7   The significance of the Polish-German territorial dispute for the Poles' changed attitude toward Russia was evaluated in my "Nationalism and Communism in Poland," *Foreign Affairs*, XL, no. 4 (July 1962), 635-43.

8   Stomma's speech in the *Sejm* as reported in *Trybuna Ludu*, 22 October 1960.

9   Among the historians of Polish political thought, two writers presented the dichotomy with special clarity. See W. Feldman, *Dzieje polskiej mysli politycznej* (2nd ed.; Warsaw, 1933), and H. Wereszycki, *Historia polityczna Polski w dobie popowstaniowej, 1864-1918* (Warsaw, 1948).

10 "Keeping Poland on the Map," *The Times Literary Supplement*, 31 August 1967, p. 779. See also the reviews by J. Rothschild, *Political Science Quarterly*, LXXXIV, no. 1; and L. Blit, *The Slavonic and East European Review*, XLVI, no. 106 (January 1968), 258-59.

11 See, for instance, Z. Rusinek, *Glos Polski* (Toronto), 23 February 1967; A. Bregman, "Idealism and Realism in Poland," *East Europe*, XVI, no. 6 (June 1967), 49-51; T. Katelbach, "Book of the Week," Radio Free Europe (Munich), No. 55790/1967 (mimeographed). There were a few critical voices too, such as Z. Stahl, "O idealizmie i realizmie w polityce polskiej," *Tydzien Polski* (London), 7 June 1969.

12 *Trwale nurty w polityce polskiej* (London, 1969); *Idealizm a realizm* (Chicago, 1977). The linguistic barrier evidently was considerable, as illustrated by the rather confused comments about the dichotomy between idealism and realism by S. Kisielewski in an interview with W. Karpinski, "Rozmowa ze Stefanem Kisielewski," *Tygodnik Powszechny* (Cracow), 2 April 1972.

13 K. Hrabyk, "O idealizmie i realizmie w polityce," *Kronika* (London), 23 August 1969; J.J. Wiatr, "Jaki realizm?," *Polityka* (Warsaw), 27 November 1976.

14 F.W., "Co jest celem Polakow?," *Jutro Polski* (London), 28 February 1973; J. Mieroszewski, "Ksiegi ugody i diaspory Adam Bromke," *Kultura* (Paris), no. 11/326 (November 1974), pp. 47-58; A. Ciolkosz, "Diaspora czy emigracja polityczna?" and "Od Bromkego do Wiatra," *Tydzien Polski*, February 26 and 5 March 1977.

15 E.H. Carr, *The Twenty Years Crisis* (3rd ed.; New York, 1964), p. 14.

16 A. Kijowski, "O wariatach i nie wariatach," *Tygodnik Powszechny*, 4 September 1977.

17 These debates are reviewed in considerable detail in my *Poland's Politics, passim*.

18 This controversy was summed up in my "History and Politics in Poland," *Problems of Communism*, XV, no. 5 (September-October 1966), 65-71.

19 For the debate's highlights in English see, "Political Romanticism: A Historical Controversy with Modern Overtones," Radio Free Europe Research/Poland, 17 February 1978 (mimeographed).

20 For the program and activities of the "Znak" deputies, see S.S. Miller, "The 'Znak' Group: 'Priests' or 'Jesters'? (1956-1970)," *The Polish Review*, XXI (1976), no. 4, 69-84.

21 S. Stomma, "Tragedie polskiego realizmu," in *Ruch Oporu* (Paris, 1977), pp. 229-35.

22 J. Herz, *Political Idealism and Political Realism: A Study in Theories and Realities* (Chicago, 1951), p. 4.

23 Evidently I have not, in my writings, explained myself sufficiently clearly on this point, for it was raised during my recent meeting with leaders of the opposition in Poland. See: "U Walendowskich: spotkanie z profesorem Bromke," *Zapis* (Warsaw), July 1978 (mimeographed).

24 W.B. Cannon, *The Wisdom of the Body* (revised edition; New York, 1939), p. 312.

25 It may be argued, of course, that unsuccessful revolutions, in the sense that they ultimately bring about the extension of freedoms, occasionally pay off. This was true in the case of the Hungarian revolution of 1848, which preceded the *Ausgleich* of 1867; and, once again, the Hungarian uprising of 1956, which led to the relative liberalization in that country in the early 1960s. It must not be forgotten, however, that the "Prague Spring" has not so far produced similar results.

26 R. Dmowski, *Niemcy, Rosja i kwestya polska* (2nd ed.; Czestochowa, 1938), p. 227.

27 *Przeglad Wszechpolski*, August 1904, as quoted by T. Bielecki in "Wyprawa do Japonii," *Mysl Polska* (London), 1 August 1964.

28 The initial improvement in Polish-German relations is discussed in A. Bromke and H. von

Riekhoff, "Poland and West Germany: A Belated Détente?," *Canadian Slavonic Papers*, XII, no. 2 (Summer 1970), 195-210; and "The West German-Polish Treaty," *The World Today*, XXVII, no. 3 (March 1971), 124-31.

29 "Polska a Niemcy," *Tydzien Polski*, 10 June 1978.

30 The impact of détente upon Poland is evaluated in my "Polish Foreign Policy in the 1970s," *Canadian Slavonic Papers*, XV, nos. 1-2 (Spring-Summer 1973), 192-204.

31 For the author's view of changes in the communist orbit see: "The Communist States and the West" in A. Bromke (ed.), *The Communist States at the Crossroads: Between Moscow and Peking* (New York, 1966), pp. 219-40; "Polycentrism in Eastern Europe" in A. Bromke and T. Rakowska-Harmstone (eds.), *The Communist States in Disarray, 1965-1971* (Minneapolis, 1972), pp. 1-19; and "The Communist States in an Interdependent World" in A. Bromke and D. Novak (eds.), *The Communist States in the Era of Détente, 1971-1976* (Oakville, 1978), pp. 287-304.

32 For an evaluation of changes in the USSR, see my "Polska 'Ost-West Politik'," *Kultura*, no. 11/326 (November 1974), pp. 28-47; and "The impact of human rights on the process of détente," *International Perspectives*, July-August 1978, pp. 12-15.

33 Socjusz, "Polityczne dzialania i programy," *Kultura*, no. 9/360 (September 1977), p. 11.

34 M. Tarniewski, *Ewolucja czy rewolucja* (Paris, 1975), p. 181.

35 "Problem demokracji," *Opinia*, March 1978, p. 6 (mimeographed).

36 U. Bartoszewska, "O rocznicy ll listopada," *Bratniak*, November 1977 (mimeographed).

37 "Ojczyzna Polakow — Tradycja niepodleglosciowa i jej wrogowie," *Tyzien Polski*, 23 April 1977.

38 M. Turbacz "Mozliwosci dzialania opozycji w Polsce," *Aneks*, 1977, nos. 16-17, p. 11.

39 *Ibid.*, pp. 10, 36.

40 A. Macierewicz "Tradycje polityczne w PRL," *Glos*, January-February 1978 (mimeographed).

41 J. Szczepanski, *Polityka*, 19 October 1974.

42 For the prospects of Poland gradually expanding its freedom in the contemporary, increasingly interdependent, world see Z. Brzezinski, *System miedzynarodowy—napiecia i przemiany* (London, 1976); and A. Bromke, *Polska Weltpolitik* (London, 1976).

II.
Poland's Political Crisis*

The fifth Congress of the Polish United Workers' Party, which took place on 11-16 November 1968, struck an optimistic note as a matter of course. It strove hard to convey the image of a party and a nation united behind Gomulka, resolutely coping with all the obstacles and purposefully forging ahead. Yet, all the ritualistic serenity notwithstanding, the Congress accomplished little. It did not come out with any new imaginative policies, it did not resolve the bitter intra-party struggle, it even failed to conceal effectively the profound dissatisfaction with the Gomulka leadership which exists in the country. If anything, the Party Congress affirmed that Poland is in the throes of the worst political crisis since the national upheaval in 1956.

The issues involved in the present crisis are basically the same as in 1956. What the Poles are pressing for is greater independence from the U.S.S.R. and a democratization of their own political system. An important difference exists, however, between the situation in 1956 and that of today. In the intervening years the mood of the country has changed a good deal. It is not only that Gomulka, who in 1956 was considered a reformer, is now regarded as an arch-defender of the *status quo*, but that in several other respects the Polish people view their tug of war with the Communist regime in a new, more assertive way.

The mood of the country in 1956 was one of thoroughgoing political realism. Three major elements contributed to it. First, memories of defeats and sufferings in the second World War were still fresh in the minds of the Poles and made them wary of military struggle as a means of winning their independence. Second, Russia's ascendancy in Eastern Europe and the inability of the West to change this situation — drastically demonstrated by the fate of the uprising in Hungary — convinced the Poles that they could count on no outside assistance. Last but not least, the revival of Germany's power, especially in view of the open claim advanced by the German Federal Republic to Poland's western territory, revived the Poles' fears of their western neighbour and made them appreciate an alliance with the Soviet Union as a protection for their national interests.

The realist sentiments of the Polish people were responsible for the restrained outcome of their 'peaceful revolution' of 1956. After the most compromised Stalinists in the party leadership were replaced by Gomulka and his followers, the popular ferment subsided. The Poles — unlike the Hungarians but like the Czechoslovaks a decade later — did not try to break away from the Soviet orbit; nor did they attempt to overthrow the Communist regime. All they strove for was to bring the political system more in line with Poland's own needs. They hoped, within the limits of an alliance with the U.S.S.R., for somewhat greater leeway in the country's foreign relations, and a fairly extensive democratization in the domestic sphere. Above all, they wanted a considerable extension of intellectual and religious freedoms, broad economic reforms, and greater popular participation in the Government — all providing more outlet for individual expression and initiative.

Their hopes of modifying the Communist system from within were largely frustrated. The reforms carried out by Gomulka proved to be half-hearted. While the most oppressive Stalinist features were eliminated, the substance of the Communist rule remained unchanged. The Communist monopoly of power was fully upheld. No major reform of the economic system took place. In the late 1950s even some hard-won religious and intellectual freedoms were withdrawn. In the realm of foreign policy Warsaw once again fell into step with Moscow.

His retrogressive course soon led to disillusionment with Gomulka among the Polish people. Yet, by the late 1950s and into the early 1960s the Poles did not press on with their political struggle. Seeing no prospect for success by open defiance of the Communist Government, in the realist vein they turned to passive opposition. By and large they sought refuge in private life and abstained from all political activity. Gomulka tried to overcome the political apathy by intensifying the Communist indoctrination. This brought exactly opposite results. Even more people became disenchanted with him and turned away from all politics. The gap between Gomulka and the Poles has widened steadily.

New Realities of the 1960s

In the last decade several changes occurred which led to the revival of at least some political aspirations among the Poles. First of all an important shift in the demographic structure of the country took place. Today's Poland is a young country — two-thirds of the population are under the age of forty. The generation gap is accentuated by differences in education. Especially in the field of technical education significant strides were made in the post-war years. The number of engineers, for example, rose from 12,000 in 1938 to 130,000 in 1968. The younger technical intelligentsia, seeking an outlet for their energies, have grown increasingly impatient with the older managerial cadre which frequently had been selected on the basis of political reliability rather than professional competence. A strong pressure for reform of the economic system, if only to achieve greater efficiency, has been emanating from this source.

Actually more than half the population is composed of people under thirty who have no defeatist memories of the second World War. They have shown a keen interest in Poland's history, including significantly its military episodes. In the 1960s two debates — the first over a collection of historiographic essays and the second over an historical film — stirred up a good deal of emotion in the country. In both, the continuity of national tradition and the need to reassert national pride were strongly emphasized.

Even history of the Polish Communist movement has been revised in a more nationalistic vein.[1] Nationalism has been clearly in the ascendant.

Last but not least, in the 1960s some hopeful signs for the Poles appeared also in the international sphere. The second and more thorough round of de-Stalinization in the U.S.S.R. in 1961, the Sino-Soviet dispute, and an at least partial *détente* in East-West relations, all contributed to the lessening of Russia's grip over Eastern Europe. The greater independence of Rumania and, subsequently, of Czechoslovakia inspired in many Poles hopes of a similar development in their country. To be sure they remained painfully aware of their difficult position in-between Russia and Germany. Thus, they continued to support the Polish-Soviet alliance but wanted to transform it into a more equal partnership. They hoped that Poland would take her place at the side of the more progressive countries in the Communist bloc and would assist in improving East-West relations.

Gomulka was slow to respond to the new realities of the 1960s. He made little effort to bring his policies into line with the changing mood of the country. He paid lip-service to the younger generation, but still relatively few young people were given more responsibility. The old cadre remained well entrenched in the key positions. The economic reforms initiated in 1963-4 moved forward at a snail's pace; in this respect Poland lagged not only behind Czechoslovakia, but also behind Hungary. At the same time Gomulka did his best to dampen the revival of nationalism. He reacted to the historical debates with the worn-out Communist stereotypes.

The Gomulka Government also did not exploit the opportunities to win more freedom from the Soviet Union in the international sphere. In his foreign policy, as if to compensate for his weakening position at home, Gomulka moved steadily closer to Moscow. In the mid-1960s he took several extremely unpopular steps. He refused to receive Pope Paul VI for the celebrations of a millennium of Christianity in Poland in 1966; he abruptly turned down the offer of Franco-Polish political co-operation made by President de Gaulle during his visit to Warsaw in 1967; and he took a militantly pro-Arab stand in the Middle East conflict of the same year. Furthermore, in the Soviet-Rumanian and then in the Soviet-Czechoslovak disputes Gomulka sided firmly with Moscow.

In the eyes of the Poles his policies amounted to stagnation at home and slavish subordination to Russia in foreign relations. He became generally regarded as a spent force — a man who could neither cope with, nor indeed comprehend, the country's needs. The dissatisfaction with his regime turned more and more frequently into open defiance. In 1964, and especially in 1966 during the millennium celebrations, bitter disputes took place between the Communist Government and the Catholic Church. Ferment among the intellectuals steadily gathered strength. In 1964 thirty-four writers and scholars came out publicly against the restrictions on freedom of expression. In 1966 in a speech at the University of Warsaw, a prominent philosopher, Professor Leszek Kolakowski, submitted the ten years of Gomulka's rule to a shattering criticism. In February 1968 the Warsaw branch of the Writers' Union protested against banning the nineteenth-century Mickiewicz play, *Forefathers' Eve*, which had some anti-Russian overtones.

It was only when the intellectual ferment merged with the unrest among the youth, however, that it resulted in an open explosion. Already in 1964 the first arrests of the students' leaders for opposing the Communist Government took place at Warsaw University. In 1966, in the wake of Kolakowski's speech, more arrests were made. In March 1968 in protest against the banning of Mickiewicz's play, the Warsaw students took to the streets. The students at the other universities throughout Poland followed their lead and the riots and sit-in strikes continued for three weeks. The youth rebellion quickly acquired a political character. The students, reflecting accurately the wishes of the nation, demanded the democratization of the political system, broadly along the Czechoslovak lines. Their slogans called for 'a Polish Dubcek'. The unrest among the youth was suppressed, but the tension in the country persisted.[2]

Struggle within the PUWP

The new political situation in the 1960s affected the ruling Polish United Workers' Party. The struggle in the party, like the tensions in the country at large, stemmed largely from the conflict between generations. In the last decade the PUWP underwent a very substantial change. Its membership more than doubled: in 1959 it was 1 million and by 1968 more than 2 million. While growing in size, the party was considerably rejuvenated. By contrast, its top leadership remained almost exclusively in the hands of old people — the pre-war Communists who had made it to the top on the revolutionary wave of the 1940s. The average age of the Politburo was sixty; its youngest member was fifty-five. Moreover, friction between generations was aggravated by an educational gap. In 1964 in a party apparatus of 7,000 workers only 1,275 had higher education.[3] This situation led to a restlessness among many younger and better educated members which provided a fertile ground for factional activity.

The present, basically three-cornered, struggle for power in the PUWP goes back to the early 1960s. Already on the eve of the fourth Party Congress in June 1964 a potential challenge to Gomulka came from the group led by Edward Gierek, and another one from the 'partisans' led by Mieczyslaw Moczar. At that time their differences were put aside as they all joined together to finish off the remnants of the factions which had played a prominent role in the 1950s: the hard-line Natolin group and the more liberal Pulawska group.[4] Once their common opponents were eliminated, however, the rivalry betwen Gomulka, Gierek, and Moczar was resumed. It was considerably sharpened after the Arab-Israeli war, when, under the guise of the struggle against the 'Zionists', the 'partisans' managed to squeeze out of the party leadership and the Government a large number of Jews — some of whom had been sympathizers of the Pulawska group, while others had supported Gomulka. After March 1968 the conflict virtually came out into the open with all three groups jockeying for position before the fifth Party Congress.

The challengers of the Gomulka *status quo* policy came forward with different programmes designed to appeal to different elements in the party and different segments of Polish society. Gierek's power base was, above all, in the quarter-million-strong Upper Silesian party organization — the 'Katanga' of Poland — which he had run very effectively for more than a decade. He also had some scattered supporters in the provincial party apparatus throughout the country. In addition, his efficient management of Silesian industry had won him considerable prestige among the technocrats. Gierek's popular appeal was directed along those lines. To his followers from the PUWP he peldged a continued prominent role for the party apparatus, especially at the provincial level. To the technical intelligentsia he promised the rationalization of the country's economy aimed at its better performance. At the same time Gierek made it quite clear that he had no taste for either democracy or nationalism. His attitude towards the Soviet Union did not differ much from that of Gomulka.

The 'partisans' led by General Moczar represented a more hetero-geneous group. In fact until Moczar made it to the Politburo in July 1968 (although only as an Alternate Member), the 'partisans' proper were not represented in that body. They had close allies, however, in the top party echelons: a group of hard-liners led by a Politburo member, Ryszard Strzelecki. Moczar's own power base lay in the security apparatus which he had controlled since 1956, first as Deputy Minister and then as Minister of Internal Affairs, and in the army, where his comrades-in-arms from the wartime Communist partisan units occupied many key posts. In addition Moczar was careful to build up his own popular base. To that end he used the organization of second World War ex-servicemen (from the Communist as well as non-Communist formations) of which he had been President since 1964.

Moczar's political programme was geared to the different tastes of his heterogeneous following. The 'partisans' also showed little sympathy for democratization, but played up Polish nationalism. They emphasized the country's proud past, including its military tradition. Poland's second World War effort was particularly strongly underlined.[5] The revision of the history of the Polish Communist movement in a more nationalistic vein was largely of their doing. Wherever expedient, the 'partisans' did not hesitate to revive the less appealing aspects of Polish nationalism, as in the crude 'anti-Zionist' campaign against their Jewish opponents which often smacked of outright anti-Semitism. As to the Soviet Union, the attitude of the 'partisans' was ambiguous. In their official enunciations they stressed their devotion to Polish-Soviet friendship and their personal bonds of comradeship with the Russians forged on the battlefields of the second World War. Yet, implicit in their programme of national self-assertion was the promise of a more independent stand *vis-à-vis* the U.S.S.R. It was this last aspect of the 'partisans'' platform which won them considerable popularity among the Polish people; but it was probably the same aspect which led to their reverse at the fifth Party Congress.

In the intra-party struggle the Russians threw their full support behind Gomulka. The upheaval in the country was hardly over when, in a speech in Warsaw on 22 April 1968, the Soviet Ambassador Aristov praised Gomulka as 'a loyal son of the Polish people'. The fifth Congress of the PUWP was attended by a high-level Soviet delegation led by the First Secretary of the CPSU, Brezhnev, and the Secretary of the Ukrainian Party, Shelest. In his speech to the Congress Brezhnev commended Gomulka's policies as faithfully adhering to the principles of Marxism-Leninism and proletarian internationalism. At the same time he defended the intervention of the Warsaw Pact Powers in Czechoslovakia and in no uncertain terms reasserted their right to such action in any country where the socialist system might be in danger. With such a blessing Gomulka could not possibly lose. He was hailed by many speakers and was re-elected First Secretary.

Gierek in his speech at the Congress went out of his way to stress the Polish-Soviet friendship. Pointing to the participation of the Polish troops in the invasion of Czechoslovakia, he declared that Poland had given the U.S.S.R. a convincing proof of her willingness to co-operate in the international as well as the military sphere. Gierek also pledged his full support to Gomulka. In exchange, the Silesian party leader played a prominent role at the Congress. He was the first speaker after Gomulka and headed the nominating committee for election of the new party officials. His close associate, Secretary of the Poznan party organization, Szydlak, was elected an Alternate Member of the Politburo and one of the Central Committee Secretaries.

The 'partisans' advanced in the spring, but in the summer and especially after the invasion of Czechoslovakia, their offensive lost its momentum. At the meeting of the Central Committee early in July, however, Moczar was elected an Alternate Member of the Poilitburo and a Central Committee Secretary. He failed, however, to be elevated to Full Membership of the Politburo at the Congress, which was particularly humiliating in view of the fact that two new men were brought into that body without having previously served as Alternates. Moczar did not speak at the Congress.

Yet, despite his formal success, not everything went well for Gomulka at the fifth Congress. It was apparent that he was no longer as fully in control of the party as during the earlier Congresses in 1959 or even in 1964, and, indeed, that at least in some respects he was now put on the defensive. First of all, he had to give in to pressure from the younger generation for a share in the top party leadership. Among the newly elected members of the Politburo, the two Full Members, Kociolek and Tejchma, are aged thirty-five and forty-one respectively, and Alternate Member Szydlak is forty-three. Among the Central Committee Secretaries, in addition to Szydlak and Tejchma, Olszowski is thirty-seven. At the same time Gomulka, in his speech at the Congress, underlined the improved educational qualifications of the party leaders. He proudly pointed out that since 1964 the number of people in the party apparatus with higher education had risen to more than 2,000.[6]

The results of the elections at the Congress also indicated the weakening of the centre and the devolution of authority to the party provincial apparatus. Three new Politburo Members are also Provincial Party Secretaries: Kociolek in Gdansk, Kruczek in Rzeszow, and Szydlak in Poznan. This might mean in the future more 'Katangas' on Gierek's Silesian pattern, and more problems for Gomulka. It might also mean more influence for Gierek as the most senior of the fief lords. And Gomulka can ill afford the further strengthening of his rival from Silesia. Gierek is already fifty-five and might not be content to wait as heir-apparent until the next Party Congress in 1972.

Furthermore, Moczar's advance was arrested but not stopped. The 'partisans' remained well entrenched in their strongholds in the administration, and now also in the party leadership. Moczar was not promoted, but neither was he demoted. In the Central Committee his supporters retained, if they did not increase, their strength. In the past Moczar has proved to be patient in waiting for his moment. To have him around might be dangerous for Gomulka. Yet to try to remove him, unless this is done by some master stroke, might be fatal. The defeat of the 'partisans' would require a purge of the first magnitude. Moreover, in view of their connections in the security apparatus and the army and, above all, of their appeal to Polish nationalism, the struggle might well spill over outside the Communist Party. And Gomulka is unlikely to survive a repetition of March 1968.

Last but not least, for Gomulka Soviet support is a mixed blessing. By putting all his eggs in one basket he has left himself little room to manoeuvre. He has compromised himself so much that, notwithstanding his record during the years when he so boldly opposed Stalinism, it would now be extremely difficult for him to retrieve his prestige among the Polish people. And Soviet support might prove to be fickle. The Russians might one day decide — as they did with Rakosi in Budapest in 1956 and Novotny in Prague in 1967 — that they prefer a Communist leader in Warsaw with more popular following.

There is little doubt that more assertive nationalism is the thing of the future in Poland.[7] The whole dynamic of the internal situation pushes the country in that direction. If it is not Moczar (who in fact as a former security chief is singularly unsuited for such a role), another Communist leader is likely to emerge who will try to make political capital by identifying himself with Polish nationalism. In the 1970s, when the younger generation will exert even more influence in the country, the pressure for emancipation from the Soviet Union will probably be intensified. At least some degree of democratization would almost inevitably go with it. In order to reassert greater independence from Moscow, a Polish Communist leader would need to strengthen his power base at home and this could be achieved only by carrying out some popular reforms. The close interdependence between the two objectives of the Poles was aptly illustrated by their reaction to the banning of Mickiewicz's play. The opposition which culminated in the students' upheaval was motivated by both Polish patriotism and the desire for cultural freedom.

The crux of the problem is the discrepancy between the internal and external dynamics of the country. At present the Russians are in no mood to ease their tight grip over Poland. If anything, after the intervention in Czechoslovakia, the order of the day in the Communist bloc is closer integration. Should this trend continue, it is fraught with grave risks. The conflict between the internal and external pressures might result in an explosion in Poland. Unless the Russians want to have another Czechoslovakia on their hands (or even a Hungary, for the Poles probably would be more prone than the Czechs to resist a Soviet occupation with arms) they would be wise to let the Poles have it their own way. Such a course would not be incompatible with Soviet interests. For Polish nationalism is not anti-Russian. In their vulnerable position *vis-à-vis* Germany the Poles have every reason to continue close co-operation with the U.S.S.R. All they want is to be regarded as a genuine ally and not a satellite.

The two views of Polish-Soviet relations, reflecting well the changing mood of the country, were presented recently in a polemic between the editors of two popular Warsaw weeklies. The editor of *Kultura*, Janusz Wilhelmi, defended Poland's participation in the invasion of Czechoslovakia in terms of thoroughgoing political realism, reminiscent of the 1950s. Poland, he argued, after the experiences of the second World War is a fatigued nation. She has no strength left to survive another possible cataclysm. The main desire of the Poles is simply to endure. Their entire policy is determined by this single objective. Poland alone could not prevent the changes in Europe which would expose her to new dangers, but the U.S.S.R. can. Thus, an alliance with the Soviet Union constitutes a guarantee of Poland's national existence. The opposite, however, is not true, concluded Wilhelmi. An alliance with Poland is not decisive to Soviet security. Here the Poles get more than they give. They can compensate for it by loyally supporting the U.S.S.R. whenever and wherever her interests are at stake:

This includes co-operation in attempts to halt changes in relations in Europe and the world which the Soviet Union deems unprofitable for itself. Thus acting, we obviously act in our own interest. The stronger the guarantor — the stronger the guarantee.[8]

Poland's Political Crisis

The editor of *Polityka*, Mieczyslaw Rakowski, articulating the more assertive attitude towards Polish-Soviet relations more prevalent in the 1960s, took up the argument with Wilhelmi. To equate political realism with mere survival, argued Rakowski, is erroneous. The philosophy of endurance is rejected by the Polish nation and its younger generation. The concept of endurance is static, while the attitude of the Poles is dynamic — they want not only to maintain but to improve their position. Rakowski, of course, readily agreed that an alliance with the Soviet Union is vital to Poland, but he rejected the view that Poland is of no importance to the U.S.S.R. The nature of the relationship between the two countries is more complex than that. He concluded:

> . . . the Soviet Union is a superpower, while we are a State of middle size; however, it would be a mistake to presume that our eastern ally treats Poland as a partner in co-operation . . . in Europe and in the world only in those actions which it deems profitable or unprofitable for itself. For the Soviet Union, Poland is a partner of equal rank . . . it is an extremely important western flank.[9]

FOOTNOTES

* Originally published in *The World Today*, March 1969.
[1] The changes in Polish historiography are assessed in my 'History and Politics in Poland', *Problems of Communism*, September-October 1966, and 'Polish Communism: The Historians Look Again', *East Europe*, December 1967.
[2] For an account of the outbreak in the spring of 1968 see a penetrating article by A. Ross Johnson, 'Poland: the End of the Post-October Era', and the selected documents published in *Survey*, July 1968.
[3] Figures given by Gomulka in his speech at the fifth Congress. *V Zjazd PZPR*, Warszawa, listopad 1968, p. 183.
[4] For an account of the factional struggle at the fourth Congress see 'Poland's Politics . . .', *op cit*, pp. 200-1.
[5] Notably in a book by Moczar himself (which already has run into nine editions) in which he depicts his wartime exploits as a Communist partisan leader.
[6] Gomulka, *op. cit.*
[7] For an early evaluation of that trend, see my 'Nationalism and Communism in Poland', *Foreign Affairs*, July 1962.
[8] *Kultura*, 8 September 1968.
[9] *Polityka*, 28 September 1968. Rakowski's position is even more significant in the light of the fact that he has been Gomulka's protégé (although a young one and relatively independently minded) and his paper has been attacked recently by the 'partisans' for presenting a defeatist interpretation of Poland's national history.

II
Beyond the Gomulka Era*

Wladyslaw Gomulka's place in Polish history is assured. He was a central, even if highly controversial, figure in Poland's politics in the postwar period. Gomulka ruled the country longer than any other Pole since the eighteenth century — including Jozef Pilsudski, who governed Poland through most of the interwar years.

Gomulka's poltical program, of course, was that of Pilsudski *à rebours*. Pilsudski epitomized the old Poland of the landed gentry. Even though he flirted with socialism he had little interest in social reform; his main concern was to maintain the country's independence. Pilsudski saw the main danger to Poland coming from the east and he was bitterly anti-Russian. Gomulka personified the new People's Poland. He was preoccupied with social progress, even if this entailed restrictions on the country's external freedom. In Gomulka's eyes the major threat to Poland was posed by Germany and he was a strong proponent of an alliance with the Soviet Union.

Yet, in terms of personal characteristics and political style, paradoxically, Pilsudski and Gomulka had a good deal in common. In private life they were both modest, almost austere, and their honesty was beyond reproach. Their public careers, moreover, showed several striking similarities. Both were men of strong views and considerable courage, who stood up for their convictions against all adversaries — both fought in the underground and knew the insides of many prisons. Pilsudski and Gomulka alike tasted moments of utter humiliation and great triumph; both were defeated and returned to power. And finally, both Polish rulers, as they grew older, became divorced from the people, intolerant of all opposition, and increasingly autocratic.

Gomulka emerged as a top political leader, on the ruins of Pilsudski's Poland, in the communist underground during World War II. From 1943 until 1948 he was Secretary General of the newly founded Polish Workers' Party. In this capacity he played a key role in helping to establish, despite formidable opposition, a communist system in the country. Yet, in contrast to the other Polish communist leaders, who were totally subservient to Stalin, Gomulka revealed himself fairly independent of Moscow. For this he was removed from power, disgraced and in 1951 imprisoned. He was spared from trial, and, in all likelihood from execution, by the death of Stalin.

His persecution had won Gomulka considerable sympathy among the Poles. The wave of popular unrest which swept the country in 1956 carried him back to power. The Poznan workers' riots in June of that year badly shook the communist régime. In July, Gomulka was readmitted to the Polish United Workers' Party and in October was reelected its First Secretary. His return to power was a moment of great personal triumph; he was given almost universal support by the people. In 1956 the Poles knew there was no way back to the prewar era. What they wanted to acomplish were reforms within the existing system. They hoped that Gomulka would introduce such changes.

The reforms adopted by Gomulka, however, proved to be half-hearted. The most oppressive Stalinist features were eliminated: the rule of terror was curbed, the persecution of the Catholic Church ended and the collectivization of agriculture was abandoned. At the same time several objectionable aspects of the communist system were maintained: intellectual freedom remained restricted and no major economic reform was carried out. Moreover, after initial attempts to assert a more independent stance in foreign affairs, Warsaw once again fell into step with Moscow.

Gomulka's retrogressive policies soon led to disillusionment among the Polish people. Throughout the 1960s dissatisfaction turned more and more frequently into open defiance. In 1964, and again in 1966, bitter disputes erupted between the communist government and the Catholic Church. Ferment among the intellectuals and the students steadily gathered strength. In 1964 thirty-four writers and scholars came out publicly against the restrictions on freedom of expression; in the same year the first arrests of students were made at the University of Warsaw. In 1966, after Professor Leszek Kolakowski openly criticized the decade of Gomulka's rule, more arrests at the University followed.

In February 1968 came the first explosion. The Warsaw branch of the Writers' Union protested against the banning of the play by the great nineteenth-century Polish poet, Adam Mickiewicz, because of its anti-Russian overtones. In March the Warsaw students joined in the protest and took to the streets. The youth at other universities throughout Poland followed their lead and the riots and sit-in strikes continued for three weeks. The students' rebellion was suppressed, but the tension in the country persisted.

Gomulka survived the crisis and at the Fifth Party Congress in November 1968 was reelected First Secretary, but his political influence was clearly waning. He was discredited among the people; dissatisfaction with the deteriorating economic conditions was mounting among the workers. Gomulka tried to stave off defeat by belatedly adopting some new policies. In 1969 he changed Poland's policy vis-à-vis West Germany. Early in December 1970, a Polish-West German treaty normalizing relations between the two countries and sanctioning the Polish western boundary was signed in Warsaw. It was Gomulka's last moment of triumph.

At the same time Gomulka attempted to cope with the catastrophic economic situation by launching substantial reforms. The move to link the cost of production with incomes was generally in the right direction, but by now the Polish economy was so run down that drastic measures were needed. The announcement of increased food prices on the eve of the Christmas holidays led to violent workers' riots in several coastal cities. As in 1956, the unrest in the country resulted in a change in the top party leadership. On December 20, 1970, Gomulka resigned as First Secretary and was replaced in that post by Edward Gierek.

II

The end of the Gomulka era, despite the swiftness with which it came, was not surprising. In a way, as is the fate of many politicians who remain in office too long, his era had ended even before he was ousted. In the last few years his program was growing increasingly obsolete. It was not only that as the years went by Gomulka had become more conservative; even more important was the fact that since he had come to power in 1956 the country had undergone a drastic transformation.

In the 1950s Poland was still badly shattered by World War II. The nation was settling down within its new boundaries and was recovering from its tremendous economic and human losses. The generation that had lived through the cataclysm of the war was wary of pushing the struggle against the communist régime too far, lest it explode into a full-scale revolution and expose them to new losses and sufferings. The fate of the 1956 uprising in Hungary — which demonstrated Russia's continued ascendancy in Eastern Europe and the inability of the West to change this situation — only strengthened those sentiments among the Poles. There was also a fear of a revived Germany, especially in view of the open claims to Poland's western provinces advanced by the German Federal Republic. At the climax of the popular upheaval in 1956, Premier Jozef Cyrankiewicz, in an address to the nation, emphasized that the alliance with the Soviet Union was necessary to protect Poland's western boundary. But, all in all, in the 1950s, the mood of the Poles tended to be quiescent.

In the 1960s several changes took place in Poland which eradicated the effects of World War II. The western territories were fully populated and integrated with the rest of the country. In the economic sphere not only were the war losses recouped, but very considerable progress was made. The old, predominantly agricultural society was transformed into an industrialized one. The human losses were also made good. The population is now approaching 33 million, but in contrast to the interwar period it is more homogeneous — there are no longer any significant minority groups. Today's Poland is a young country; almost half of its population is composed of people born since the war. While in the entire interwar period 85,000 people received university degrees, in the years 1945-66 over 400,000 pursuded higher education.

The changes which took place in the last decade have led to a marked revival of political aspirations, especially among the younger generation. They, of course, have no defeatist memories of the last war. They do not share the pessimism of their fathers and their passive acceptance of restrictions on freedom. It is by no means accidental that the first rebellion against the Gomulka régime was staged by the students. It is also characteristic that during the recent workers' outburst the fiercest fighting was in Szczecin which has the youngest population in the country.

The generation gap is accentuated by differences in education. The young intelligentsia, seeking an outlet for their energies, have grown increasingly impatient with the narrow dogmatism and sheer incompetence of the older managerial cadre which frequently was selected on the basis of political reliability rather than professional competence. Although few people had the courage to say it openly, many would have readily agreed with a statement made in 1968 by a well-known writer, Stefan Kisielewski, that the country was run by ignoramuses. The realization that the new technetronic age, which Poland is still ill-prepared to enter, is at hand, made the young technocrats even more restless. In 1970 there was an animated debate in the press criticizing in no uncertain terms the economic stagnation of the country.

The young people also seem to be intensely nationalistic. They show a keen interest in Poland's history. In the 1960s two debates — the first over a collection of historiographic essays and the second over an historical film — stirred up a good deal of emotion in the country. In both, the continuity of national tradition and the need to reassert national pride were strongly emphasized. Even some aspects of the history of the Polish communist movement were rewritten in a more nationalistic vein. All in all, in the last decade a more assertive political climate emerged in Poland; from the point of view of domestic dynamics, the country was increasingly ripe for political changes.

In the 1960s, moreover, some hopeful changes for the Poles took place in the international sphere. The new round of de-Stalinization in the U.S.S.R. in 1961, the Sino-Soviet dispute, and at least a partial détente in East-West relations all contributed to the lessening of Russia's grip over Eastern Europe. The greater independence in foreign policy which has been assumed by Rumania, and the reforms which were undertaken in 1967-68 in Czechoslovakia made many Poles hope for similar developments in their country. The students' slogans in 1968 called for "a Polish Dubcek." Indeed, had the new trends in Eastern Europe not be abruptly reversed by the Soviet intervention in Czechoslovakia, Gomulka probably would have been removed from power earlier. The suppression of Czechoslovakia, however, only postponed, but did not eliminate, pressure for changes in Poland.

With the resumption of efforts toward an East-West détente in 1969, and especially with the launching of a new Eastern policy by West Germany, an international climate more favourable to Poland has been largely restored. The conclusion toward the end of 1970 of the Polish-West German treaty, sanctioning Poland's western boundary, was particularly important. It was characteristic that during the recent upheaval, in striking contrast to his attitude toward Germany in 1956, Premier Cyrankiewicz singled out the treaty with the German Federal Republic as an achievement of the Polish communist government. Obviously, it would not have been credible to play up the German threat several days after the widely publicized visit of Chancellor Brandt to Warsaw.

In the new circumstances Gomulka was increasingly at a loss. He was totally devoid of new ideas and made little effort to adjust his policies to fit the 1960s. He paid lip service to the younger generation, but the old cadre remained well entrenched in the key positions. Economic reforms were frequently debated, but moved forward at a snail's pace. Gomulka also did his best to dampen the revival of nationalism. He responded to the historical debates with the worn-out communist stereotypes. In foreign policy, the Gomulka government did not exploit the opportunities to win more leeway for Poland from the Soviet Union. Both in East-West relations and in the disputes among the communist countries — including participation in the suppression of Czechoslovakia — Warsaw trailed along after Moscow at every turn.

Seen in retrospect, the turning point in Gomulka's political fortunes probably came in 1961. The second, more thorough de-Stalinization campaign launched in that year by Khrushchev, and the split between Russia and China, created a situation which could well have been used by Polish leaders to carry out substantial reforms in the country. Gomulka, however, failed to exploit this opportunity; he was simply not interested in introducing any more changes in Poland. His stand in 1961 cost him public support. Until then many people still had believed that his course was influenced by pressure from Moscow. With this illusion gone, Gomulka was now seen by the Poles for what he really was — not a Stalinist, but still a communist in the old international tradition. From then on the gap between the Polish people and Gomulka widened steadily. He became increasingly regarded as a spent force — a man who could neither cope with, nor indeed comprehend, the country's needs. Eventually, he had to give way to new people more attuned to contemporary circumstances.

III

The new political forces affected the ruling Polish United Workers'Party (PUWP) and gradually eroded the delicate equilibrium underlying Gomulka's position. The struggle in the party, like the tensions in the country at large, stemmed largely from the conflict between generations. In the last decade the PUWP membership more than doubled: in 1959 it was one million and by 1968 more than two million. While growing in size, the party was considerably rejuvenated, but its top leadership remained almost exclusively in the hands of old people. The key positions were occupied by the men who made it to the top with Gomulka in the 1940s: Kliszko, Spychalski, Loga-Sowinski and Strzelecki. In 1968 the average age of the members of the Politburo was 60. Moreover, friction between generations was aggravated by the educational gap. In a party apparatus composed of some 7,000 officials, in 1964 only 1,275 — and even by 1968 only around

2,000 — had completed their higher education. This situation led to a restlessness among many younger and better educated members which provided fertile ground for factional activity.

In the 1960s the challenge to Gomulka's *status quo* policy came from two groups within the PUWP: one led by Edward Gierek and the other by the 'partisans' led by Mieczyslaw Moczar. Each faction put forward a different program designed to appeal to different elements in the party and different segments of Polish society. Gierek was an influential figure in the PUWP — since 1956 he had been one of its Secretaries and since 1959 a member of the Politburo. His main power base was the quarter-million strong Upper Silesian Party organization which he personally had led since 1957. Gierek never revealed any taste for either democracy or nationalism, in fact his attitude toward the Soviet Union did not differ much from that of Gomulka. However, his efficient management of the Silesian region, which was contributing roughly a quarter of Poland's industrial production, had won him considerable prestige among the technocrats and the workers.

General Moczar's power base lay in the security apparatus which he had controlled since 1956, first as Deputy Minister and then as Minister of Internal Affairs, and in the army, where his comrades-in-arms from the wartime communist partisan units occupied many key posts. In addition, since 1964 Moczar had been President of the 300,000-strong organization of the World War II veterans — from the communist as well as non-communist formations. The 'partisans' also showed little sympathy for democratization, but played up Polish nationalism. They emphasized the country's proud past, including its military tradition. Whenever expedient, they did not hesitate to revive the less appealing aspects of Polish nationalism, as in the crude anti-Zionist campaign of 1967-68, aimed at compromising Gomulka's Jewish supporters. As to the Soviet Union, the attitude of the 'partisans' was somewhat ambiguous. In their official enunciations, of course, they stressed their devotion to Polish-Soviet friendship and their personal bonds of comradeship with the Russians forged on the battlefields of World War II. Yet, implicit in their program of national-self-assertion was the promise of a more independent stand vis-à-vis the U.S.S.R. It was this last aspect of the 'partisans'' program which won them popularity among a good many Poles.

The internal conflict in the PUWP was greatly intensified after the riots in March 1968. In the spring the 'partisans' virtually openly challenged Gomulka. In July Moczar was elected to the Secretariat and, although only as an alternate member, to the Politburo; it appeared that he would soon make a try for the top party post. Yet later in the summer, and especially after the invasion of Czechoslovakia, the 'partisans' lost their momentum. At the Fifth Party Congress in November, with Gierek's full support, Gomulka was reelected First Secretary.

Despite his formal success at the Congress, it was clear that Gomulka was no longer fully in control of the party. First of all he was dependent on continued support from Gierek. Second, Moczar's advance was arrested, but not reversed — he was not promoted to full membership in the Politburo, but neither was he demoted. Last but not least, Gomulka had to give in to pressure from the younger generation for a share in the top party leadership. Among the newly elected members of the Politburo two full members, Stanislaw Kociolek and Jozef Tejchma, were 35 and 41 respectively. The new men did not produce any coherent political program of their own, but they represented a new style of leadership. They were better educated and although they did not exhibit any liberal sympathies, they were reputed to be more pragmatic than the older generation.

The defeat of Gomulka in 1970 was administered by a coalition of those three groups and the spoils were divided among them. Gierek, as a reward for withdrawing his support from Gomulka, was given the post of First Secretary. In the place of the ousted Gomulka supporters — Kliszko, Spychalski, Strzelecki and the economic expert, Jaszczuk — the 'partisans' and the pragmatists introduced their own men. Moczar was elevated to full membership in the Politburo. Tejchma remained in his post; while two younger men, Jan Szydlak and Stefan Olszowski — who are 45 and 39 respectively — also entered the Politburo as full members. Indeed, to emphasize the broad base of the new leadership, the Army Chief General Wojciech Jaruzelski and Professor Henryk Jablonski, former Secretary General of the Academy of Science, were included in the top party body as alternate members.

The new leadership is truly "collective" and as such, probably rather unstable. Several former followers of Gomulka managed to remain at the top, but their days may be numbered. Trade unions' boss Loga-Sowinski, Foreign Minister Jedrychowski, formerly responsible for economic affairs, and former Premier Cyrankiewicz — all are likely to go. In their places both Gierek and Moczar will try to put their own men, and the rivalry between the two leaders may be revived. Yet it is unlikely that either one of them will be able to consolidate fully his position. Both Gierek and Moczar are 57, and time is not on their side. The more they quarrel, the sooner they will be replaced by the pragmatists of the younger generation. The future in the PUWP clearly belongs to the Tejchmas and the Olszowskis.

The struggle in the Communist Party will be tied to the pressures in the country at large. In order to win popular support the various competing factions will have to attune themselves more closely to the wishes of the people. In this respect the early policy of the Gierek régime is symptomatic. Not only have the unpopular economic measures been withdrawn, but the workers' rights to participate in the process of political decision-making have been explicitly recognized. The adoption of effective methods of communication and even consultation with the masses has been promised. Gierek has also gone out of his way to assure the intellectuals that their opinions will be taken into account. And the new Premier, Piotr Jaroszewicz, in his inaugural address to the Sejm has called for full normalization of relations between the communist government and the Catholic Church.

Gierek has thus succeeded in temporarily appeasing the workers, but his position remains difficult. He has no choice but to continue with economic reforms in one form or another. The drastic overhaul of the economic system in the direction of greater market influence on production is a necessity. Otherwise, Polish products will not meet international competition, foreign trade will not expand, and without it the country's economy will remain stagnant. To undertake such reforms, however, would require that production be linked once again with wages and prices. This, at least in the short run, is going to be painful for the workers. In the economic sphere things will get worse before they get better.

The political situation in the country, moreover, continues to be tense. Despite the fact that the upheaval in 1970 was shorter and not as widespread as that in 1956, its long-term effects may be more profound. The Polish people could not fail to observe that by taking to the streets, for the second time they succeeded in removing from power unpopular communist leaders. Should conditions become unbearable, they may try to do it once again. Moreover, remembering how they were deceived by Gomulka in 1956, they are now unlikely to be satisfied by mere promises. They will judge the new leaders not by words but by deeds. Their expectations were well articulated by the Polish Primate, Stefan Cardinal Wyszynski, who in response to Premier Jaroszewicz's appeal, called for the adoption of true democracy.

IV

The dynamics of the internal developments also push Poland toward a more assertive nationalism. The revival of aspirations for a more independent stance in foreign affairs was already evident in the last decade; in the 1970's, with the younger generation on the ascendancy, Polish nationalist sentiments are likely to grow. This may well bring them into conflict with Soviet objectives in Central and Eastern Europe, with the resulting delicate interlocking of internal and external pressures.

Contemporary Polish nationalism is not anti-Russian. After the cataclysm of World War II the Poles have no desire to return to the Pilsudski era. They are conscious of their extremely vulnerable position between Russia and Germany. They are certainly mindful of immense Soviet power in Central and Eastern Europe. Since the occupation of Czechoslovakia in 1968, and with a large Soviet force present in East Germany since the end of World War II, Poland is surrounded by Soviet armies on all sides; a small Soviet garrison is also stationed on Polish soil. The Poles are not necessarily adverse to Soviet influence in that part of the world. They remember that the Russian armies freed them from occupation by Nazi Germany, even though this is tempered by recollection of the sufferings inflicted on them by the Russians. They certainly have appreciated constant Soviet support of the Polish western boundary. They are aware, no doubt, that even before its acceptance in the Polish-West German treaty the border had already been sanctioned by the Soviet-West German pact of August 1970. It is not, then, the intention of the Poles to cut their ties with the U.S.S.R. What they strive for is to readjust relations between the two countries to fit the new situation of the 1970s.

Paradoxically, if anti-Russian sentiments were to be revived among the Poles, this could be brought about most easily by the Soviet Union itself. By refusing to adjust Polish-Soviet relations to fit the new aspirations of the Poles, and especially by trying to intervene in their domestic affairs, Moscow might well make Polish nationalism acquire a sharply anti-Russian edge. Such a development might prove tragic. Soviet efforts to suppress changes in Poland could lead to another Czechoslovakia, or even a Hungary — for in line with their tradition the Poles would be prone to resist Russian military intervention, with arms. The appointment of General Jaruzelski to the Politburo during the recent crisis may have been intended as a subtle hint to the Russians that, no matter what comes, the Polish Communists can better handle the situation on their own.

Good relations between the two countries, however, are important to the Soviet Union too. Poland is located on the strategically crucial border of the U.S.S.R.; she is also a lynchpin of the present international system in East-Central Europe. Deprived of access through Poland to East Germany and Czechoslovakia, the Soviet position in those countries would become untenable. This situation greatly restricts Poland's freedom of manoeuvre in the international sphere, but it also provides her with a certain leverage vis-à-vis Moscow. Provided the Poles do not go too far, the Russians have every reason not to push them beyond the point of no return.

In the past, the Russians seemed to have appreciated the extreme delicacy of their relations with the Poles. In the late 1950s Poland occupied a unique place among the communist states in Eastern Europe. Despite the fact that no similar innovations were tolerated in other countries, the Russians closed their eyes to various internal changes which were adopted in Poland — notably the de-collectivization of agriculture and the special position of the Catholic Church. Had Gomulka tried to widen the scope of domestic reforms in the 1960s, especially by linking them to Khrushchev's de-Stalinization campaign, he probably would have succeeded in getting away with them. And it was precisely his failure to keep probing the outside perimeter of their freedom which led to the Poles' disillusionment with Gomulka, and ultimately brought about his defeat.

The Soviet leaders were probably sorry to see Gomulka go. Only two years before, while attending the Polish Party Congress, Brezhnev had warmly commended Gomulka's policies. Yet, when the Polish leader had outlived his usefulness in keeping the country quiescent, the Russians did nothing to help him. During the crisis in 1970 they abstained from any overt interference in Polish affairs, and when Gierek visited Moscow in January he was warmly received by Brezhnev. Given the internal dynamics of the country, Gierek seems to have little choice but to revive the probing of the outside perimeter of Polish freedom. He has to win from Moscow a new lease on Poland's domestic reforms. Should he fail do do so, he is likely to be replaced by another communist leader who will identify himself more closely with the aspirations of the Poles. And in the process of readjustment in Polish-Soviet relations, the situation at each step will threaten to get out of hand.

Whether Poland and the Soviet Union will be able to evolve a stable equilibrium, and in so doing avoid an explosion of major proportions, will depend to a large extent on the future course of European diplomacy. For the problems in the relations between the two countries are more susceptible to resolution in a broader political framework than on a stricly bilateral basis. Indeed, in the past few years, and especially since the Budapest appeal of the communist leaders in March 1969, Polish diplomacy has been actively trying to promote such a framework in Europe. Taking its cue from the Soviet call for increased cooperation among all the European states, Poland has considerably expanded its contacts with various countries. The marked improvement in relations between Warsaw and Paris, and more recently beween Warsaw and Bonn, has contributed to the emergence of a more relaxed climate in Europe. Poland has also assumed a major role as the proponent of a European conference. Polish diplomats have been canvassing support for such a meeting in the Western capitals on both sides of the Atlantic.

By applying themselves with such enthusiasm to the task of reducing East-West tensions in Europe, the Poles, it seems, are not only running errands for the U.S.S.R. but have reasons of their own. They see in these various diplomatic initiatives an opportunity to overcome, with Soviet approval, the barriers dividing them from the West. They want to obtain access to Western markets and technology, both of which they badly need in order to get their economy moving once again. They also seem to hope that a progressive de-emphasis on the formal alliance structure, especially if accompanied by troop reductions, and its replacement by growing multilateral cooperation among all the European states, offers them the best way to resolve their political difficulties with the Soviet Union. In this way bilateral Polish-Soviet ties would be gradually transcended by an emerging all-European system. The revival of traditionally strong Polish bonds with Western Europe, side by side with her continued cooperation with Russia, would go a long way to meet the objectives of a more assertive Polish nationalism in the 1970's.

Poland's return to Europe would also be of great importance in resolving East-West conflicts in that part of the world. Precisely because she is a lynchpin of the present system in East-Central Europe, such a development would have far-reaching repercussions throughout the entire continent. Conversely, a major explosion in Poland could be extremely damaging to the prospects for an East-West détente. For there can be no stable European system without Poland's active participation. Whatever the final outcome of the present political crisis in Poland, for better or for worse, one thing seems to be certain—with the end of the Gomulka era, Poland will play an increasingly significant role in the international sphere, as befits this dynamic and proud nation.

*Originally published in *Foreign Affairs*, April 1971.

IV.
Poland Under Gierek: A New Political Style*

When Edward Gierek came to power in Poland in December 1970, his position was extremely difficult. The uprisings that had broken out in the coastal cities and precipitated the fall of Wladyslaw Gomulka left the atmosphere in the country very tense, and spreading unrest among the workers manifested itself in new work stoppages at the shipyards in Szczecin and Gdansk toward the end of January and at the textile mills in Lodz in mid-February. There was a distinct danger that the strikes might result in renewed violence and bloodshed. Indeed, as one Polish commentator observed, the country was like a volcano that might erupt at any moment.[1]

Gierek's situation was complicated by several factors, not the least of which was the critical state of the economy resulting from fifteen years of inept management under Gomulka.[2] Sorely-needed reform of the economic system had been delayed so long that by 1970 drastic measures had to be introduced, inflicting severe hardships on the population. The Poles, however, after over two decades of extensive industrialization and limited consumption, were in no mood to accept further deprivations and instead demanded to have their sacrifices tangibly rewarded by an improved standard of living. Against this background, it was hardly surprising that the Gomulka regime's ill-timed move to increase food prices sparked the December 1970 workers' riots. Gierek quickly reversed his predecessor's harsh action, but as for further economic relief to the population at large, he could do little more than promise better things sometime in the future.

Gierek also had to cope with the fact that the credibility of the Communist regime had been seriously undermined. The vast majority of Poles, who had supported Gomulka in 1956 only to become thoroughly disillusioned with him over the ensuing decade and a half, were not disposed to place much trust in the promises of his successor. "Gierek," wrote one of the readers of the weekly *Polityka*, "arouses considerable sympathy; yet it cannot be compared with the feelings which most of us had toward Gomulka in 1956. After such a letdown one has to watch the authorities."[3] The people, in short, demanded action rather than mere promises, and the new leadership could no longer count on their unlimited patience.

Even more important was the fact that Gierek lacked an effective political instrument with which to carry out any new policy. The ruling Polish United Workers' Party (PUWP) was torn by internal dissension. While Gomulka and his top lieutenants Zenon Kliszko, Ryszard Strzelecki, Bolelaw Jaszczuk, and Marian Spychalski had been removed from the Politburo in December 1970, many other former Gomulka supporters remained entrenched in key party posts. In addition, Gierek faced a potential challenge from the 'partisans,' led by Mieczyslaw Moczar. This faction, which controlled the security forces, had helped Gierek remove Gomulka, but it was doubtful that Moczar's elevation to full membership in the Politburo in December 1970 was enough of a reward to satisfy his political aspirations. He clearly expected to share power with Gierek and could at any moment change from a collaborator into a rival. Thus, it was not without reason that in February 1971 the Warsaw daily *Zycie Warszawy* reported "an acute struggle...going on between the old and the new at many levels" in Poland.[4]

Last but not least, Gierek had to carry out his policies in Poland with one eye on Moscow. True, the Soviet Union had acted with unusual restraint during the December 1970 crisis, carefully avoiding any impression of overt interference in Polish affairs. The new Polish leaders were promptly endorsed by Moscow, and in February 1971 the Russians even extended credits to help Gierek cope with the country's most urgent economic problems. Yet, heightened Soviet sensitivity to political changes in the Communist countries of Eastern Europe in the aftermath of the events of 1968 in Czechoslovakia was doubtless a factor that Gierek could not ignore. There was the danger that, if the situation in Poland were to get out of hand, the Russians might shed their restraint and intervene militarily. Some Polish Communist leaders clearly had this possibility in mind when, at the meeting of the Central Committee in February 1971, they spoke of the need to avoid "a catastrophe" and "a great tragedy."[5]

The combined effect of all these factors was to impose severe restrictions on Gierek's room for political manoeuver. Whichever road he took, his course was fraught with grave perils. Yet, within little more than a year, he managed to bring the situation in the country pretty well under control.[6] He acted energetically and with great political skill, moving on a broad front to attack the most urgent problems first, while not ignoring the others. In this way he not only effectively defused existing tensions but also began—almost imperceptibly—to formulate and implement a long-range program of economic and social reform. At the same time he left no doubt that he remained in full charge of the reform process.

The first problem to which Gierek directed his attention was the consolidation and legitimation of his own power position. In a series of swift political moves, he disposed of his rivals one by one to emerge, toward the end of 1971, as undisputed leader in the ruling bodies of the PUWP. His authority was sanctioned by the parliamentary elections which were held in March 1972, also a year ahead of schedule.

Consolidation of Power

The purge of Gomulka's former supporters progressed in piecemeal fashion throughout 1971. In February, the trade union boss, Ignacy Loga-Sowinski, and one of Gomulka's younger aides, Stanislaw Kociolek, were removed from the Politburo; and in June, Artur Starewicz was released from the Party Secretariat. At the Sixth Party Congress, former Premier and State Council Chairman Jozef Cyrankiewicz and Foreign Minister Stefan

Jedrychowski also lost their Politburo seats, and after the March 1972 elections the former was dropped altogether from the government, while the latter was demoted to the lesser post of Finance Minister. At the same time two other younger Gomulka followers, while remaining members of the Politburo, were relieved of their positions in the Secretariat and transferred to the government: Jozef Tejchma as Deptuy Premier and Stefan Olszowski as Foreign Minister.

Gierek had meanwhile begun moving against Moczar in the spring of 1971. Moczar was excluded from the PUWP delegation which attended the Soviet 24th Party Congress in April. When Gierek returned from Moscow, he quickly relieved Moczar of his Secretariat duties in charge of security affairs, transferring that responsibility to a close follower, Stanislaw Kania. In June, after being demoted to the politically insignificant post of Chairman of Supreme Chamber of Control, Moczar resigned altogether from the Party Secretariat, and at the same time Kania launched a wholesale purge of Moczar's supporters in the security apparatus. Deputy minister of Interior General Ryszard Matejewski and several other high-ranking officials in the Ministry were arrested in June and charged with gross corruption (they were eventually tried in February 1972, Matejewski receiving a 12 year prison sentence and five other defendants getting lesser sentences). The purge continued, and by the fall of 1971 some 200 people had been summarily dismissed from the security apparatus.

The next move against Moczar came at the Sixth Party Congress, when he was ousted from the Politburo. (At the same time, one of his supporters, Warsaw Party Secretary Jozef Kempa, was retained as an alternate Politburo member but was denied promotion to full membership.) In May 1972, Moczar lost yet another of his power bases when he was removed from the presidency of the influential Association of World War Veterans. Although he remained a member of the Central Committee and a deputy in parliament, his political influence had virtually disappeared.

To replace the Gomulkaites and Moczarites, Gierek meanwhile moved in his own supporters, mostly younger men. By the conclusion of the Sixth Party Congress, only seven of the eighteen people who had been serving in the Politburo and Secretariat in December 1970 remained, and none of these had served in either body prior to 1968. The Sixth Congress also effected a drastic change in the composition of the Central Committee, with roughly half those elected—again mostly young men—entering the Committee for the first time. Of the 115 full members, only some 30 had reached this rank prior to 1968. The rejuvenation of these key party organizations also clearly establishes Gierek, who has been in the Politburo since 1959 and in the Central Committee since 1954, as a senior figure in the top echelon of the PUWP.

From the top, the purge gradually descended to the lower party ranks. By February 1972, twelve out of eighteen provincial secretaries had been replaced by new men. The party also began a massive screening of its general membership. In the first half of 1971, individual interviews were conducted with about 1,150,000 persons—i.e., roughly half the PUWP membership—resulting in the removal of some 100,000 from the party rolls. Early in 1972, another round of screenings was undertaken, this time covering about one-third of the membership. Its stated objective was "to mobilize party activists to a still better execution of tasks arising from the resolutions of the Sixth PUWP Congress"[7]—in other words, to make the PUWP a more effective instrument for implementing Gierek's policies.

Perhaps the most significant result of these developments has been a radical change in the social profile of the Polish ruling elite. Gierek, himself, is symbolic of this change. His whole background differs strikingly from that of the predominantly intellectual-ideologue types who ran the party under Gomulka. In the first place, he is of genuine proletarian origins: son of a Silesian miner who perished in a mine accident, he himself worked in the mines from the age of 13 until he was about 30 (only later, when he was already in his forties, did he earn a degree in mining engineering). Second, Gierek's career with the PUWP, which he joined in 1948, has been centered in Silesia. He served as secretary of the Katowice Provincial Committee in 1949-54 and as First Secretary of that body in 1957-70. It was his reputation there as a first-class administrator that led to his selection to succeed Gomulka in December 1970. Gierek's pragmatic Silesian background was intensified during his youth when he spent long periods in Western Europe—working as a miner and participating in trade union activity. Expelled from France in 1934 for participating in a miners' strike, he later went to Belgium and again worked in a coal mine, also becoming active in the Communist movement. He returned to Poland only in 1948, at the age of 35.

The New Elite

Not only is Gierek himself, at 59, eight years junior to Gomulka, but he has forged a leadership team that is conspicuous for its relative youth. Of nineteen key individuals elected by the Sixth Party Congress to the Politburo and Secretariat, fifteen were born after 1920, with the result that the average age of full Politburo members has been reduced from 57 years as of 1968 to 51 as of 1971, while the average age of Politburo alternates and Central Committee secretaries has dropped to only 45. This makes the present Polish ruling elite one of the youngest in age composition not only in the Communist orbit but also in Europe as a whole.

Many of these new additions to the top echelon have had relatively short experience in Communist ranks. Only two out of the nineteen top PUWP leaders participated in the Communist movement prior to World War II,[8] while three others date their membership back to the war years. The rest joined the PUWP only after the war, several of them not until the early 1950's (although they had previously belonged to Communist youth organizations). The new elite's claim to rule is thus based not—as was that of the Gomulka group—on long participation in the revolutionary struggle, but rather on educational achievement and administrative experience.[9] The educational qualifications of the Gierek group are good, with five out of nineteen top echelon officials holding doctorates and all the younger ones having university degrees or at least diplomas from party schools. They acquired their administrative experience by serving as provincial party secretaries, as heads of Central Committee departments, or as leaders of Communist youth organizations.[10]

At the pinnacle of the PUWP leadership is a group with close links to Upper Silesia. In addition to Gierek, five of the nineteen members of the Politburo and Secretariat are Silesians from miners' familes, and four hold degrees in mining engineering. One of them boasts a background strikingly similar to Gierek's having entered the Communist movement in his youth while working as a miner in France and Belgium; and four served under Gierek in the Katowice party apparatus. Together with Gierek, these persons constitue the "inner circle" of the present Polish leadership. They occupy five out of nine posts in the Central Committee Secretariat, while four of them (Gierek, Edward Babiuch, Franciszek Szlachcic, and Jan Szydlak) are also full members of the Politburo. Significantly, the latter are the only members of the top leadership who combine these two key party posts.

The different background of the new ruling elite undoubtedly accounts for the fact that their social philosophy and political style also differ radically in many respects from those of the Gomulka group. The Gierek people are not professional revolutionaries but administrators; and as such they are less ideological and more pragmatic than their predecessors. This does not mean that they are not loyal Communists—in their youth (during the Stalinist period) they were exposed to intense political indoctrination, and they have since made their careers within the party.

None the less, they are Communists of a new vintage, less concerned with a distant vision of proletarian paradise than with everyday practical issues. Products of an industrial society, they understand its functioning well; of proletarian background, they are genuinely concerned about bettering the workers' lot. Their exposure to Western influences—not only French and Belgian, but also German(which remains strong in Silesia)—has impressed upon them that the path to improved living standards is improved economic performance. Their first priorities, then, are to increase production and modernize the Polish economy.

In the realm of foreign policy, the new party leaders—not only as Communists but also as Poles—regard the maintenance of a close alliance between Poland and the Soviet Union as axiomatic. The members of the inner circle in particular, having their roots in western Poland, exhibit less anti-Russian bias than their compatriots from the eastern provinces; indeed, if anything, they look to the U.S.S.R. as an effective counterforce to keep

Germany in check. This pro-Soviet inclination may be further strengthened by close ties with the French Communist Party, which has a record of firm loyalty to Moscow—at times bordering on idolatry. Thus, in contrast to the Gomulka group, whose attitudes toward Moscow were often a complex mixture of *Hass und Liebe*, the Gierek team reveals no such ambivalence. They favor close bonds between Poland and the Soviet Union out of choice rather than compulsion, and in turn they expect the Russians to treat Poland not as a satellite but as an ally capable of playing an important role in European politics.

Economic and Social Objectives

The main thrust of Gierek's domestic policy has been directed toward improving the living conditions of the Polish population. This effort has evolved through a first stage of basically stopgap measures into a broader program of more fundamental social and economic changes.

The immediate moves of the Gierek team to defuse the December 1970 crisis included: scrapping the objectionable wage-incentive system (which had entailed a two-year wage freeze for most workers while expanding bonuses for a few) and—a short time later—the unpopular December increases in food prices; raising pensions and minimum wages; and accelerating housing construction. In agriculture, the government abandoned Gomulka's fruitless quest for self-sufficiency in grain (which had adversely affected meat and dairly production) and raised procurement prices for meat and milk.

A comprehensive reform in agricultural policy announced in April 1971 went into effect in January 1972. The unpopular system of compulsory deliveries of animals, grain, and potatoes to the state was abolished; property laws were revised giving an individual farmer a greater sense of security; a fundamental change in land taxes was introduced; and finally health services were extended to farmers and their families, a total of 6.5 million persons.

These initial changes in the socio-economic sphere brought about a tangible improvement in the standard of living. In contrast to 1961-70, when individual income on the average increased 1.8 percent annually, the average increase in 1971 was over 5 percent. At the same time the supply of consumer goods increased substantially: the shortages of meat and butter were largely eliminated, and a greater variety of clothing, including imported goods, was made available. Yet, the government acknowledged that these gains by themselves were insufficient. The year 1971 was described as a period of convalescence after which many new efforts would be needed to attain full economic recovery.[11]

The shape of the next stage in Poland's economic development— through 1975—was worked out during 1971 by a commission of experts headed by Jan Szydlak and was adopted in December by the Sixth Party

Poland Under Gierek: A New Political Style

Congress.[12] The new program for 1971-75 stood in sharp contrast to that put forward by Gomulka in December 1970. The essence of the new approach was outlined in a pamphlet delineating Polish aims in the 1970's:

The new socio-ecomomic policy is based on the assumption that it is already possible for the present generation to benefit from the economic progress of Poland.... The crux of the problem is, while not ignoring economic growth, to attain the maximum possible standard of living. In short, the objective is to promote parallel social and economic development of the country.[13]

In fact, the new PUWP leadership has accepted the unlikely (for a socialist state) concept that "increased consumption is an important and necessary factor in economic growth."[14]

The social goals for 1971-75 are very ambitious. Average income is to increase by 18 percent at the same time that working time is reduced. Full employment is to be maintained, requiring the creation of jobs for some 1.8 million young people scheduled to complete secondary or university education in the next four years. A committee of experts headed by the internationally famous sociologist, Professor Jan Szczepanski, is reviewing the entire school system in the interest of improving its functioning. The variety and quality of consumer goods is to be improved, in part through imports, and 600,000 inexpensive automobiles are to be produced and marketed. An estimated 1,080,000 apartments are to be built, and the construction industry is to be modernized in order to handle even larger housing programs in the latter half of the decade. New hospitals with a total of 16,000 beds are to be built, and 500 health centers are to be established in the countryside.

Success in achieving these ambitious goals, of course, depends on the performance of the economy, and the PUWP has targeted a 38-percent growth in Polish national income by 1975 (compared with 1970). The results for 1971 were encouraging but reflected a number of nonrecurring favorable phenomena—in particular, the utilization of existing reserves of credit within Comecon (the Council for Mutual Economic Assistance) and an upturn in the prices of some Polish exports on world markets. In the long run, a more fundamental step is required: the drastic revision of the system of economic planning and management in order to increase efficiency and productivity. However, no comprehensive reforms have been forth-coming. In March 1972, a Warsaw daily highlighted the need for reform and indicated that the Polish government might soon begin to move with more determination on this front:

In the last fifteen months...the efforts of the government concentrated mainly on the reorientation of the development of the country, overcoming stagnation in the economy and adjusting it to fit the needs and aspirations of the society.... This is, however, only the beginning of the road. Progress in this sphere must be based on the reorganization of the entire system of planning and management. Premier Jaroszewicz has (in his speech of March 28) announced such changes.... More elastic planning and more effective distribution of income, better organization of foreign trade, strengthening the responsibility of managers, improvements in the financial system—these are the directions where basic changes are under way.[15]

Yet, so far, no concrete steps have followed. Only time will tell whether Gierek will, indeed, introduce the comprehensive, far-reaching reforms which the Polish economy requires.

The Credibility Gap

A highly important adjunct to the Gierek leadership's moves to resolve social and economic problems has been its effort to remedy the credibility gap separating the party and the general public—a legacy of the skepticism built up during the 14 years of Gomulks's ineffective rule. The new leadership has publicized its "new methods of political work"[16] designed to demonstrate its accessibility to the public and its genuine concern for popular wishes and opinions. The practice of conducting direct discussions with workers to review their grievances, initiated by Gierek with his dramatic personal visits to the shipyards in Szczecin and Gdansk in January 1971, has been continued, if under less critical circumstances. Gierek and his top lieutenants frequently travel around the country to visit factories and villages and hold informal talks with local people. Some 160 major industrial enterprises have been singled out for special attention. Specific issues, such as the best methods of increasing the incomes of the lowest-paid categories of personnel, were submitted to the workers for discussion and recommendations.

Regular channels of information about the activities of party and government leaders have also been established. Short communiques are now issued after each Politburo meeting. A government spokesman was appointed in March 1971 to act as a regular liaison between the Council of Ministers and the press. A journalist from the Communist weekly *Polityka* was invited in the fall of 1971 to sit in on three Cabinet meetings with a view to stripping away the "unnecessary veil of secrecy and unapproachability."[17] In June 1971, a highly successful open-line television program called "The Citizens' Tribune" was launched. This format, in which the top party leaders answer questions from all over the country, has been repeated at regular intervals. Also, soon after Gierek came to power, an October 1970 law restricting the release of information to the press by local officials and enterprise managers was rescinded. As a result of all these measures, the tone of the press has changed considerably. Many sensitive issues are now being openly discussed and highly unorthodox articles—not only critical of current government policies but posing fundamental questions about the nature of the political system itself—have appeared, especially in the Cracow Catholic weekly *Tygodnik powszechny* and in *Polityka*.

Nevertheless, information made available to the public is still carefully screened. The regime's promise to reveal all the facts about the brutal repression of the workers' demonstrations in December 1970 was not kept. A special issue of the party monthly *Nowe drogi* containing a record of the debate that took place on this subject in the Central Committee on February 6-7, 1971, was never put on sale and was circulated only to a very restricted number of party activists.[18] (Politburo member Szydlak was greatly embarrassed when he appeared on national television on June 2, 1971, and was repeatedly asked to explain this.) Press censorship, though perhaps less rigorous, continues, and foreign newspapers are no more easily available in Poland now than in Gomulka's days. Indeed, in at least one respect, Gierek has outdone Gomulka: jamming of Radio Free Europe, abolished in 1956, was resumed in March 1971.

Courting the Intellectuals

Although clearly most concerned about improving the PUWP's image among the workers, Gierek has also moved to mend the party's fences with the intellectuals. To be sure, he has never repudiated the repressive measures taken by Gomulka against students and writers in 1968, and at the Sixth Party Congress he explicitly condemned "revisionist tendencies" among these groups.[19] Nevertheless, during 1971 he made a number of conciliatory gestures aimed at achieving a *modus vivendi* between the government and the intellectuals. The youth leaders who had been jailed for opposing Gomulka's policies were released; writers who had been jailed for opposing Gomulks's policies were released; writers who had been barred from publishing under Gomulka—notably Antoni Slonimski and Stefan Kisie-lewski—once again appeared in print; a new historial book by the late Pawel Jasienica was published, and émigré playwright Slawomir Mrozek was invited to return to Poland from the West. Late in the summer, Gierek personally met with Igor Newerly, Chairman of the rebellious Warsaw Branch of the Polish Writers' Union, and soon thereafter the new Minister of Culture, Stanislaw Wronski, met with several well-known writers.

In February 1972, on the eve of the Congress of the Polish Writers' Union, Slonimski published an article which praised "the change in the style of relations between the authorities and the public" and noted the possibility of "an agreement between the authorities and creative circles." He argued, "It would be irresponsible to pretend that there are no conflicts, but it would be equally irresponsible to pretend that no compromise is possible."[20] Indeed, some sort of compromise did seem to emerge at the Congress, which subsequently took place in Lodz. While voicing his preference for ideologically-committed works, Minister of Culture Wronski emphasized that, barring fundamental political objections, "we do not and will not restrict the freedom of creative cultural activity,"[21] and as an evidence of good will he promised improved working facilities and higher remuneration for writers. Several speakers voiced continued apprehension about the government's cultural policies, but on the whole their criticism was quite restrained. The elections to the new board of the Writer's Union also reflected the effort to achieve a *modus vivendi*. While the key posts remained in the hands of people loyal to the party, several figures who had taken a hard-line stance in 1968 lost their seats on the board and were replaced with well-known liberals. Soon after the Congress, a new weekly, *Literatura*, was launched in Warsaw. Its chief editor is a party stalwart, Jerzy Putrament, but the editorial board includes several people known for their liberal views, notably Gustaw Gottesman, the former editor of *Przeglad kulturalny*, an outspoken weekly shut down by Gomulka in 1963.

On the other hand, it has been made plain that the regime, while willing to tolerate somewhat greater freedom of expression, fully intends to keep a firm grip on the reins. Though the first edition of Jasienica's new book quickly sold out, the authorities have yet to authorize a second edition. Publication of a biography of the national democratic leader Roman Dmowski, written by the Catholic writer Andrzej Micewski, has been considerably delayed. The scholars who were involved in the disturbances of March 1968 have not yet been allowed to resume university teaching. And the members of an underground youth group called "Ruch," who were brought to trial in 1971, were given prison sentences even harsher than those handed down in the Gomulka period,[22] evoking a joint protest by seventeen noted Polish intellectuals. In sum, the truce between the regime and the intellectuals remains extremely fragile.

Toward a Broader Base

Besides trying to better the regime's relations with the intellectuals, Gierek has also sought to broaden his base of popular support by taking actions specifically designed to win mass support outside the party rank and file. One such action, calculated to appeal to Polish nationalist sentiment, was the decision to rebuild the Warsaw Royal Castle, which had been demolished during the war and which Gomulka saw no need to restore in the capital of People's Poland. A public committee, which included the Bishop of Warsaw and several well-known intellectuals, was established in January 1971 to solicit support and funds for the project from Poles both at home and abroad. The reconstruction work was soon started and is to be completed by mid-1974.

The regime has also promised to promote greater participation in the government by people from outside the ranks of the PUWP. In February 1971, an independent deputy, Mrs. Halina Skibniewska, was elected a

Poland Under Gierek: A New Political Style

Deputy Speaker of the *Sejm* (Poland's parliament), and at the same time Jozef Tejchma declared the strengthening of all representative bodies, particularly the *Sejm* to be a major party goal.[23] In June of the same year, the Presidium of the National Unity Front—an umbrella organization through which the PUWP supervises the political participation of two residual parties, the United Peasants' Party and the Democratic Party, as well as of other less structured groups—was reorganized to provide for stronger representation of non-party people. Breaking with the tradition that a Communist should hold the post, the Front elected unaffiliated Professor Jan Szczepanski and Konstanty Lubienski, a noted Catholic intellectual and vice-chairman of the Church-sponsored "Znak" circle of *Sejm* deputies, to be deputy chairmen.

Notwithstanding these friendly gestures, however, the Gierek leadership has made few changes that enlarge concretely the political opportunities afforded non-party people. The parliamentary elections of March 1972 were particularly revealing in this regard. Although the make-up of the *Sejm* was altered (and rejuvenated) by the election of more workers and scientists, the voters were not given any greater leeway for expressing their preferences, and the party's screening of candidates was as tight as in the Gomulka days. In fact, the new *Sejm* compared unfavorably with that of 1957—elected in the early liberal phase of Gomulka's rule. Among the 460 deputies elected in 1972, only 49 were unaffiliated (the same number as had served since 1961) compared with 62 in the *Sejm* elected in 1957. Likewise, representation of Catholics remained at ten seats—five each for the "Pax" group (fostered by the PUWP) and the Church-supported "Znak" group—which was less than the twelve seats (divided three and nine, respectively) which the Catholics held in 1957. Nor is there any convincing evidence of concrete steps to effect the promised increase in the powers of the *Sejm*.

There has also been little visible progress toward increasing the opportunities for non-party persons to function in lower-level administrative positions, despite considerable public discussion of the problem and official pledges to improve the situation. In a July 1971 article which drew heavy reader support, Mieczyslaw Rakowski, editor-in-chief of *Polityka,* noted the absurdity of trying to require that every director of a small factory, every schoolmaster, or every manager of a local savings bank be a PUWP member. Rakowski wrote:

> *Among the millions of non-party people there are many individuals superior in intelligence and performance to many party members....A wise cadre policy must strictly observe the principle of equal opportunity for party and non-party people.*[24]

Two months later, possibly in response to Rakowski's criticism, Edward Babiuch, Politburo member in charge of cadre policy, pledged to "emphasize even more strongly the need for placing highly qualified non-party specialists in executive positions."[25] Little seems to have been accomplished, however, apparently because local party authorities, jealously guarding their influence, have continued to discriminate against non-party specialists. As the leader of the "Znak" group of Catholic *Sejm* deputies, Stanislaw Stomma, complained in the spring of 1972:

> ...*efforts to release social energy at the bottom are still unsatisfactory. This restricts social activity and adversely affects progress in the country.*[26]

A Modus Vivendi with the Church

A particularly important aspect of the Gierek leadership's drive to gain broad popular acceptance has been its effort to improve relations with the Church, the institutional focus of Poland's millions of Catholics. In his very first speech to the *Sejm* after taking office in December 1970, Premier Jaroszewicz announced the government's readiness to normalize relations.[27] Stefan Cardinal Wyszynski responded cautiously but positively the next day in his Christmas Eve sermon in Warsaw's St. John's Cathedral. On March 4, the two men met in the first state-Church encounter at this level since 1963. Although little was revealed of the substance of the three-hour negotiations, they presumably paved the way for several government concessions to the Church that followed. In June, ecclesiastical property in the former German territories was formally returned to the Church, and in February 1972 the regulations requiring the Church to keep a complete inventory of all its property, including that used for purely liturgical purposes, were abolished. The government also began to grant permission for the construction of new churches; some 30 permits had been granted by mid-1972. In another open gesture of accommodation, the Polish authorities helped airlift some 1,500 Polish Catholics to Rome for the ceremonies beatifying the Polish martyr of Auschwitz, Father Maksymilian Kolbe.

The concessions to the Polish Church were linked to negotiations looking toward the establishment of diplomatic relations with the Vatican. In April 1971 and again in November, Aleksander Skarzynski, Polish Deputy Minister in charge of religious affairs, conferred with Archbishop Agostino Casaroli, Secretary of the Vatican's Council for Public Affairs, but nothing concrete emerged from the discussions. The major obstacle was apparently Warsaw's insistence that the Vatican officially recognize Poland's western boundary—the Oder-Neisse line, established by the 1945 Potsdam Agreement. The Holy See was unwilling to take this step before ratification of the Polish-West German treaty terminating the territorial dispute between the two countries. The FRG's ratification of the treaty facilitated a breakthrough in these negotiations. On June 28, 1972, the Vatican appointed Polish bishops to six western dioceses of Poland, thereby acknowledging the ecclesiastical control of the Polish Church over these areas and implicitly recognizing the territories as part of Poland. The most significant appointment was that of Boleslaw Kominek as Archbishop of Wroclaw, an area which was still listed in the 1972 Vatican yearbook as "Breslavia" (the Latin version of its former German Name, "Breslau").[28]

These developments do not indicate, however, that all issues in Church-state relations in Poland have been resolved. The Episcopate still complains that the situation in regard to the issuance of permits to erect churches—especially in newly-built workers districts of the cities has been far from satisfactory, and that, even when such permits have been granted, actual construction has been held up in some places by local PUWP officials. As if delays in the construction of new churches were not enough, on March 22, 1972, a provisional chapel in the village of Zbroza Duza, south of Warsaw, was demolished by the militia—an incident strongly condemned by Cardinal Wyszynski in his Lenten sermon in the Warsaw Cathedral.

The PUWP's clumsy efforts to manipulate and control the token Catholic representation in the *Sejm*, have also antagonized the Church. In the selection of candidates for this year's election, the party successfully had Tadeusz Mazowiecki, a member of the Church-approved Znak group in the previous *Sejm*, dropped from the lists. He was replaced by the Secretary of the Warsaw Club of the Catholic Intelligentsia, Ludwik Aulajtner. But after his predictable election to the *Sejm*, Aulajtner was removed as Secretary of the Warsaw Club—a clear rebuke to the PUWP and its meddling. A further affront to independent Catholic opinion was the election by the *Sejm* of Boleslaw Piasecki, leader of the PUWP-sponsored Pax group among Catholic deputies, to membership in the State Council. Despite these symptoms of continuing tension, however, Premier Jaroszewicz, in his first address to the *Sejm*, repeated his call for normalization of relations for an agreement based on mutual concesssions by the state and the Church.[29]

Polish-Soviet Relations

Although they have been heavily involved in demestic affairs, the new Polish leaders have not neglected foreign relations. Immediately after coming to power, Gierek was quick to stress the continuity of Polish foreign policy, particularly with respect to close friendship and alliance with the Soviet Union. In his message to the nation on December 20, 1970, Gierek stressed "fraternal and cordial cooperation" with the U.S.S.R. and promised to consolidate it even further in the future.[30] He has reiterated this theme in virtually all his major pronouncements and in terms no less exuberant than those used by Gomulka. At the same time, however, there have been evidences of a new and more self-confident approach to Polish-Soviet relations. Commenting on Gierek's visit to Moscow in January 1971, a writer in *Polityka* rebuked those who, in looking at Poland's alliance with the Soviet Union, "stubbornly cling to yesterday's patterns while ignoring the passage of time and the changes which come with it."[31] Similarly, a well-known Warsaw commentator on international affairs, Ryszard Wojna, stressed the importance of Poland's role as a member of the Warsaw Pact. "Our contribution to the Warsaw Treaty is by no means unimportant," he wrote. "Taking into account of demographic, economic and military potential, we are, next to the Soviet Union, the second strongest power in the socialist bloc."[32]

The new Polish leaders may, in fact, be in a better position than their predecessors to put relations with the Soviet Union on a more equal footing. Gierek's team appears to be more attuned to the present Soviet leadership than the Gomulka group ever was. While Gomulka had good rapport with Khrushchev, Gierek—even though he speaks Russian poorly—probably finds it easier than Gomulka did to get through to Brezhnev. Despite the difference in their ages, both Gierek and Brezhnev belong to the same first post-revolutionary Communist generation, and they both talk the language of practical administrators rather than of doctrinaire ideologists.[33] Indeed, their partnership seems to work well. In February 1971, the U.S.S.R. extended badly-needed credits to Poland; in the spring of the same year, Moscow threw its support behind Gierek in his power struggle against Moczar; and in December, Brezhnev made a personal appearance at the sixth Polish Party Congress to signify his approval of Gierek's course.

Poland has also cultivated good relations with the other East European countries. Immediately after his takeover, Gierek dispatched leading members of his team to various East European capitals to establish contact with the local communist leaders. Polish-East German relations, which had been seriously strained under Gomulka and Ulbricht over the shift in Polish policy toward reconciliation with the FRG, have visibly improved since the present East German leadership's decision to fall into line with Moscow and the rest of the bloc on the issue of European détente. Indeed, the new atmosphere of friendliness in Polish-East German relations was underlined in January 1972 by the opening of the boundary between the two countries to tourist traffic for the first time. (A similar opening of the Polish-Czechoslovak border was contemplated but apparently has run into difficulties.) Poland's relations with Romania and with Yugoslavia, whose President Tito was accorded a warm welcome when he visited Warsaw in June 1972, have also undergone marked improvement. On the other hand, Poland's relations with China have remained cool. In evident solidarity with the Soviet position, the Polish leaders, including Gierek himself, have harshly denounced the Chinese for splitting the international Communist movement.

While preserving or cultivating good relations with Poland's Communist neighbors, the Gierek leadership has stressed from the very outset its intention to pursue the course initiated by Gomulka in 1969, looking toward a rapprochement with West Germany and détente in Europe. In the present international situation, it maintains that Poland's continued alliance with the U.S.S.R. and a policy of improving relations with the Western powers are not only compatible but indeed complementary. "The effectiveness of our policy in the West," wrote foreign affairs commentator Ignacy Krasicki, "depends upon our position in the solialist system....In the present constellation of forces in Europe, our country is the first ally of the strongest European power—one of the two world superpowers—the Soviet Union."[34] The Catholic writer, Andrzej Micewski, was even more explicit:

> We are faced with a completely new situation in which Poland's pro-Russian course is no longer incompatible with other international associations. At present the Polish-Soviet alliance is helpful to us in expanding relations with other countries....Our participation in the eastern bloc provides us with an opportunity to reach a Polish-German reconciliation and to revive ties with our traditional friends in the West.[35]

Polish advocacy of European détente is clearly more, however, than a dutiful seconding of Moscow's current policy. Rapprochement and détente promise not only to give Poland access to important Western markets and technology, but also to restore traditionally close cultural ties with Western Europe. Even more important perhaps, the Poles no doubt hope—even if they do not say so publicly—that the emergence of an all-European system will servce to strengthen Warsaw's position vis-à-vis Moscow within the framework of the Polish-Soviet alliance.

Warsaw and the West

A key part of the Gierek leadership's effort to promote a general European détente has, of course, been its persistent endeavor to bring the rapprochement with West Germany to fruition. During 1971 the new leadership continued active contacts with West German representatives, welcoming to Warsaw not only supporters of Chancellor Brandt but also several ranking members of the opposition Chrtistian Democratic Union, including the party's head, Rainer Barzel. The regime meanwhile continued to permit Germans living within Poland's boundaries to emigrate to West Germany if they desired to do so, and bilateral talks were held on mutual steps to correct inaccuracies in history and geography textbooks of the two countries. During the bitter debate in Bonn over ratification of the West German treaties of 1970 with Poland and the U.S.S.R., the Polish leadership reacted with moderation and restraint, although the press did not conceal its apprehension. When, in mid-May 1972, the treaties were finally ratified by the West German parliament, Warsaw was quick to follow suit, ratifying the Polish-FRG treaty on May 26.[36] On June 5, Deputy Foriegn Minister Jozef Czyrek went to Bonn to exchange the ratification documents with his West German counterpart, and it was announced that formal diplomatic relations would be inaugurated in the near future with an exchange of ambassadors. *Trybyna Ludu*, commenting on the event, hailed it as "opening new perspectives, and even a new chapter, in the postwar history of Europe."[37]

The Gierek regime has also continued to develop broad contacts with several other West European countries with the dual objective of expanding bilateral relations—especially economic—and paving the way for a conference on European security and cooperation. Poland's relations with France, which has chilled appreciably since President de Gaulle's 1967 visit, have begun to warm, and Gierek has received an invitation to pay an official visit to France in the fall of 1972. In October 1971, Poland signed an agreement with Italy providing for the mass production of small Fiat cars in Poland, and in November a protocol guaranteed long-term Italian credits for the project. In late 1971, a Polish-British venture in the coproduction of machine tools was agreed on, and in mid-1972 a contract was negotiated with the British Petroleum Company for the joint construction of an oil refinery at Gdansk. The Swedes, in turn, are to build a luxury hotel in Warsaw.

Particular attention has been paid to Finland, which has been in close consultation with the Poles on preparations for the proposed conference on European security and cooperation. Early in 1972, Warsaw appointed a senior diplomat, Adam Willman, as Ambassador to Helsinki, obviously with an eye to the possibility of having the conference convened in the Finnish captial. The idea of a European conference has also been promoted by numerous informal contacts; by discussions with foreign diplomats, scholars, and journalists at the Polish Institute of International Affairs; and by the airing of Western views on European problems in the Polish press.[38]

Not the least important part of the Gierek leaderships's foreign policy program has been an effort to bring about a thaw in the frigid climate that prevailed in U.S.-Polish relations during the last years of Gomulka's rule. This effort centered first in the economic sphere. Warsaw's interest in developing commercial and technical cooperation with the United States was emphasized by the appointment early in 1971 of one of Poland's leading economists, Witold Trampczynski, as Ambassador to Washington. This was followed in the spring by the dispatch of two high-level Polish missions to the U.S., one headed by the Minister of Chemical Industry and the other by the Chairman of the government's Committee on Science and Technology. In June, Gierek and Premier Jaroszewicz, paying a personal visit to the American pavilion at the Poznan trade fair, chatted with U.S. Ambassador Walter Stoessel and expressed their interest in increasing trade with the U.S. and gaining access to American technological know-how. Washington's response to Warsaw's overtures was both positive and swift. In August 1971, reversing a decision which had been made shortly before Gomulka's ouster, the U.S. government agreed to grant an export license allowing Poland to purchase an American catalytic cracking plant; in October, a small credit was extended for the purchase of American agricultural produce; in November, U.S. Secretary of Transportation John Volpe visited Warsaw to sign an agreement for cooperation in research on transportation problems; and in December, U.S. Secretary of Commerce Maurice Stans also went to Warsaw to explore further the prospects for expanding trade between the two countries. During his visit, Stans hinted at the possibility of easing current U.S. restrictions on the provision of long-term credits to Poland.

By early 1972, the road was clear for even more dramatic steps. In an address to the *Sejm* of March 28, Premier Jaroszewicz welcomed "the interest of the United States in expanding economic, scientific and technical relations with Poland."[39] President Nixon reciprocated with a congratulatory message to the newly-elected Chairman of the Polish State Council, Henryk Jablonski, in which he voiced satisfaction over the improvement in relations between the two countries during 1971 and voiced the hope that this trend would continue in the future.[40] On April 17, at a meeting described as "elaborate and warm," Polish Ambassador Trampczynski extended to the U.S. President an invitation to visit Poland,[41] which resulted in Mr. Nixon's brief stopover in Warsaw on May 31 and June 1 on his way back from Moscow.

The official reception accorded to the President during his visit was entirely proper but not demonstrative, although he did receive a tumultous welcome from the crowds that gathered to see him lay a wreath at the tomb of Poland's Unknown Soldier in Victory Square. The President then had two meetings with the Polish leaders, an official communique describing the talks as "frank, business-like and constructive."[42] The communique acknowledged differences, especially over the war in Vietnam, but also recorded agreement on various matters of common interest, notably the holding of regular bilateral consultations to develop trade and expand scientific cooperation, increased personal contacts, and steps to establish air and sea connections between the two countries. A consular agreement clarifying the status of the Polish-Americans were also signed, and Mr. Nixon extended an invitation to the Polish leaders to visit the United States. In the area or broader international issues, President Nixon place the U.S. on record as welcoming the treaty between Poland and West Germany (including its border provisions) and as endorsing the Polish view that multilateral consultations should soon be started to prepare for a conference on European security and cooperation Speaking at a state dinner in the Radziwil Palace, the President stressed his expectation that Poland would plan an important role in coming negotiations on Europe.[43]

The Poles had good reason to be pleased with the results of Mr. Nixon's visit, which no doubt enhanced the prestige of the Gierek leadership both at home and abroad. The visit was hailed by one Polish commentator as the beginning of "a new chapter in relations between Poland and the United States," although he hastened to add that the way had been "paved by the historic results of the Moscow accord."[44] Another well-known writer on international affairs, Janusz Stefanowicz, saw a broader significance in the visit, which he said demonstrated that "the role of the middle powers... .increases proportionately to the progress of détente in East-West relations."[45]

The Regime and Public Opinion

By and large, then, the policies of the Gierek leadership appear to have achieved a substantial degree of success to date. The emergency, stopgap measures taken to surmount the immediate domestic crisis worked. The regime's subsequent moves toward instituting longer-range reforms have gone far toward overcoming the apathy and stagnation of the last Gomulka years and instilling a new sense of direction in the population.

Yet there is no doubt that Gierek's credit with the people is not unlimited and that his ultimate success will depend on whether or not he demonstrates the will and ability to carry out an effective long-range program of reform. On this question, Polish public opinion appears to be divided into three camps. The first—and perhaps largest—segment of the population believes that Gierek will take effective steps to assure continued improvement of the situation. A second group also has trust in Gierek's leadership but feels that he is unlikely to succeed in view of the seriousness of the obstacles in his path. A third group simply has no confidence in Gierek and believes that, once he has consolidated his power, he will revert to the conservatism and inertia of the later Gomulka period.[46]

These divergent trends of public opinion harbor elements that are at once conducive and inimical to change in Poland. On the one hand, the existence of widespread enthusiasm generated by expectations of real progress is a positive force that not only pushes the leadership to fulfill its pledges of reform but also contributes materially to the effectiveness of the reforms themselves. On the other hand, the fact that the expectations of many Poles exceed the capabilities of the regime to fulfill them creates a dangerous situation. The Poles, still disillusioned by Gomulka's betrayal of their aspirations for reform in the late 1950's, may adopt a *déja vu* attitude which interprets any slackening of Gierek's course as an abandonment of the promise of reform. Such skepticism could lead in turn to a shirking of effort that could jeopardize the very reforms the majority of the nation desires to see come about. For without massive popular support and effort Gierek's chances of successfully implementing the reforms must necessarily be greatly reduced. Indeed, in an article published in June 1971, the popular Polish writer Wieslaw Gornicki already warned of the emergence of the latter syndrome in these terms:

The truth about the past six months is as follows: productivity has not increased, while absenteeism, work stoppages, and unfulfilled plans have mounted. Tragic and unrealistic demands, the realization of which would mean economic suicide, have arisen.

Gornicki went on to blame these shortcomings on "the buddy in the beer shack" who wants more money but refuses to work, and who will soon say, "See now what has come of all the promises made by Gierek? Are we once more to toil for a measly 2,000 zlotys a month and keep waiting for Godot?"[47]

Gornicki's article evoked a strong reaction. The well-known Catholic columnist Stefan Kisielewski ridiculed paying so much attention to "the buddy in the beer shack" and called the presence of such people "merely a symptom and not the cause of the disease." Instead, he urged concentrating all efforts on reform of the economic system.[48] Professor Szczepanski, too, has made the same point, coupling it with an appeal for stronger leadership. Observing that there are in Poland "many strong hands and able minds which for a long time have been waiting to be used effectively and creatively." he added:

It is not the lack of opportunities, but the inability of the leaders to exploit them which has been responsible for the stagnation of our economy.... For it is the quality of political leadership which determines also the moral climate prevailing in the country.[49]

Gierek's Prospects

There thus appears to broad recognition that the key to the success of Gierek's course lies in effective reform of Poland's economic system. This, in turn, is closely linked to two crucial ancillary problems: placing the most competent people, whether or not they carry a party card, in responsible positions in the economy; and overcoming the strong resistance in the middle echelons of officialdom to the adoption of such criteria. Mieczyslaw Rakowski may well have put his finger on the main threat to Gierek's internal policies when he pointed to the existence of powerful vested interests in the administrative bureaucracy:

On various levels in the government, and especially at the intermediate level, there exist indolence and inertia, organizational paralysis, inability or unwillingness of men in the positions of responsibility to abandon routine, disregard of human needs, and infringement upon the rights of the citizens. [There are still] those who are saying to themselves: "Never fear, we shall also outlast this reform."[50]

Resolution of Poland's key domestic problem of economic reform also hinges to a considerable extent on what degree of systemic change Moscow will tolerate. Soviet criticism of even the economic phases of the 1968 Czechoslovak experiment in liberalization, and more recently of the Hungarian economic reforms, must make the Poles wary of proceeding with a major overhaul of the economic system especially one that would involve a major purge of the economic bureaucracy so as to entrust greater responsibility and authority to non-party people. This might well antagonize the Soviet leadership, which still regards preservation of the leading role of the Communist Party as the *sine qua non* of a true socialist system. Gierek must, therefore, tread carefully with his internal reforms.

The recent changes on the international scene, however, seem to have enlarged Warsaw's scope of maneuver vis-à-vis Moscow. In the new climate of European détente that is beginning to prevail, Moscow will probably be more reluctant to risk a rift with its immediate neighbor and ally to the west. The Kremlin leaders, moreover, must be aware that given the situation existing in Poland, Gierek really has no choice but to proceed with substantial internal changes. Therefore, provided the Poles do not move too far or too fast, there is a fair chance that the Russians—in order to maintain tranquility on their western flank—may overlook minor ideological deviations by their Polish comrades.

This brings us to the more fundamental question of whether or not the Gierek team will be disposed to exploit this situation in order to expand the perimeters of political freedom within Poland. Certain factors that may inhibit them from doing so come immediately to mind. In the first place, although the present Polish leaders differ radically from the Gomulka group, they represent only the second post revolutionary generation, while—as Professor Szczepanski has sagely observed—it requires at least three generations for any ruling elite to develop a political culture of its own.[51] Consequently, there may still be a strong tendency for the Gierek leadership to revert to the ingrained habits of its predecessors. After all it is not easy for anyone to divorce himself from a system in which he has been indoctrinated from youth and to which he owes most of his personal advancement, no matter how completely that system may be compromised.

Secondly, the very success initially achieved by the new leadership may—again paradoxically—strengthen rather than restrain the inherited autocratic tendencies of the new Polish leaders. A certain degree of intoxication is already evident. After the Sixth Party Congress, *Zycie Warszawy* made a comment about Gierek that sounded like an ominous echo of the Gomulka era:

> *One would like to add a word about the First Secretary, about his modesty, simplicity, and straightforwardness in dealing with the people, and at the same time about his sense of responsibility... responsibility before history for the fate of the Poles and People's Poland. But these are unnecessary words....*[52]

Even if Gierek should personally disapprove of such exaggerated hero worship, there is the danger that it may lead him to become isolated from the people in the same way Gomulka did. Nor should it be forgotten that there are as yet no institutional checks that would stand in the way of such a tendency on the part of Gierek and the new ruling elite. The Communist Party remains the sole guarantor that the party will not abuse its rule.

Finally, it must be remembered, that the pressure which Polish public opinion can be expected to exert to push the regime along the path of genuine reform also has its limits. It is not only that the masses are handicapped when faced with a tight and determined group of rulers; even more important is fact that the legacy of history inhibits the Poles from exerting their full pressure. As this writer has observed elsewhere, today's Poles are in the grip of political realism.[53] The memories of their defeats and sufferings during World War II are still quite strong among the present generation, and they do not want to be exposed again to the same bitter experience. As the restraint of even the rebelling workers in December 1970 clearly demonstrated, the Poles today are clearly not prepared to push the regime so far that it may feel compelled to invite Soviet military intervention. When the next generation comes to the fore, however the situation could change. The attitudes of Polish youth differ markedly from those of their parents because of their different life experiences.[54] Their impact on Polish political life, however, will not be fully felt before the 1980's.

Thus, with regard to the possibility of political as well as economic liberalization, it seems probable that the present Polish leaders will continue to give priority to socio-economic over political reform and that they will make concessions in the political sphere only insofar as they deem it necessary in order not to impede progress in the socio-economic sphere. Even so, the Gierek leadership can make an important contribution. If it succeeds only in rationalizing and modernizing the country's economy, it may yet carve out for itself an honored place in Poland's history. At least it will have a just claim to having handed over to the next generation of Poles a better and healthier country than it inherited.

Gomulka's Legacy:
Two Vantage Points

Problems of the Workers

Below are statements made by striking workers at the Adolf Warski Shipyard is Szczecin during a meeting with Polish party leader Edward Gierek on January 24, 1971. A tape of this session was published in Ewa Wacowska, Ed., Rewolta szczecinska i jej znaczenie *(The Szczecin Revolt and Its Significance), Paris, Institut Literacki, 1971.*

DELEGATE K-4: Work in our division is harmful to one's health. At present every second worker who works on the ships is blind, deaf, rheumatic, or afflicted with some form of lung disease, and all for so little money....An assistant makes 1,800 to 2,000 zlotys [a month]. Let's look at his expenditures. In a family of five: for breakfast each has a roll with water—cost, 2 zlotys; for supper the same, a total of 4 zlotys: the least expensive lunch is 12 zlotys per person i.e., 60 zlotys. [This comes to an overall] total of 64 zlotys a day. In a month this amount to 1,800-1,900 zlotys—for mere subsistance....

DELEGATE W-6: In our division the average wage is 2,000 zlotys....This is really very little. Very little! After paying rent, electricity, gas, etc., a worker is left with 1,600 zlotys. No family can survive on it. So, to make more money we work overtime....I know many people who regularly do 150 or even 200 hours overtime a month. This means that they are virtually visitors in their own homes.

DELEGATE ZGW:....there have emerged men who live off the efforts of manual workers, but who sit behind their desks and decide our wages. Is this democracy? (Pounding his fist on the table.) No! (Applause.)

MEMBER OF THE STRIKE COMMITTEE: I do not know whether this is just gossip or a lie, but I have heard that Director Skrobot makes 18,000 zlotys a month. If so, this has to be changed. For some live in luxury while others have barely enought for bread....

DELEGATE SOWI: Here we had a Comrade Skrzydlowski. During eleven months, it is said, he was paid over 170,000 zlotys. Not as basic salary, of course, but from all sorts of bonuses. But all the evil is not at the bottom! Our manager is like an estate overseer in the interwar period....People frequently blame the party and the system for all of this....

DELEGATE W-4: The average income in our division is 2,600 zlotys for eight hours a day...2,600 or even 3,000 zlotys at the current prices amounts to very little, especially if one has three or four persons to support....This should be taken into account by those comrades from the Central Committee who are here today. It is necessary to understand the position of the people who earn so little—for what can they do? We have a saying: "When a Pole is hungry, he is angry"—hence the present upheaval. (Strong applause.) It stems directly from our dissatisfaction. (Applause.)

DELEGATE K-2: Many young people were killed [in the December rioting]—they were shot in the back. There is evidence of that. So many people were killed, so many people....People who were killed were put in nylon bags and buried like animals. This is true! Nothing can change this....

DELEGATE K-1: We are not going to count bodies, for it is difficult to count exactly how many fell on the streets. We were given the figure of 17 for Szczecin....Well, I am not going to contradict this, but I know there were more—for sure! For where bullets fly, people die. But it is sad that our hard-earned money paid for these very bullets which were used against us....How is it possible for the working class [i.e., the party] to turn against the working class?

DELEGATE W-2: I ask for a frank answer from the First Secretary of the Central Committee of the PUWP. Is it necessary to shed blood to change the Central Committee and the government? It is not possible to consider a fixed term of office in order to avoid a repetition of 1956 and 1970.

DELEGATE MAMOR....we demand that the guilty ones—both those who actually did the shooting and those who gave the orders to shoot the workers—be punished. (Applause.) Regardless of who they are or what positions they occupy....

DELEGATE K-3: We must give Comrade Gierek a chance....We must have confidence in him, as we had confidence in Gomulka. Except that the latter failed us....

DELEGATE W-4: The situation in our division is that everybody wants to continue the strike. Comrade Gierek, Comrade Jaroszewicz, your arguments did not convince the people from our division. Yet, after long and stormy discussion, we have come to the conclusion that alone we cannot continue the strike. We are ending the strike not because we think we should but because all the others are doing it. That's all.

DELEGATE MKP: We have to give the government a chance for a year or two...We must do it! If in a year or two there is no improvement, then we will say: Comrades, we were deceived.

CHAIRMAN OF THE STRIKE COMMITTEE: The strike is over! The strike is over! As of tomorrow the shipyard is back at work.

UNIDENTIFIED VOICE: Sorry, I would like to say something about those who will not report for work tomorrow. I would like to ask everybody to pay a tribute to their memory observing a minute of silence....(37 seconds of silence)

Problems of the Party

Below are statments made by members of the Central Committee of the Polish United Workers' Party at its Eighth Plenum, held February 6-7, 1971. The transcript was published in a special,undated issue of Nowe drogi *(Warsaw) which was distributed to a select group of party activists but later leaked to outside sources.*

WINCENTY KRASKO (Head of the Central Committee's Cultural Department): The tragedy of the December days is behind us, but the drama is not yet over. It goes on in the form of intense discussions in each factory, each village, in each Polish family. These are discussions full of pain and bitterness not only because of the confidence that was abused but, above all, because of the missed opportunities for quicker development of our country, the losses which could have been avoided, and the moral damage which Poland has suffered.

The [December] events signaled that our country was threatened with a serious disease. The brain of the party suffered from serious disorders.... There was a sharp contradiction between the intellectual and educational achievements of the people, and the anachronistic (not to use a stronger expression) working style of the leaders.... Their work was characterized by subjectivity, dilettantism, lack of systematic information, and insufficient preparation before making decisions.

ANDRZEJ WERBLAN (Head of the Department of Science and Education, Central Committee): We were faced with a situation in the party where the top political leaders remained too long—until their intellectual potentialities were totally exhausted, until they were totally unable to deal with new problems and were more and more inclined to make irrational decisions.

JAN OSSOWSKI (Member of the Central Planning Commission): The comrades from the former leadership cut themselves off from reality. They denied it. They did not understand the daily affairs of the working man. They did not know about his living conditions, the difficulties in getting to work, the lines at the shops, the shortages of goods, etc.

Poland Under Gierek: A New Political Style

HENRYK SZAFRANSKI (Secretary of the Warsaw Provincial Committee): For a long time one could sense that there was something terribly wrong with the party.... Doubts were repressed by using the authority of the Politburo and especially that of Comrade Gomulka... We got entangled in the mechanism of power which we ourselves had created. Authority became transformed into autocracy.

JOZEF CYRANKIEWICZ (Politburo Member, Chairman of the State Council, and former Premier): In the leadership of the party...there was almost complete decline the principle of collectivity....It was not possible to present one's views...at the meeting of the Politburo, for it only aroused the egotistic sensitivity of Gomulka and assailed his sense of authority....

MIECZYSLAW MOCZAR (Politburo Member and Secretary of the Central Committee): Comrade Wieslaw [Gomulka] ... was an autocrat. He could not stand independent people around him.... In such a situation, as usual, some "helpful" people emerged and they did "help" Wieslaw....[They] presented him with all sorts of statistics and tables, arguing that these were truths which only his enemies would contradict.

PIOTR JAROSZEWICZ (Premier): It is generally known and well documented that the former Economic Secretary of the Central Committee [Boleslaw Jaszczuk—Ed.], by exploiting the authority of the First Secretary and by referring to opinions and decisions which had been influenced by himself, interfered in all the activities of the government....

WIESLAW BEK (Head of the Central Committee's Press Department): Any critical remarks in the newspapers, even the most innocuous, if they contradicted the views of the people who had been responsible for the economic decisions, immediately aroused their nervousness. This was illustrated by the government decision, made in mid-October 1970, to stop supplying [the press with] essential information. This, in effect reduced the task of the journalists to the mere reiteration of the ideas...of the former leaders.

WLADYSLAW KRUCZEK(Politburo Member and Chairman of the Central Council of the Trade Unions): With the complete abandonment of the principles of socialist democracy within the party and the state, the trade unions played little part in the decisions affecting vital problems of the working people.

WLADYSLAW KOZDRA (First Secretary of the Lublin Provincial Committee): Among the many problems...which the political crisis revealed to the party and the nation, one is foremost in our minds: How to avoid tragic upheavals in the future. How to achieve an effective way to formulate and implement the best methods of development; how to create the conditions in which the party and the society, in a natural simple and obvious way, without pain, riots and upheavals, can select new leaders; how to ensure that the rights of the ruling class, the working class, are secure; and how to make certain that the constitutional rights of all citizens of People's Poland are observed. What sort of checks are needed to prevent the inherent tendencies of some individuals to restrict the process of collective decision-making and abuse democracy both within and without the party?

—translated by Adam Bromke

Footnotes

* Originally published in *The Problems of Communism*, September-October 1972.

1 Karol Malcuzynski, *Kultura* (Warsaw), April 4, 1971. For the evaluation of the situation in Poland at the time of Gierek's takeover see Stanislaw Staron, "The Winds of Change in Poland," *East Europe*, (New York), April 1971, pp. 2-10; A. Ross Johnson, "Polish Perspectives, Past and Present," *Problems of Communism* (Washington, DC), July-August 1971, pp. 59-72; and V. C. Chrypinski, "Poland," in Adam Bromke and Teresa Rakowska-Harmstone, Eds., *The Communist States in Disarray*, 1965-1971, Minneapolis, University of Minnesota Press, 1972, pp. 95-120.

2 For analysis of Gomulka's economic policies in the 1960's, see Stefan Markowski, "Mr. Gomulka's Legacy: The Roots of Dissent," *The World Today* (London), February 1971, pp. 56-67.

3 Quoted in Mieczyslaw F. Rakowski, "Perspektywa" *Polityka* (Warsaw) Feb. 13, 1972.

4 Feb. 19, 1971.

5 See comments by Jozef Cyrankiewicz and Mieczyslaw Moczar in *Nowe drogi* (Warsaw), special number [undated], pp. 208, 215. Circulation of this issue of the PUWP's theoretical monthly was limited to a select circle of party officials, although several copies have made their way to the West.

6 For early evaluation of Gierek's policies see Michael Costello, "Poland Today: Political Prospects," *Survey* (London), Summer 1971, pp. 53-73; Richard Davy, "Changing the Face of Polish Communism," *The Times* (London), May 25-26, 1971; Adam Bromke, "A Better Way of Life Comes to Poland," *The Globe and Mail* (Toronto), Dec. 1, 1971; and John J. Lenaghan, *The Limits to Freedom: Poland in World Affairs*, 1964-1972, Occasional Papers, School of International Affairs, Carleton University, Ottawa, May 1972.

7 *Zycie partii* (Warsaw), March 1972.

8 In fact only one, Wladyslaw Kruczek, belonged to the interwar Communist Party of Poland, whereas Gierek had been a member of the French, and then, Belgian Communist Party. In addition, Henryk Jablonski belonged to the prewar Polish Socialist Party.

9 Ryszard Strzelecki highlighted the contrast between the two types of background in his speech of self-defense at the Central Committee meeting in February 1971: "I have devoted all my life to the country and the party. I have served faithfully at a time when one could not count on the promotion from one armchair into another, but when the only reward was ... imprisonment, tortures or death." *Nowe drogi*, Special Number, pp. 145-46.

10 Indeed, as such the new elite is the first since the 18th century to reach the top in Poland through regular channels. The interwar elite based its claim to rule the country on participation in the struggle for Poland's independence during World War I.

11 "Rekonwalescencja", *Polityka*, Jan. 29, 1972.

12 "Vl Zjazd Polskiej Zjednoczonej Partii Robotniczej, Uchwala o dalszy socjalistyczny rozwoj Polskiej Rzeczypospolitej Ludowej," Warsaw, *Trybuna ludu*, December 1971. The 1971-75 plan was finally adopted in June 1972.

13 Natalia Swidzinska, *Polska lat siedemdziesiatych*, Warsaw, Ksiazka i Wiedza, 1972, p. 8.

14 See the speech of Jan Szydlak printed in *Tribuna ludu* (Warsaw), Oct. 14, 1971.

Poland Under Gierek: A New Political Style

15 In *Zycie Warszawy*, March 30, 1972.
16 "Procesy posytywne, nowy styl pracy, problemy do dyskusji" *Polityka*, Sept, 25, 1971.
17 Daniel Passent, "Jak pracuje rzad? Piatek, od dziesiatej do piatej", *ibid.*, Jan. 1, 1972.
18 In this respect Gierek proved to be even more secretive than Gomulka, for the deliberations of the Central Committee of October 19-21, 1956, reviewing the political crisis in the country of that year, had been published in the regular issue of the party monthly. See "VIII Plenum Komitetu Centralnego PZPR, 19-21, X, 1956 r." *Nowe drogi*, October 1956.
19 *Trybuna ludu*, Dec. 7, 1971. For a comprehensive account of the intellectual ferment in 1968 see two volumes of documents: *Wydarzenia marcowe*, 1968, and *Polskie przedwiosnie*, Paris, Instytut Literacki, 1969.
20 "Kompromis", *Tygodnik powszechny* (Cracow), Feb. 6, 1972.
21 *Trybuna ludu*, Feb. 6, 1972.
22 For a systematic review of political trials in 1971, see "Nowe procesy polityczne," *Kultura* (Paris), December 1971.
23 See the report of Tejchma to a plenary session of the *Sejm*, *Zycie Warszawy*, Feb. 14, 1971.
24 "Dobry fachowiec ale bezpartyjny," *Polityka*, July 3, 1971.
25 *Nowe drogi*, September 1971.
26 *Tygodnik powszechny*, April 14, 1972.
27 *Trybuna ludu*, Dec. 24, 1970.
28 *The Washington Post*, June 29, 1972.
29 *Trybuna ludu*, March 31, 1972.
30 *Ibid.*, Dec. 21, 1970.
31 S. K., "Zawsze blizej", *Polityka*, Jan. 16, 1971.
32 "Nasze funkcje europejskie", *Zycie Warszawy*, Jan. 17, 1971.
33 It is widely believed in Warsaw that Brezhnev's dislike of Gomulka, who at the international Communist meetings had bored the Soviet comrades with lectures on ideology, was probably one of the reasons for Moscow's signal lack of interest in the fate of the Polish leader in December 1970.
34 "Nasze miejsce w sojuszu", *Zycie Warszawy*, Jan. 26, 1971.
35 "Historyczne warianty i teranzniejszosc polityki polskiej", *ibid.*, Dec. 27, 1970.
36 It is interesting to note a significant difference between the Polish and Soviet interpretations of Bonn's obligations under the treaties. While the U.S.S.R. implicitly accepted the *Bundestag* resolution which held that the treaties do not prejudice the ultimate settlement of German boundaries at a peace conference, Poland made it clear that it regards the territorial settlement as final. Indeed, at the joint session of the Foreign Affairs and Legislative Committees of the *Sejm*, Foreign Minister Olszowski explicitly stated that "all of the reservations of the unilateral resolution of the *Bundestag* have no validity in international law." *Krajowa Agencja Informacyjna* (Warsaw), May 31, 1972.
37 Karol Malcuzynski, "Sukces i egzamin dojrzalosci", *Trybuna ludu*, May 21, 1972.
38 See, for example, articles by the editor of *The Economist*, Alastair Burnet, in *Polityka*, June 19, 1971, and by the present author in *Tygodnik powszechny*, Dec. 12, 1971.
39 *Trybuna ludu*, March 29, 1972.
40 *Krajowa Agencja Informacyjna*, April 12, 1972.
41 *The New York Times*, April 20. 1972.
42 *Ibid.*, June 2, 1972.
43 *Krajowa Agencja Informacyjna*, June 7, 1972.
44 Ryszard Wojna, "W kierunku wytyczonym porozunieniem moskiewskim", *Zycie Warszawy*, June 3, 1972.
45 Janusz Stefanowicz, "Wizyta wazna i owocna", *Slowo powszechne* (Warsaw), June 3, 1972.
46 A survey conducted by Radio Free Europe in late 1971 indicated that the division among the three groups was as follows: 39 per cent supporting the first view; 25 per cent the second; and 34 per cent the third. It is significant that a considerable difference was revealed in the attitudes of the different age groups, with the younger people displaying considerably more confidence in Gierek than the older ones. Radio Free Europe, Audience and Public Opinion Research Department, *Polish Confidence in Gierek*, Munich, December 1971.
47 "Chocholy", *Zycie Warszawy*, June 13, 1971.
48 "Kwasno", *Tygodnik powszechny*, Aug. 29, 1971.
49 *Rozwazania o Rzeczypospolitej*, Warsaw, Panstwowy Instytut Wydawniczy, 1971, pp. 98-99.
50 "Gory i doly", *Polityka*, May 29, 1971.

[51] Jan Szczepanski, *Polish Society*, New York, Random House, 1970, p. 75.
[52] Dec. 12, 1971.
[53] *Poland's Politics, Idealism vs. Realism*, Cambridge, Harvard University Press, 1967.
[54] Such a possibility was explicitly pointed out in a letter by a young listener from Poland to Radio Free Europe. Polish youth, he reports, "is rebelling against the order established by the PUWP.... Despite indoctrination in the schools, youth is looking for other ideals.... One can expect that in the next decade, when the influence of the present young generation increases, there will be serious upheavals in Poland." *Na antenie* (London), May 1972, p. 2.

V
A New Juncture in Poland

On October 13, 1975, shortly before the Seventh Congress of the Polish United Workers' Party (PUWP), Communist chief Edward Gierek visited the shipyards in Gdansk. It was a nostalgic visit, for it was there, in January of 1971, that he had faced rebellious workers as the newly appointed First Secretary of the PUWP and pleaded for their support of his program. This meeting was different: it was carefully staged, and its mood was joyful. One speaker after another hailed the successful completion of the 1971-75 Five-Year Plan and emphasized the substantial improvement in the Polish standard of living. They all heaped praise upon the First Secretary as a leader "closely bound up with the working class." In turn, Gierek promised further improvement in living conditions and urged the workers to intensify their efforts to meet the targets assigned to them by the party under the new Plan for 1976-80.[1]

There is no doubt that since 1971 there has been considerable economic progress in Poland. Yet on June 24, 1976, when new food price increases were announced, the workers once again promptly went on strike. The laborers from the Ursus tractor factory south of Warsaw blocked the railroad tracks, stopping trains to the capital, and in Radom there was widespread rioting. To avoid a bloody confrontation, perhaps more serious than that of December 1970, the Communist government backed down. In a terse television statement, Premier Piotr Jaroszewicz announced that the bill in question had been withdraw for further consideration.

The disturbances were barely over when the Communist Party staged a counteroffensive. In the next several days, massive rallies in support of the government policy were organized throughout the country. On June 28, more than 100,000 people demonstrated in Warsaw,[2] and on July 2 more than 200,000 people gathered to listen to speeches by Gierek and Jaroszewicz in Katowice. The latter assemblage was characterized by public media as a "powerful patriotic demonstration of trust in the party and state leadership."[3]

At the rallies, the demonstrators criticized the strikers and denounced the rioters as "firebrands and hooligans." The press claimed that there was "universal condemnation of those who had disturbed public order in Radom and Ursus"[4] and demanded that they be severely punished. Indeed, trials were soon staged for seven of the workers from Ursus and six from Radom. All were found guilty and were sentenced to terms of imprisonment ranging from three to ten years.

At the same time, the government stuck to its argument that food prices must be increased. In his speech in Katowice, Premier Jaroszewicz claimed that "the present structure of prices has become a barrier to further development." However, he did soften his statement by promising that the increases will be smaller than originally planned and will be introduced only after extensive consultation with the workers.[5]

In recent years, and especially since 1974, economic progress has slackened, and inflation has made inroads in Poland. The government thus had valid reasons for seeking to raise food prices, which had remained frozen since 1970. Yet it aggravated the impact of this highly unpopular decision by serious errors—both political and psychological—in its approach to the public. In a period when it needed the people's trust, the Gierek regime has managed to undermine its own credibility and has helped to create a climate of apprehension and stress in Poland.[6]

Gierek's blunder has been to develop a program that contains an inherent discrepancy between its economic and its political goals. He has not matched his economic pragmatism with political liberalization; if anything, in recent years there has been a return to doctrinal orthodoxy in Poland. Gierek has rightly acknowledged that an improvement in the standard of living represents an important stimulus to economic growth; however, he has failed to perceive that freedom also can contribute to creative economic activity. In this respect, he has very badly misjudged the Polish national character.

The present article will look at trends in the economic and political spheres that have led to the current tensions in Poland. Then it will weigh the country's prospects for the future.

Economic Pragmatism

Overall, Gierek's policies in the economic realm have been both innovative and practical. However they have also helped to create new economic problems which have intensified sharply in the last two years.

Ever since he came to power, the main thrust of Gierek's policies has been to promote Poland's economic growth and to improve the living conditions of the population.[7] Unlike his predecessor, Wladyslaw Gomulka, who concentrated on the former and ignored the latter, Gierek believes that advancement toward these two objectives should be simultaneous. In his eyes, a higher standard of living not only keeps the people contented but also induces them to work harder. In short, Gierek has rehabilitated the profit motive—although strictly within the limits of a socialist system—as a valuable stimulus to economic growth. He made his view clear at a party conference held toward the end of 1973:

The objective of our system is equality. Socialist equality means, above all, the equality of opportunity in life. Beyond that, the share of each citizen in the goods produced by the society must correspond to the quantity and quality of his work. Those who work better, who have higher qualifications and contribute more to the society, deserve greater moral and material satisfaction.[8]

A New Juncture in Poland

To promote these goals the Gierek government introduced two major innovations in the economic system[9]. First, a so-called "small economic reform" was adopted.[10] Unlike some of the economic experiments in other Communist countries, this reform did not aim at a modification of centralized planning and management; if anything, Warsaw's control over major industrial enterprises was strengthened. Central guidance , however, was combined with a greater scope for initiative in the key industries, in which the principle of the interrelationship of efficency and remuneration was established. In January 1973, this new system was introduced on an experimental basis in 28 industrial units responsible for 20 percent of national production. By mid-1974, units accounting for nearly half of Poland's industrial production had already adopted the new scheme, and it was still continuing to spread into many other branches of the national economy.[10]

Second, and once again in striking contrast to the Gomulka era, foreign trade was recognized as an important instrument of economic advance. A strategy of stimulating growth through imports was adopted to modernize Polish industry. To obtain modern technology, Poland turned primarily to the West. The Gierek government strove to expand trading relations with various Western countries and to obtain extensive credits from them. A temporary disequilibrium in Polish foreign trade in favor of imports was accepted, but it was hoped that with industrial progress Polish exports to the West would increase and that ultimately a balance would be restored.

Detente with the West

In developing economic relations with the West, Poland has used the overall climate of East-West détente as a protective umbrella. At every turn, the Poles have emphasized that they are following in the footsteps of their powerful eastern neighbor, and Gierek has never tired of proclaiming his unswerving loyalty both to the U.S.S.R. and to Brezhnev personally. Indeed, Poland has stayed safely within the limits of solidarity with the rest of the Communist bloc. But at the same time, Warsaw's relations with the various Western capitals have expanded beyond purely commercial contacts into cultural, dipomatic, and even political spheres.

Poland's interest in reducing East-West tensions in Europe was already evident under Gomulka; the Gierek regime's commitment to détente, if only because of the regime's economic program, has been beyond doubt. The Poles were in the forefront of the move to promote the Conference on European Security and Cooperation—which culminated in the summit meeting in Helsinki in July 1975—and they played a constructive role (although more as a matter of style than of substance) during the preceding intricate negotiations in Geneva.

Since 1970, Poland's relations with most of the West European countries have undergone substantial improvement. Warsaw's contacts with Paris have turned into what the Poles like to label a model of relations between countries with different socio-political systems. In October 1972, Gierek paid a visit to Paris, and in June 1975 President Valéry Giscard d'Estaing visited Warsaw. Close relations have also developed between Poland and the Scandinavian countries, especially Sweden, highlighted by Premier Olof Palme's trip to Warsaw in April 1974 and Gierek's return visit to Stockholm in June 1975. There has been noticeable improvement, too, in Poland's relations with Britain, Belgium, Austria, and several other countries in Western Europe. Last but not least, since the visit to Poland of Archbishop Agostino Casaroli early in 1974, working diplomatic contacts have been maintained between Warsaw and the Vatican through the regular exchange of diplomatic visits.

It has taken longer to improve Poland's relations with the Federal Republic of Germany (FRG), owing to the burden of some legacies of World War II. The Poles initially assumed a hard negotiating stance but subsequently showed considerable flexibility. Particularly thorny problems, having to do with the repatriation from Poland of ethnic Germans and indemnification by pensions of Poles who had worked during the war for German companies, were resolved in a personal meeting (stretching into the small hours of the morning) between Gierek and Chancellor Helmut Schmidt early in August 1975 during the summit in Helsinki. After the agreement was finally signed and ratified, Gierek paid a visit to West Germany in June 1976. To enhance the symbolic importance of the visit, Gierek stayed overnight at Schmidt's personal residence in Hamburg before proceeding to Bonn.

Polish-American relations took a dramatic turn for the better soon after Gierek came to power. In the spring of 1972, on his way back from a summit session in Moscow, U.S. President Richard Nixon stopped over in Warsaw. In October 1974 Gierek paid a visit to the United States, and in July 1975 Nixon's successor, President Gerald Ford, visited Poland. On all of these occasions, manifold agreements providing for broad cooperation between the two countries were concluded. Relations between Warsaw and Washington clearly went beyond purely businesslike contacts; the historic tradition of friendship between the two nations was emphasized by both sides.[12]

In its efforts to improve relations with the West, the Gierek regime did not ignore the Polish ethnic communities in the Western countries. Travel restrictions for people of Polish origin visiting Poland and for Poles visiting their relatives in the West were eased. The activities of the "Polonia Society," whose task is to maintain cultural contacts with Poles abroad, were considerably expanded. During his visits to France and the United States, Gierek paid tribute to the achievements of people of Polish background in those countries.

In general, détente with the West has paid off handsomely for Poland. Not only has foreign trade been dramatically expanded, but Warsaw has also obtained substantial Western credits. West Germany has become Poland's fourth trading partner, with France and Britain occupying the next two places. Polish commerce with the United States, which in the early 1970's was negligible, climbed to over $700 million in 1974. While economic cooperation with the Communist countries has been simultaneously advanced (in 1970-74, Polish-Soviet trade rose by approximately 50 percent), economic relations with the West have expanded even more rapidly. As a result, in 1970-74 the Comecon countries' share of Poland's trade was reduced from 63.2 to 47 percent, while that of the capitalist countries rose from 27 to 44.3 percent.[13]

One price which Poland has had to pay for its expansion of trade with the West is a serious imbalance between imports and exports. While in 1971-75 the former increased four times, the latter rose only two and a half times.[14] This gap, however, has been covered by Western credits, which in the period of recession were readily available and relatively inexpensive. In 1972, U.S. Export-Import Bank credits were granted to Poland. Since then the Poles have obtained many other government and private loans, by now totaling some $7 billion, from the United States and Western Europe.[15]

Economic Progress and Problems

In the first years after Gierek's assumption of power, his new economic policies brought about highly positive results. As early as 1971, there was a noticeable improvement in economic conditions, and in the next few years Poland underwent a veritable boom, unprecedented in the entire postwar period. Summing up the economic progress on the eve of the Seventh Congress, an editorial in the party daily *Trybuna ludu* boasted:

Never in the past have we achieved so much within such a short period of time. This is true of our efforts both to develop the material base of socialism and to improve living conditions in the society.[16]

In point of fact, Poland's rate of economic growth in the early 1970's was one of the highest in the world. During the 1971-75 Five-Year Plan, national income increased by about 60 percent (amounting to over $65 billion in 1975), and industrial production by over 70 percent.[17] The level of investments stayed very high, at about 20 percent a year. Some branches of Polish industry were completely modernized. About one-third of the industrial machinery is less than five years old. Equipment for entire factories was often acquired in the West.

During the plan period, there was also a marked improvement in living conditions. In the later years of the Gomulka regime, real wages had increased by 1.8 percent annually; by contrast, in 1971-75 they rose at an average of 8 percent a year. Throughout this entire period, the prices of basic foodstuffs remained frozen. The regime also made an effort to provide more and better consumer goods. Production in the consumer sector increased by 79 percent over five years, and additional goods, including Western items, were imported from abroad. Gierek's belief that an improved standard of living should accelerate economic growth was apparently confirmed: 70 percent of the increase in wages in the plan period was attributed to higher labor productivity under the new economic system—although there is little doubt that improved technology, imported from the West, also played a key role in the upswing.

Not only was full employment maintained during the entire period, but close to three million young people were absorbed into the economy. Various social services were expanded. Old-age pensions were increased, maternity leaves were extended, and free medical services were offered to 6.5 million people in the countryside. All in all, these were impressive results— in many respects, they even exceeded the original targets of the 1971-75 Plan.

Yet, at the same time—especially since 1974—there has been evidence of mounting economic problems and consequent growing dissatisfaction among the Polish people. These economic difficulties have not been unexpected. To a large extent, they stem from the very success of Gierek's policies. The greater interaction with the West has made Poland more vulnerable to changing trends in the world economy, and the dynamic growth of earnings has brought about inflation and severe market dislocations.

Since 1974, several developments in the world economy have adversely affected Poland. Inflation in the West has increased the price of imports, while the simultaneous recession has reduced the demand there for Polish exports, making it more difficult for Poland to close the gap between the two. Moreover, Poland's indebtedness has already reached a relatively high level. To make matters worse, the oil crisis in 1973 led the Soviet Union drastically to increase the price of crude oil, which hitherto had been available to the Comecon countries at preferential rates.

The spillover of Western inflation into Poland has aggravated the already severe inflationary tendencies created by the discrepancy between rapidly rising incomes and an insufficient quantity of consumer goods. In 1974 and again in 1975, agriculture—already lagging badly behind industry (in 1971-75 agricultural production increased by only 27 percent)—was hit by severe droughts. Serious shortages of food, and especially of meat, ensued.

To compound the Poles' frustrations, a housing shortage has continued unabated. There are at present some one and a half million families without their own separate dwelling space, and with the postwar generation reaching marriageable age, the situation is becoming even more acute.[18] The waiting period before obtaining one's own apartment is frequently ten years. The fortunate people who finally get their own place to live still have to wait for furniture. With the drastic gasoline price increases of 1974, the dream of early motorization—which in 1971 Gierek had enticingly dangled before the Poles—also largely faded away.

The short-lived economic boom in the early 1970's produced a climate of rising expectations in the country. The Poles believed that they would not only maintain their newly-won prosperity but improve it. When this did not happen, the credibility of the Gierek government increasingly came into question. The situation has been made worse by the postures struck in domestic propaganda. On the one hand, economic difficulties have been minimized. Inflation has been blamed on fluctuations in world prices, and its rate of increase under-reported at 2-3 percent a year, while shortages of food have been explained away as a consequence of temporary bad weather conditions.[19] On the other hand, economic achievements have been exaggerated beyond all reality. In the mass media, the PUWP has been touted as a force capable of building "the second Poland" (in the sense of doubling the country's national capital), and Gierek has emerged as a veritable superman who could cope with any adversity.

In the new economic plan for the remainder of the 1970's, which was announced at the Seventh Party Congress in December 1975, the policies and priorities of the past five years continue basically unchanged. Yet, significantly, among the targets which are to be scaled down, the most substantially reduced are wage increases, which in 1976-80 are to be only half as great as in 1971-75.[20]

Under these circumstances the population's frustration has increasingly manifested itself in open demonstrations of discontent. In the summer of 1974, there were labor disturbances among the dockers in Gdynia, and in the fall of the same year, there were reports of unrest among the miners in Katowice. In the spring of 1975, exasperated housewives demolished a grocery store in Warsaw.[21] And in the autumn, when a series of fires broke out in the capital, rumors of arson by a mysterious anti-Gierek group were widely circulated. The outbreaks in June 1976 suggest the volatile nature of the tensions that continue to mark the atmosphere in Poland today.

Gierek's Consolidation of Power

In the political domain, Gierek has sought to consolidate his power and has pursued a vigorous program to promote ideological conformity and firm allegiance to the Soviet line, both within party ranks and in Polish society at large. While he has succeeded in establishing his supreme authority in the top echelons of the PUWP and in streamlining the middle levels of the party organization to assure adherence to his leadership, his efforts to impose ideological orthodoxy and his pro-Soviet policies have provoked controversy and strong opposition. The latter in particular have worked to the regime's disadvantage in relations with key elements in Polish society, most notably the intellectuals and the Catholic Church.

To turn first to party developments, the recent Seventh Congress, held

December 8-12, 1975, confirmed Gierek's dominant position in the PUWP. From the beginning to the end of its proceedings, the First Secretary occupied a central role, and his leadership was hailed by many speakers. Gierek also received warm praise for his achievements from Leonid Brezhnev, who came to Warsaw for the occasion.[22] In contrast to the Sixth Congress in 1971, when many former supporters of Wladyslaw Gomulka and of ex-security chief Mieczyslaw Moczar had to be eliminated, there were few changes in the top echelons of the PUWP.

The only significant exception was the removal from the Politburo of Franciszek Szlachcic, a final step in the eclipse of a man who earlier seemed to pose a potential challenge to the party chief. Szlachcic, as Minister of Interior, had helped Gierek to consolidate his position during the political crisis in 1970-71 and had been rewarded with seats on both the Politburo and the Secretariat at the Sixth Congress. An intelligent and dynamic person, Szlachcic soon emerged as one of the key figures in the Communist leadership. Perhaps to compensate for his security background, he assumed a relatively liberal stance, cultivating connections with intellectual circles and letting it be known that he might advocate Poland's greater autonomy from the U.S.S.R. At the same time, through political patronage, he nourished his own base in the party and the administration.

In 1974 the leadership moved against Szlachcic, and his fall from power was swift. From February onward, he largely disappeared from public view, and in June he was shifted from the Party Secretariat to a relatively insignificant position as one of several deputy premiers. After his removal from the Politburo he was also dropped from the government and has since been relegated to complete obscurity. Meanwhile, an extensive purge of Szlachcic's supporters (The "Franciscans," as they were called in Poland) has been conducted in the administration, especially in the security apparatus.

In the present leadership, Gierek's supreme position is clearly unchallenged. There is no one who stands out as his deputy; instead, the responsibility for political decisions is divided among several individuals. The "inner" leadership is composed of five persons: Gierek; the three other Politburo members who, like him, combine this position with a seat on the Secretariat—Edward Babiuch, Jan Szydlak, and Stanislaw Kania; and Premier Piotr Jaroszewicz. Their authority is in many respects interlocking. Babiuch, who is in charge of party affairs, is responsible directly to Gierek. Szydlak is entrusted with the overall supervision of the government on behalf of the PUWP. Kania has responsiblity for security affairs, although the present Minister of the Interior, Stanislaw Kowalczyk, is likewise a full member of the Politburo.

The diffusion of authority immediately under Gierek was reflected in decisions at the Seventh Congress expanding the size of the Politburo from fourteen members (eleven full members and three candidates) to seventeen (fourteen full members and three candidates). The Central Committee was also expanded to increase the number of full members from 115 to 140 and of deputy members from 93 to 111.[23] The Committee is now predominantly filled with men who can be presumed to be Gierek loyalists. Close to three-fourths of the full members and almost all of the deputy members have been elected since his rise (i.e., in 1971 or 1975). The province of Katowice, where Gierek served for many years as provincial secretary, is particularly well represented on the Central Committee—topped only by Warsaw, where many CC members are from the party's central apparatus.

In advance of the Seventh Congress, the Gierek leadership also acted to bring the middle ranks of the PUWP under more effective control. A reform of the territorial administration in the spring of 1975 provided the opportunity for a drastic shake-up of party personnel at the district and provincial levels. The districts were altogether eliminated, while the provinces—which have often been the power bases of ambitious local secretaries—were increased in number from 17 to 46.[24] The obvious aim of the new two-tier organization is to make the party apparatus more responsive to the center.

Thus, in contrast to the 1960's and even the early 1970's when the PUWP was repeatedly torn apart by factional struggles, Gierek has largely restored party unity. At present, there are no visible groups in the PUWP which could pose a challenge to his authority, and as long as the country stays calm, there is little chance that any will arise. However, the situation could change overnight in the event of a major crisis, since the consolidation of the party has been imposed artificially from the top and since many of the First Secretary's former opponents are still around.

The Ideological Offensive

Gierek's ventures in the ideological realm have been something of a surprise. When he came to power, his image in the eyes of the Poles—an image he had gained as the successful Secretary of the industrial province of Katowice— was that of an able administrator. At the same time, he was know for his paternalistic—if not autocratic—political style, and he was generally not expected to undertake any major liberalization. However, the Poles did hope that his economic pragmatism might spill over into the cultural sphere, in that while carrying out his economic program he would probably deem it expedient to avoid confrontations over ideology. Indeed, in the first few years of Gierek's rule it appeared that a compromise along those lines was feasible. A fragile, but nevertheless real, *modus vivendi* was worked out by the party with Poland's intellectuals as well as with the Catholic Church, and at least for a time some degree of pluralism of opinions was tolerated.

As soon as Gierek established his dominant position in the Communist Party, however, he began moving toward greater ideological conformity. The political indoctrination of PUWP members was gradually accelerated.

In 1971, the Higher School of Social Sciences, attached to the Central Committee and responsible for the training of party cadres, was reorganized to expand its program.[25] At the lower levels of the party, political education was also stepped up. By the end of 1972, out of 125,000 members of the Warsaw party organization, 80,000 were undergoing some part-time political training.[26]

In this revived ideological activity, special attention was paid to the role of U.S.S.R. The Soviet Union was presented in PUWP propaganda as a leader of the socialist commonwealth whose experience should be emulated by all the Communist countries. As East-West détente progressed, Poland's close attachment to its powerful neighbor was repeatedly and ostentatiously emphasized. Gierek himself set the tone. In an address at the Kremlin on the 50th anniversary of the U.S.S.R., he declared:

> *Our most important task is to strenthen ideological and political unity with the CPSU and with the Soviet state.... The international position and future prospects of People's Poland are inseparably linked to our alliance and friendship with the Soviet Union, which...is the keystone of our ideological education and the chief element in the thinking of the majority of our citizens.*
>
> *Solving the present era's most significant problem—the question of war or peace—is closely linked with the historical experiences and the leading role of the Soviet Union and with the great personal contribution made by the CPSU's leader, Comrade Leonid Brezhnev.*[27]

There was little surprise, then, when—soon after a conference in Moscow of the East European party secretaries for ideological affairs in December 1973—a so-called "ideological offensive" was launched in Poland. In February 1974 a new Institute for Basic Problems of Marxism-Leninism, attached to the PUWP Central Committee, was established under the direction of the ideologist Andrzej Werblan, who was simultaneously promoted to the rank of Party Secretary. The Institute's task was to develop the theory of Marxism-Leninism with particular reference to "socialist construction" in Poland.[28]

In March 1974, a national conference of ideological activists was convened in Warsaw. In his keynote address, Politburo member Jan Szydlak hammered out the theme that East-West détente does not reduce but, on the contrary, intensifies ideological conflict:

> *Peaceful coexistence cannot be identified with the termination of class struggle, either now or in the future. It does not remove the antagonistic contradictions between socialism and capitalism. It is a form of class struggle, a form of historical strife between socialism and capitalism in many different spheres.... Under conditions of peaceful*

coexistence the significance of ideological struggle increases considerably, and its outcome will more than ever affect the nature and the rate of social transformation.[28]

The "ideological offensive" of the PUWP, according to Szydlak, should have two major objectives. On the one hand, it should "present Poland as an integral part of the socialist commonwealth, inseparably linked by ideology, alliance, and many-sided cooperation with the U.S.S.R."; on the other hand, it should "unmask the false image of capitalism by revealing its internal contradictions and the many manifestations of its advancing crisis." Szydlak criticized academe as well as the mass media for not following these precepts. He castigated the historians for trying to rehabilitate bourgeois political movements while not paying enough attention to the achievements of the Communist Party; and he chided the social scientists for not resisting—and for even espousing—Western ideas.

Szydlak reserved a particularly vicious denounciation for what he called the "reactionary" core of the Catholic Church:

The main organized anti-socialist power in our country, a veritable center uniting all the anti-state currents while at the same time representing their last hope, is the reactionary wing of the Episcopate deriving its support from the institutional structure of the Roman Catholic Church. It is the only center of social rightist forces which has at its disposal a coherent philosophic outlook, a strong organizational base and numerous cadres....Its political strategy is aimed above all, at exploiting our difficulties and failures.[30]

A Countertide of Protest

As the party's "ideological offensive" gathered momentum, its relations with intellectual circles deteriorated. The intellectuals not only refused to be intimidated but more and more often resorted to open defiance of the Communist authorities. Despite valiant efforts made by the Minister of Culture Jozef Tejchma, one of the moderate Politburo members, to mitigate the conflict, the situation soon went from bad to worse.

The ferment in the intellectual milieu first came into the open toward the end of 1974. In a petition addressed to Tejchma, written by the noted poet Antoni Slonimski and signed by fifteen well-known writers, scholars, and artists, the sensitive issue of the fate of Poles in the Soviet Union was raised. The signatories argued that parallel with the expansion of relations with the Polish communities in the West, contacts should be estasblished with Poles in the U.S.S.R. The petition also demanded freedom of culture, education, and religion for the Soviet Poles.[31] The Communist authorities responded with petty administrative measures against some of the signatories but otherwise refrained from confrontation over this highly sensitive issue. Indeed, in November 1975, on the occation of Slonimski's 80th birthday, Tejchma ostentatiously sent him a congratulatory message.[32]

In September 1975, a letter by the popular Catholic writer, Stefan Kisielewski, bitterly denouncing the restrictions imposed on the study of history in Poland appeared in the émigré historical quarterly *Zeszyty Historyczne*, published in Paris. Kisielewski gave many specific examples of books on Polish modern history which had been either banned for publication or substantially revised by the censors. He ironically observed that the ban extended to many episodes in the history of the Polish Communist Party—nothing could even be said, for instance, about Wladyslaw Gomulka! Kisielewski concluded that for all practical intents and purposes,

> *...the study of recent Polish history is nonexistent. In its place there is a superficial and one-sided compilation, artificially put together,... geared to political propaganda, and exclusively serving to mold the minds of the students in a way desired by the party. The speciality of our system, as Orwell envisaged it, is history in the service of politics, adjusted and transmuted backward.*[33]

The Catholic Church was not silent either. In a series of sermons delivered in 1974, Stefan Cardinal Wyszynski castigated various aspects of the Gierek regime's policies.[34] The Primate of Poland complained about obstacles impeding the creation of new churches and decried incidents in which the Communist authorities had closed down provisional chapels. He voiced concern that a planned reform of education did not provide sufficent room for religious instruction. He also criticized the amalgamation of all youth organizations into a single union of Polish Socialist Youth directly subordinate to the PUWP.

The Polish Primate did not restrict himself to religious matters but touched upon political issues as well. He asserted that in view of the role which the Church had played for over 1,000 years in Poland's history, it was entitled to voice concern over crucial problems affecting the nation's future. He demanded respect from the Communist government for several basic democratic freedoms:

> *A wise organization of society precludes application everywhere of the same narrow schemata; on the contrary, it provides the opportunity for free and unrestrained activity by various social groups and strata.... This requires a courageous defense of the right to free association as well as the rights to freedom of the press, expression of opinion, and unrestrained scientific research....*[35]

Cardinal Wyszynski also challenged Communist claims of the identity of Poland's interests with those of the Soviet Union. In a passionately patriotic sermon, he declared:

For us, next to God, our first love is Poland. After God one must above all remain faithful to our Homeland, to the Polish national culture. We will love all the people in the world, but only in such an order of priorities.

And if we see everywhere slogans advocating love for all the peoples and all the nations, we do not oppose them; yet above all we demand the right to live in accordance with the spirit, history, culture, and language of our own Polish land—the same which have been used by our ancestors for centuries.[36]

By 1975 the Gierek regime was clearly on a collision course with both the intellectuals and the Catholic hierarchy. The former climate of moderation had largely evaporated, and the stakes were increasing on both sides. It was not surprising, therefore, that when the PUWP came out with a proposal to amend the country's Constitution—ostensibly to bring it more into line with advanced "socialist construction"—the opposition took on the government directly.

The Constitutional Conflict

The regime's intention to change the Constitution was first publicly announced in the "Guidelines" for the Seventh PUWP Congress, published in October 1975. The document referred to the need to affirm the socialist character of the Polish state, which it defined as "derived from the same class-revolutionary principles which originally triumphed in the Great October Socialist Revolution."[37] On December 19, 1975, Edward Babiuch revealed in the *Sejm* (the Polish parliament) that the amendments would also enumerate the basic principles of Poland's foreign policy and, above all, its "unshakable fraternal bond with the Soviet Union."[38]

The first reaction came even before the text of the proposed amendments was made public. On December 5, a group of 59 intellectuals, led by the respected senior economist Professor Edward Lipinski, sent a petition to the *Sejm* elaborating the principles which they felt should be included in the new Constitution. The memorandum, which invoked the Helsinki Declaration in support, amounted to a plea for the restoration of democratic liberties. It stopped short of endorsing a multiparty system and free elections, but it called for freedom of conscience and religion, freedom to work, freedom of expression and information, and freedom of scholarly pursuit and learning. Among specific proposals, it advocated admission of people with religious beliefs into all state positions, independence for the trade unions, the abolition of censorship, and autonomy for the universities.[39]

The petition of the 59 was followed by a veritable flood of protests. Several hundred people of all ages and from all walks of life—writers, scholars, artists, soldiers, priests, and lawyers—publicly expressed their support, in the form of open letters addressed to the *Sejm*. When the text of the proposed constitutional revisions was made available, new protests against its formulation on Polish-Soviet relations took place. A proposal to have the leading role of the Communist Party enshrined in the Constitution and a clause making citizens' rights contingent upon fulfillment of their duties came under especially heavy fire. In January 1976, Cardinal Wyszynski threw his enormous authority behind the dissenters and in three Warsaw sermons voiced strong concern over the proposed constitutional changes.

The Communist leaders were clearly taken aback by the strength of the opposition. The government's official spokesman, Wlodzimierz Janiurek, tried to minimize the amount of protest by claiming that 90 percent of the people supported the constitutional changes (by Communist standards, this less-than-unanimous figure was an unusual admission in itself).[40] Nevertheless, in response to popular presure the party backed down. The Constitutional Committee of the *Sejm* modified the amendments by removing several particularly objectionable phrases. In the next text, Poland was still defined as a socialist state; however, no reference was made to its similarity with the U.S.S.R., and the name of "Polish People's Republic" was retained.[41] The controversial phrase about the "unshakable fraternal bond" with the Soviet Union was eliminated in favor of a watered down statement that "Poland strengthens its friendship and cooperation with the Soviet Union and other socialist states." The PUWP was acknowledged as a "leading political force in society in the construction of socialism," but it was not given any formal role in the state. The linking of citizen's rights and duties was dropped altogether; indeed, a clause explicitly providing for the possibility of participation by people with religious beliefs in the Front of National Unity was added. Still, when the constitutional amendments were submitted for approval by the *Sejm* on February 10, the leader of the Catholic Znak group, Professor Stanislaw Stomma, abstained from voting.

The Communist leaders had met the opposition halfway, but it was a grudging compromise. Once again, administrative measures were applied against some signatories of the petitions, and Professor Stomma was ostentatiously omitted from the list of candidates for the new parliament. Gierek himself did not conceal his irritation over the protest. At a conference with Polish journalists, he characterized the petition of the 59 as "...a miserable attempt to revive obsolete Polish bourgeois concepts...and to try to apply long-dead ideas to a new era."[42]

A New Juncture in Poland

Continuing Ferment

The Communists' lack of grace in conceding their defeat only widened the chasm between the PUWP and the opposition and led to still further polemics. In April 1976, the Episcopate issued a tersely-worded communique elaborating its position on the recently enacted constitutional changes. The communique, pointing to the Helsinki Declaration, strongly endorsed both the principle of respect for human rights and the principle of the right to national self-determination. It also explicitly cautioned the Communist authorities not to use sanctions against signers of the various protests.[43]

In an open letter addressed to Gierek, Professor Lipinski answered the First Secretary's charges against the signatories of the appeal of the 59. As a veteran socialist, Lipinski asserted that he had a right to be concerned about the nature of socialism in Poland. Declaring himself in favor of the pluralistic model of socialism espoused by the Italian and the French Communists, he repudiated the Soviet totalitarian model as incompatible with Polish democratic traditions. The old professor did not mince words in describing the negative aspects of Soviet influence on Poland:

> The imposition of the Soviet system has devastated our social and moral life. It represents a great misfortune in the history of the nation. We are being compelled to support Soviet foreign policy unconditionally, and we have ceased to be an independent element in world politics. This is often contrary to Polish national interests. We took part in the military invasion of Czechoslovakia, helping to suppress the process of renewal in that country at the very time when it was emancipating itself from Soviet influence....
>
> Today there is no more important goal for Poland then the reassertion of its sovereignty. Only after regaining political independence will it be possible to undertake systematic economic reform and to restructure the political and social system, which will release the creative potential of the nation.[44]

Another open letter to the Communist leadership, highly critical of the constitutional changes, came from Wladyslaw Bienkowski. Bienkowski is a veteran Communist and was a close collaborator of Gomulka until the late 1950's when he resigned from the PUWP and subsequently wrote several books critical of various aspects of the political system in Poland. Never in the past, however, had he been so outspoken in his denunciation of Soviet interference in Polish domestic affairs. In a direct attack on the Soviet Ambassador in Warsaw, Stanislaw Pilotowicz, Bienkowski compared the present situation with that which existed in Polish-Russion relations toward the end of the 18th century, just before Poland's final partitioning:

*We have our own censors, but...the position of main censor is now
occupied by the representative of the Soviet Union in Poland, whose
main function, it seems, is to oversee the ideological purity of the allied
country. He does not even conceal his mission and often intervenes
personally. Under his pressure, books are refused publication, and
books which have already been published...are withdrawn from
circulation. In historical works entire sections are deleted, even when
they deal with long-ago Polish Russian relations—as if the Soviet
authorities identified themselves with policies of the Russian Tsars. It
closely resembles the situation of two centuries ago, when, in a still
independent Poland, the representative of the Russian Empress acted
as a de facto governor and with the assistance of corrupted elements
and the support of the Russian army...suppressed any attempt at
renewal in the country.*[45]

Dissident opinion of a more radical nature is reflected in an interesting
document which has recently been circulated in Poland in *samizdat* form—
the Program of the Polish Coalition for Independence. It goes beyond
anything that has emanated from opposition circles in the past in that it is
issued in the name of an organized political group (though its members are
not identified) and proposes a totally different alternative to Poland's
present political and economic system.

The program asserts that the Communist leaders are not interested in
cooperation with Polish society but simply manipulate the people to stay in
power. It calls for resolute opposition to communism and advocates the
restoration of parliamentary democracy and at least a partial return to
capitalism. The anonymous authors have no illusions that their objectives
can be accomplished immediately, but they claim that the Communist
countries, including the U.S.S.R., are already in the throes of a grave crisis
They write:

*It is impossible to anticipate when the crisis will come into the
open....[But it] may begin in Poland. We must be ready for this, and
consequently we should be conscious not only of what we reject, but
also of what we want to accomplish....*

*The opposition must not be reduced to mere grumbling and
gossiping. We must at all times be prepared with alternative plans and
goals. This is above all the duty of the Polish intelligentsia, which
historically has been burdened with responsibility for the spiritual
fortunes of our nation. It is also the task of the most numerous social
group, namely, the industrial workers, who command the greatest
power.*[46]

Parallels and Portents

The confrontation between the government and the workers in June 1976

78

gravely deepened the political crisis in Poland. Ironically, its scenario was somewhat similar to the upheaval in 1970. Gomulka had raised prices shortly after his great success in foreign policy—the visit to Warsaw by the then West German Chancellor, Willy Brandt; Gierek took the same step soon after his triumphant visit to Bonn. In one important respect, however, Gierek's position is worse than that of Gomulka. The intellectuals came out openly against Gomulka in March 1968, but at that time the workers remained passive. Conversely, when the workers struck in December 1970, the intellectuals were taken by surprise and played no role in the crisis whatsoever. By contrast, in the present situation both intellectual circles and the working class are opposing Gierek's policies.

In comparison with Gomulka, Gierek has been handicapped from the very start. When Gomulka came to power in 1956, he enjoyed considerable prestige among the Poles for his opposition to Stalinism, while Gierek in 1970 has no such record to his credit. Also, the Poles' eventual disillusionment with Gomulka made them more reserved toward his successor. In January 1971, the rebellious Szczecin workers told Gierek this to his face:

> We must give Comrade Gierek a chance....We must have confidence in him, as we had confidence in Gomulka. Except that the latter failed us...
> We have to give the government a chance for a year or two...we must do it! If in a year or two there is no improvement, then we will say: Comrades, we were deceived.

In 1956, the mood of the Poles was one of political realism. The memories of their immense but futile losses during World War II was fresh in their minds, and they were wary of staging another costly revolt. Thus, they eagerly embraced the compromise offered by Gomulka—which gave them at least a modicum of freedom after years of Stalinist oppression. The present mood of the Poles is different; they have shifted markedly toward political idealism. The losses wreaked by the war have been made up, and today the members of the young generation are no longer under the defeatist spell of the 1940's. They are more assertive and impatient. The spontaneous reaction of a major segment of the workers to the recent price increases clearly illustrated this. By taking to the streets in 1956, the workers brought Gomulka to power, and in 1970 they overthrew him. At present, the workers seem to be confident that they can depose Gierek in the same fashion. The government's prompt retreat from food price increases probably only confirmed them in this conviction.

When he came to power in 1970, Gierek tried to play his own game. He cultivated his image as an able administrator. He gave his first attention to economic progress. His objective, it seems, was to buy the workers' political acquiescence with an improvement in their standard of living. Yet, economic progress produced other results. It helped increase the Poles' confidence, and it intensified their economic as well as their political demands.

With the first sign of economic difficulties in 1974, Gierek abandoned his earlier stance and tried to overcome the crisis by political means. He sought to arouse the workers to greater efforts by a renewed stress on Communist propaganda. Yet, by resorting to practices which had been thoroughly compromised under Gomulka, Gierek damaged his credibility even more. Soon the country was caught up in a vicious descending spiral. The more popular dissatisfaction the Communists encountered, the more they intensified their proaganda drive; and the wider the gap between the slogans and the existing facts became, the less authority the PUWP commanded.

Since the confrontation in June, there has been an impasse between the Communist government and the workers. Sooner or later, for economic reasons, food prices will have to be increased. This however, is likely to lead to new strikes and conceivably even to a large-scale workers' rebellion. Resolving the conflict by replacing one Communist leader with another might be difficult, for at present there are no figures in the top echelon of the PUWP who enjoy a stature comparable to that of Gomulka in 1956 or even to that of Gierek in 1970. Yet crushing a rebellion by force—if it could be done at all—would compromise the PUWP even more. At the same time, it would disrupt economic progress and worsen the workers' plight. It would also adversely affect Poland's cooperation with the West, which is crucial to the country's progress.

The intellectuals and the Catholic leaders are well aware of the dangers inherent in the present situation. They watch the government's impasse with the workers with a certain *Schadenfreude* (a mixture of sorrow and satisfaction), but they would not like to see the situation deteriorate to the point of no return. Most of them have not forgotten the lesson of Czechoslovakia in 1968. The Program of the Polish Coalition for Independence does not seem to represent the views of the general intellectual milieu, for most intellectuals appear to believe that in Poland's present position democracy and capitalism are unrealistic goals. Yet, there is no question that more and more of the intellectuals have been pushed to embrace extreme positions. Their mood of frustration seems to have deepened into one of desperation.

In the last few years Polish society has thus become larely polarized, with emotions on both sides running high. The parallel escalation of demands has made compromise increasingly difficult, and it seems very possible that a major explosion threatens. By 1976, the situation in the country has come dangerously close to the pessimistic prediction offered two years ago by Professor Jan Szczepanski:

Polish politics is governed by emotions. We still believe that

A New Juncture in Poland

development of the country is a function of patriotic involvement, devotion, readiness to sacrifice, etc., and in education and propaganda we emphasize emotions.... This is playing with fire, for aroused emotions often can product quite unexpected results.

The basic question is whether our society will have enough determination to continue the efforts undertaken in 1971...or whether it is going to be carried away by the emotional traditions which worked with such regularity in our history....

The Test of Helsinki

The Poles' more assertive mood has been reflected not only in domestic developments but also in their attitude toward foreign relations. They have been pleased by the expansion of Poland's contacts with the West; Gierek's exchange of visits with various Western statesmen has undoubtedly enhanced his prestige at home. However, many Poles also hoped that in the climate of international détente they would be able to improve their position vis-à-vis the Soviet Union. They would have liked the Helsinki Declaration's provisions for noninterference in domestic affairs to apply to Polish-Soviet relations. Yet, since 1971 the trend has been in the opposite direction. As if to compensate for his expanded contacts with the West, Gierek has gone out of his way to demonstrate his unconditional loyalty to the Kremlin.

Warsaw undoubtedly was put under pressure by Moscow to conform with the general ideological tightening in the Soviet bloc in the wake of East-West détente. But Gierek apparently needed no urging. His repeated discourses about Poland's unshakable bonds with the U.S.S.R. and his profuse praise of the CPSU and of Brezhnev personally have gone far beyond what is expected of a loyal ally. His statements have annoyed the Poles no end and have become the object of widespread scorn in the country. Soviet Ambassador Pilotowicz's overbearing behavior has only added insult to injury. In such a climate, the proposal to enshrine Poland's subordinate position with respect to the Soviet Union in the Polish Constitution was viewed by many Poles with genuine alarm. They regarded it as a first step toward incorporation of the Polish People's Republic into the Union of Soviet Socialist Republics.

The Poles are well aware of the necessity of maintaining good relations with the U.S.S.R.; however, they want Poland to be Russia's ally, not its satellite—even less a Soviet republic.[48] A popular saying in Warsaw, attributed to disgraced Communist leader Franciszek Szlachcic, has it that Polish-Soviet friendship should be like "good Russian tea—strong, warm, but not too sweet." It is important to remember that several leading figures now in the ranks of the opposition—notably, Stomma, Slonimski, Bienkowski, and Kisielewski—have been known in the past as strong supporters of the Polish-Soviet alliance. They were driven to their present positions by sheer dismay. Instead of a gradual improvement in Poland's position vis-à-vis Russia, they have seen a steady deterioration—even as compared to the Gomulka era.

The Polish people have no illusions about the prospects of any assistance from the West should a crisis develop. Among all the various documents emanating from opposition circles, not a single one anticipated direct Western support for Poland. The Poles do expect, however, that the climate of East-West détente will have a restraining influence on Moscow, reducing the chances of Soviet intervention. They also hope that the prospect of criticism from the influential Italian and French Communist parties—who were openly indignant over the Soviet invasion of Czechoslovakia in 1968—will be a similiar deterrent to rash action on Moscow's part. While these attitudes seem realistic enough, many Poles have a distorted picture of the internal situation in the U.S.S.R. Under the influence of the Western media and émigré publications, they tend to exaggerate the impact of the Soviet dissidents, and many even seem to believe that a major upheaval is imminent in that country.

The growing divergence between internal and external trends in Poland is potentially threatening to détente in Europe. Should the internal political situation culminate in an open rebellion, the Polish Communist regime might be unable to cope on its own and might turn to Moscow for assistance. Yet Soviet military intervention, which would almost certainly encounter armed resistance in Poland, would doubtless be viewed by the West as a flagrant violation of the Helsinki Declaration. The last several years of painstaking progress in East-West relations would thus be gravely imperiled.

The tug-of-war between the Communist regime and the Polish people has by now gone on for a generation. The latest workers' strikes occurred almost twenty years to the date after the "Black Thursday" in Poznan on June 28, 1956. There were popular upheavals in Poland in 1968 and again in 1970. Today the Polish people are in a more assertive mood than ever before, and the present confrontation—unless handled with great caution— could evolve into a more acute crisis than those in the past.

Footnotes

* Originally published in *The Problems of Communism*, September-October 1976.
1   Radio Warsaw, Oct. 17, 1975.
2   *Trybuna ludu*, (Warsaw), June 29, 1976.
3   Radio Warsaw, July 2, 1976.
4   *Slowo powszechne* (Warsaw), June 20, 1976.
5   Radio Warsaw, July 2, 1976.
6   For an analysis of the situation in Poland in the fall of 1975, see Thomas E. Heneghan, "Poland on the Eve of the Seventh Party Congress," *Radio Free Europe Research* (Munich), Dec. 3, 1976.
7   For evaluation of early Gierek policies, see Adam Bromke, "Poland Under Gierek: A New Political Style," *Problems of Communism* (Washington, DC), September-October 1972; and M. K. Dziewanowski, *The Communist Party of Poland*, 2nd ed., Cambridge, Mass., Harvard University Press, 1976, Chap. 17.

8 *Trybuna ludu*, Dec. 10, 1973.

9 In addition to substantial revision of agricultural policy which is discussed in the previous paper.

10 For an analysis of Gierek's economic policy, see Stanislaw Gomulka, "The Present Economic Situation in Poland," *Kultura* (Paris), November 1975. For earlier evaluations, see Michael Gamarnikow, "Poland under Gierek: A New Economic Approach," *Problems of Communism*, September-October 1972; also Zbigniew Fallenbuchl, "The Strategy of Development and Gierek's Economic Maneuvre," in Adam Bromke and John W. Strong, Eds., *Gierek's Poland*, New York, Praeger, 1973.

11 *Zycie gospodarcze* (Warsaw), July 28, 1974.

12 See, e.g., the pamphlet *Edward Gierek's Visit to the United States*, Warsaw, Interpress Publishers, 1974.

13 Thomas E. Heneghan, "Polish Trade and Polish Trends: Economic and Political Considerations," *Radio Free Europe Research*, Nov. 13, 1975.

14 *Contemporary Poland* (Warsaw), November 1975.

15 Toward the end of 1975, Poland's foreign debt was estimated at over $6 billion (*The New York Times*, Dec. 14, 1975). Since that time, Poland has obtained substantial additional credits from West Germany, the United States, and some other Western countries.

16 *Trybuna ludu*, Dec. 8, 1975.

17 Most of the figures quoted in this and the next several paragraphs are from *Wytyczne Komitetu Centrainego na VII Zjazd PZPR*, Warsaw, Edition *Trybuna ludu*, 1975. Wherever possible, they have been checked against various other Polish as well as Western sources.

18 *Tygodnik powszechny* (Cracow), July 21, 1974.

19 *Contemporary Poland*, November 1975.

20 See *Wytyczne....* For a pessimistic evaluation of Poland's future economic prospects, see the statement by Z.M. Fallenbuchl in "Poland in the Last Quarter of the 20th Century," *Slavic Review* (Urbana, Ill.), December 1975.

21 *Glos wybrzeza* (Gdansk), Aug. 28, 1974; *Polityka* (Warsaw), March 14, 1975.

22 *Trybuna ludu*, Dec. 10, 1975.

23 *Ibid.*, Dec. 16, 1975.

24 *Polish Perspectives* (Warsaw), September 1975.

25 *Trybuna ludu*, May 22, 1971.

26 *Ibid.*, July 1 and Aug. 14, 1973.

27 As quoted by J. Lukaszewicz in *Nowe drogi* (Warsaw), February 1974.

28 *Trybuna ludu*, Feb. 27, 1974.

29 *Nowe drogi*, July 1974.

30 *Ibid.*

31 For the text of the petition in English, see *Radio Free Europe Research*, Dec. 20, 1974.

32 *Krajowa Agencja Informacjina* (Warsaw), Nov. 19, 1975. Slonimski, it should be noted, died in a car accident in the summer of 1976.

33 *Zeszyty historyczne* (Paris), No. 34, 1975.

34 *Mysl Polska* (London), April 1, 1974.

35 *Ibid.*

36 *Polonia* (Chicago), June 6, 1974.

37 *Wytyczne....*

38 *Zycie Warszawy* (Warsaw), Dec. 20-21, 1975.

39 For the text of the memorandum in English, see *Radio Free Europe Research*, Dec. 31, 1975.

40 *Zycie Warszawy*, Feb. 5, 1976.

41 The modifications discussed in this paragraph were published in *Trybuna ludu*, Jan. 27, 1976. While the original amendments had contained no explicit reference to changing the name of "Polish People's Republic," their allusion to Poland's advance to the higher stage of "building socialism" implied that Poland might be declared a "socialist republic," as all the other East European countries have been. Moreover, in Polish there is a distinction between *republika* and *rzeczpospolita*—the latter being a traditional historical term used even when the country was a kingdom. Since *socjalistyczna rzeczpospolita* would not fit well together, many people feared that the state would become a *socjalistyczna republika*, which would follow closely the Soviet terminology.

42 *Trybuna* (London), No. 23/79, 1976.

[43] *Polonia*, May 30, 1976.
[44] *Trybuna*, No. 23/79, 1976. This letter circulated in Poland in *samizdat* form.
[45] *Kultura*, April 1976. This letter circulated in Poland in *samizdat* form.
[46] *Glos Polski* (Toronto), May 27-June 24, 1976.
[47] *Polityka*, Oct. 19, 1974.
[48] For fuller treatment of this subject, see Andrzej Micewski, "Polish Foreign Policy: Historical Perspectives," in Bromke and Strong, *op cit.*

VI
Poland at the Crossroads*

The Polish People's Republic is in the throes of the most serious crisis in its entire existence. The present difficulties reflect not just erroneous policies, but strike at the roots of the system itself. The ruling Communist Party seems uncertain as to how to cope with the situation, and its leader, Edward Gierek, is fighting for his political life. The opposition, in contrast, displays a mood of self-assurance, perhaps over-confidence. For the first time since the 1940s demands for a change of the system itself are openly and boldly articulated.

The workers' riots in Ursus and Radom in June 1976, in protest against drastic food price increases, left the Gierek regime badly shaken.[1] For several months afterward the Government conveyed the impression of being totally disoriented—moving in different, and often contradictory, directions at once. The objectionable price increases were hastily revoked, but the authorities insisted that they were still necessary and would have to be reintroduced at a later date. The need for closer consultations with the workers was acknowledged, but severe reprisals were nevertheless applied against the participants in the June demonstration. Amid widespread rumours of police brutality, several groups of workers from Ursus and Radom were tried and sentenced to lengthy terms of imprisonment. At mass rallies staged to demonstrate support for the communist authorities, Gierek emphasized the need for national unity, while at the same time the press mounted a campaign against "hooligans and firebrands." Despite the admission of a major error of judgment on its part, no changes in the Government were forthcoming.

Economic retrenchment

It was only late in the year that the Gierek regime regained its composure and tried to come to grips with the problems. A meeting of the Central Committee held on 1-2 December 1976 addressed itself to the task of bolstering the sagging economy. In his speech on that occasion Gierek defended the economic policies of the first part of the 1970s as "fruitful and creative," but he admitted that tensions had developed in the Polish economy.[1] These he blamed on adverse climatic conditions, which had resulted in poor grain harvests and a decline in livestock, and difficulties in foreign trade because of the recession in the West. There were also other shortcomings, such as an obsolete price structure, a tendency towards over-investment, a lack of co-ordination among various branches of industry, and inefficiencies which often resulted in the poor quality of goods. To cope with the deteriorating situation a "New Economic Manoeuvre" was adopted. In the next few months several further meetings of the Central

Committee were devoted to elaborating and expanding this economic adjustment.

The New Economic Manoeuvre was directed as much towards the preservation of calm in the country as to economic recovery. The price increases of basic foodstuffs were shelved and top priority for 1977 was given to improving the supply of the home market. To that end a drastic reduction in the overall level of investments, but an allocation of a greater proportion to consumer industries, was announced. Substantial additional funds were allocated to housing construction. Imports of industrial equipment, but, significantly, not of meats and grain, were cut down. More authority over distribution of profits was delegated to industrial units. At the same time, encouragement was given to private farming. Prices of agricultural produce were increased. Individual farmers were offered pension plans, and their prospects of acquiring more land were underlined. The small private enterprises that provide many crucial consumer goods and services were also promised more support.

All these measures were in the right direction, but they failed to bring about the desired results. If anything, in 1977 the situation at the market deteriorated even further. In addition to chronic shortages of meat, many other foodstuffs such as coffee or citrus fruits were in short supply. Although Poland is the world's largest per capita producer of coal, there was also shortage of this commodity. For the first time since the war, sugar was rationed and the queues became a familiar sight all over the country. Dissatisfaction and grumbling were evident. There were reports of scattered strikes in the coal mines, steel works and other factories.

Obviously, the Government had overestimated the speed with which it could accomplish economic recovery. Another bad harvest in 1977, due to heavy rainfalls, resulted in increased grain imports from the West. Poland's staggering debts to various Western countries—estimated at some 12 billion dollars—not only reduced the country's imports but also compelled it to export many goods badly needed at home.[2] Moreover, the effects of some of the newly adopted measures, such as the re-allocation of funds from heavy industry to agriculture and housing, are to be felt only in the long run. What the Government hopes for is that the results of the New Economic Manoeuvre, combined with the coming to fruition of the substantial investments in industry made in the past, will eventually ease the crisis. But this is not going to take place soon. Several lean years are clearly ahead for Poland.

There are signs that the roots of the crisis go deeper and reach beyond specific policies into the heart of the economic system. When in October 1977 the Central Committee met to review the results of the New Economic Manoeuvre, its mood was sombre. There were still complaints about poor co-ordination of various industrial activities and gross waste due to inefficiency. On 5 November an influential Warsaw weekly, *Polityka*, proposed as a remedy a greater decentralization of economic decision-making. In an article written by the Editor-in-Chief, Mieczyslaw Rakowski, this was stated very clearly: "Excessive centralization may result in harmful curtailing of individual initiative...Overcoming the existing difficulties ought to be linked as much as possible to decentralization."

There is no evidence, however, that *Polityka's* advice was heeded. At the Party Conference held on 9-10 January 1978, Gierek once again criticized the economy for inefficiency and insufficient co-ordination among its various branches, but he proposed no new measures to cope with these problems. Price increases of basic foodstuffs were once more postponed. No reforms of the price-wage structure or of the methods of planning and management were undertaken. Evidently "muddling through" in the Polish economy is to be continued.

The rise of opposition

After his coming to power in 1970, Gierek adopted a new political style which emphasized greater respect on the part of the Communist authorities for the citizens' rights and a readiness to enter into dialogue with the Polish people. This, coupled with improvements in the standard of living, won the Gierek regime a measure of genuine popular sympathy. In the mid-1970's, however, with the return to more orthodox Communist policies, the good will among various segments of the society was largely squandered. There was a tightening of religious freedom and Church-State relations visibly deteriorated. Cultural freedom was also curbed, and when, early in 1976, amendments to the Polish Constitution were introduced, bringing it closer to the Soviet document, there were massive protests by the intellectuals. The persecutions of the Ursus and Radom workers, after the Government had withdrawn the controversial food price increases, were the last straw. At that stage, various discontented groups coalesced into a united opposition.

On 27 September 1976 the "Committee for the Defence of the Workers" (KOR) was openly formed. Among its original fourteen members there were several distinguished intellectuals, a few elderly social democrats, and a group of younger people consisting of the leaders of the 1968 students' rebellion. The Committee appealed for the release of the imprisoned workers and demanded that a parliamentary committee be established to investigate the charges of police brutality. In its communiques, issued regularly in *samizdat* form, the Committee asked for support for its activities from the Polish people. This was not long in forthcoming. Funds for legal and medical aid for the persecuted workers were collected all over the country. Many intellectuals sent appeals to the Government, demanding the release of the prisoners. The Primate of Poland, Cardinal Wyszynski, also threw his enormous authority behind the Committee. Although stressing the need to preserve calm in the country, he strongly denounced the workers' persecutions. "It is painful," he declared in one of his sermons, "when workers must struggle for their rights under a workers' government."

The Government responded to the new challenge by zig-zagging between concessions and repression. Special efforts were made to appease the Catholic Church. On 3 August 1976, the Prime Minister, Piotr Jaroszewicz, ostentatiously sent Cardinal Wyszynski a bouquet of white and red flowers for his seventy-fifth birthday. In a speech in Mielec on 3 September, Gierek declared that there was no conflict between the State and the Church and that all the outstanding problems could easily be resolved. The Church reacted coolly to the Communist overtures. Late in November the Episcopate issued a letter complaining about "a secret conspiracy against God" and presented a veritable litany of grievances. In exchange for its co-operation the Episcopate demanded the removal of obstacles against building new churches, the unimpeded right to hold catechism classes for children, the termination of atheistic propaganda in schools and universities, access to public media and an end to discrimination against Catholics holding public office.

Conciliatory gestures were also made toward the intellectuals. Late in January 1977 Gierek received the Chairman of the Writer's Union, and a few weeks later he held "frank and open" discussions with a group of representatives of artistic circles. Early in March a film by Andrzej Wajda, "The Marble Man"—highly critical of the Stalinist era, and not without some contemporary political overtones—was shown in all the major cities in Poland. Some overtures were made towards the workers too. On 3 February Gierek visited the factory in Ursus and promised clemency for the imprisoned workers. Indeed, most of them were soon quietly released. On 26 March *Polityka*, in an article entitled "The roots of democracy," emphasized the need for more effective consultations with the workers. Meanwhile, however, five workers remained in prison. A campaign against the Committee for the Defence of Workers was mounted in the press, and the younger members of KOR were systematically submitted to police harassment and intimidation.

On 7 May Stanislaw Pyjas, a Cracow student and an active supporter of KOR, was found dead. The circumstances strongly suggested (although it is doubtful that it was in fact a premeditated murder) political assassination. Students all over the country rose in protest. Requiem masses were celebrated in all the university cities and some 2,000 Cracow students staged a candlelight procession. Tension was high—it was feared that clashes between students and police might spark an open revolt. The Government responded by promptly arresting ten persons: six younger members of KOR and four of its active supporters. This led to new protests from the intellectuals and the church hierarchy. In the face of the mounting wave of popular indignation the Government relented. On 30 June, in a speech to the Polish Parliament, Gierek pledged to respect the citizens' dignity and to uphold the rule of law. On 23 July the KOR people, as well as the remaining five workers, were all released from imprisonment.[3]

The opposition activities, however, did not stop there. If anything, they were even further intensified. In September KOR transformed itself into a permanent "Committee for Social Self-Defence," whose goals were defined as combating violations of the law and fighting for institutional guarantees of civil rights. Meanwhile, a similar group, called the "Movement for the Defence of Humand and Civil Rights," came into existence. It has opened offices in five cities where people aggrieved by the Communist authorities are offered free counsel. During the events in Cracow the "Students' Solidarity Committee" was formed, and soon it established branches at virtually all the universities in the country. At the same time the *samizdat* periodicals proliferated. At present there are some fifteen publications which appear regularly in mimeographed form, ranging from the purely literary to the avowedly political. In September a new periodical, *The Worker*, addressed to the industrial labourers, was launched. By now it is clear that several thousand people, a good many of them young, have become involved in the opposition activities in Poland.

Disarray in the Party

In the face of the mounting economic and political difficulties, the leadership of the Polish United Workers' Party has maintained an outward façade of unity. To some extent, in fact, the unity has been there. After his coming to power Gierek skilfully disposed of all his potential rivals in the Party and at the Seventh Congress in December 1975 he filled the key positions with his own men. Since that time there have been surprisingly few personnel changes. The only event of any consequence was the shifting in December 1976 of a young and able Politbureau member, Stefan Olszowski, from the post of Minister of Foreign Affairs to the Party Secretariat, where he was entrusted with the task of overseeing the New Economic Manoeuvre. Premier Piotr Jaroszewicz, despite the fact that since the fiasco of the price increases his popularity in the country plummeted, has managed to retain his post. Gierek evidently has been reluctant to oust the Prime Minister, perhaps fearing that the changes at the top might not stop there.

It has been a *secret de polichinelle* in Warsaw, however, that beneath the surface serious differences exist among the leaders of the Polish United Workers' Party (PUWP). There has been no revival of clearly identifiable factions, such as existed in the 1960s, but there have been increasingly sharp divisions in the Politbureau and the Secretariat over some specific issues. The most significant among them, of course, have been the methods of dealing with the ecomonic crisis and of coping with political opposition. The moderate wing has favoured economic decentralization, expansion of cultural and religious freedoms and more consultations with the workers. In contrast, the hard-line wing had advocated centralized economic planning and management and tougher measures towards the opposition. The split has often, although not uniformly, reflected the professional preoccupations of various individuals. Persons responsible for culture, science, agriculture and foreign affairs have leaned towards a moderate course, while those concerned with ideology, Party affairs and internal security have favoured the hard line. Gierek and his closest supporters have oscillated between the two groups, although, since the spring of 1977, they have moved closer to the moderate wing.

The tug-of-war between the opposing Party wings has from time to time surfaced in the press. The showing of the "The Marble Man" resulted in a controversy over permissible limits of cultural expression. On 4 April 1977 the Warsaw daily paper identified closly with the hard-liners, *Zycie Warszawy*, denounced the film as a one-sided and distorted presentation of the Stalinist era. It was also revealed in the press, no doubt intentionally, that the attack continued at the meeting of the Central Committee on 14 April. On that occasion the Secretary of the Party organization in Lodz, where the main centre of the Polish film industry is located, criticized "The Marble Man" for serious ideological errors.

Even more heated polemics ensued over Rakowski's article in *Polityka* in which he advocated a decentralization of the economic system. On 8 November 1977 *Zycie Warszawy* published an article in which Dr. Wladyslaw Ratynski, an obscure social scientist, but one who was evidently well connected among the Party hard-liners, viciously attacked Rakowski. He even accused the Editor-in-Chief of *Polityka* of an ideological deviation. In a pointed allusion to the economic reforms in Czechoslovakia during the Dubcek era, Ratynski equated "decentralized socialism" with a "market economy socialism" which, he concluded, inevitably leads to "revisionism." In the 19 November issue of *Polityka*, Rakowski, clearly stung by the gravity of the charges, hit back hard at Ratynski. He categorically repudiated the accusation that he wanted to go beyond the limits of the socialist system. If all the proposals to improve the existing situation were branded as political deviations, he argued, harmful stagnation would result. Indeed, Rakowski turned the tables on Ratynski and charged him with an attempt, by reviving the atmosphere of mutual recriminations, to undermine the unity of the Party. Such practices, Rakowski concluded, had been compromised and repudiated a long time ago, while for the past several years PUWP unity had been fully restored.

Rakowski's posing as a representative of the dominant trend in the Party may have been tactically sound, but it does not accurately reflect the constellation of forces in either the top leadership or among the PUWP rank and file. *Polityka's* line undoubtedly has a broad appeal among the technical intelligentsia—the managers and engineers who would like to free themselves from the shackles of the central planners. They are, however, counterbalanced by a powerful Party bureaucracy, especially well entrenched in the middle echelons, jealous of its prerogatives and reluctant to amend its autocratic ways. At the Party's top, for the time being, the moderates and the hard-liners are stalemated too. The zig-zagging in government policies has largely reflected the struggle between them. As the economic situation in the country deteriorates and popular pressure for changes intensifies, however, sooner or later the hard choices will have to be made. At this point the internal struggle in the PUWP is likely to be intensified with, ultimately, either one wing or the other gaining the upper hand.

The tug-of-war in the Communist Party is delicately interlinked with the activities of the opposition. Popular pressure, as long as it remains confined to proposals of reform within the existing system, is useful to the moderates. Too much pressure, however, could be counter-productive. The demands for a change of the Communist system itself play into the hands of hard-liners. In an article in *Polityka* on 10 September 1977, Rakowski subtly warned the opposition against this danger. He noted that there are people in Poland who, by presenting an excessively pessimistic picture of the situation, create a climate of nervousness and tensions. Such activites, in Rakowski's opinion, were not in the interests of the country.

Prospects and portents

Both the Communist Government and the democratic opposition are well aware that the outcome of their confrontation may be determined not only by internal but also by external forces. The opposition is confident that, if the danger of Soviet intervention in Poland were removed, they would prevail over the Government.[4] The opposition leaders also believe that, if pressed to the wall, Gierek would not invite Soviet troops, but that he would offer substantial concessions to the Polish people. This is because he understands that he could not survive such a major crisis. Soviet intervention would be a tragedy for the Polish nation, but it would be a catastrophe for the Gierek regime. In this respect their interests run parallel.

Furthermore, the opposition is convinced that even if the Polish Communists did turn to Moscow for help, in the present international climate the Soviet leaders would be extemely reluctant to oblige. If Moscow refrained from intervening in Poland with force in 1956, and again in 1970 (when, reportedly, Gomulka pleaded with Brezhnev for assistance), it is even less likely to take such a step today. The Poles would resist the invasion with arms and this would lead to a small-scale Soviet-Polish war. Poland, of course, would lose the conflict, but it would have grave consequences for the progress of East-West détente. Indeed, at least so far, Moscow's response to the new crisis in Poland has been remarkably circumspect. The Soviet leaders have continued to voice their full confidence in Gierek,[5] and have abstained from any public references to the activities of the Polish opposition. In November 1976 Moscow even offered substantial economic aid to Warsaw. In addition to the granting of a low-interest loan of one billion rubles, Soviet deliveries of grain and of some raw materials and consumer goods were considerably increased.

Nevertheless, there are limits beyond which Soviet patience had best not be tried by the Poles. Moscow probably would tolerate substantial changes in the existing system in Poland, as long as they were carried out in an orderly fashion and under the aegis of the Communist Party. Yet, the U.S.S.R. is unlikely to accept, as some of the Polish opposition groups have demanded, Poland's assertion of sovereignty and adoption of democracy. The Russians, who are at present flexing their muscles in such far away places as Ethiopia and Angola, would not easily suffer, regardless of the consequences to East-West détente, a major setback in their own backyard. Should the need arise, as Ratynski's article clearly illustrated, they would also have little difficulty in finding the Polish Husaks in Warsaw.

It is not only the opposition but also the Communist Government which has been using East-West détente to its advantage. Gierek is well aware of the fact that rubbing shoulders with the Western leaders enhances his prestige in the eyes of the Poles, and this he has been exploiting to the full. Since mid-1976 he has exchanged visits with President Giscard d'Estaing and has received at home Chancellor Schmidt and President Carter. During his visit to Italy on 1 December 1977, Gierek had an audience, especially widely publicized by the Polish media, with Pope Paul VI.

Gierek's visit to the Vatican marked a new relaxation in State-Church relations in Poland. Even earlier, on 29 October, Gierek held talks with Cardinal Wyszynski. This was their first meeting, and it was conducted in a style as if negotiations between two sovereigns were take place. The offical communique issued on this occasion emphasized that the Polish Communist leader and the Primate of Poland exchanged views on "the most important problems of the nation." The formal aspect of the meeting accurately reflected polical reality. Cardinal Wyszynski today is undoubtedly the most respected man in the country. His courageous defence of religious freedom and human rights has won him enormous prestige among the Polish people. At the same time he had consistently followed a thoroughly realistic course, and whenever the danger of the Soviet intervention has arisen, as in 1956 and 1970, he has appealed to the Poles for calm and restrain.[6] At present Cardinal Wyszynski is probably the only person in the country who could effectively check excessive demands on the part of the opposition.[7] Yet, he is unlikely to do so, unless, in return, Gierek would curb the hard-liners in the Party and introduce popular reforms in the country.

As one of the writers for the *samizdat* paper *Opinion*, Andrzej Woznicki observed, Poland now stands at the crossroads. There is no return to the situation which existed prior to June 1976. The Communist regime has little choice but to offer meaningful concessions to the Polish people. Nothing short of this will defuse the present crisis. This reality was recently underlined by a group of veteran Communists, headed by a former PUWP First Secretary, Edward Ochab. In a letter issued in October 1977 they urged the present Party leaders to adopt a broad programme of democratization.

Poland at the Crossroads

Should the Gierek regime fail to carry out popular reforms, pressure from the opposition will probably increase. In such a situation political forces in the country would become sharply polarized, with the danger that political events might overtake them all and necessitate Soviet intervention. Yet, this would not solve anything. Moscow's direct involvement in Poland would only defer, but not eliminate, the existing problems. Indeed, by intensifying the Poles' resentment against the Russians, it would precipitate another, even more bitter, political confrontation in the future.

It was almost exactly ten years ago, in March 1968, that the Polish students took to the streets in defence of cultural freedoms and their own national traditions. They protested against the banning by the Communist authorities of a nineteenth-century patriotic play by Adam Mickiewicz. The Gomulka regime responded with repressions and many students' leaders were thrown into jail. Two years later Gomulka was ousted from power, and today the students' leaders of 1968 are in the fore-front of democratic opposition in Poland. The lesson of these events for Gierek is obvious.

Footnotes

* Originally published in *The World Today*, April 1978.
1 An excellent analysis of economic developments in Poland in the 1970s is presented by Zbigniew M. Fallenbuchl, "The Polish economy in the 1970s" in *East European Economies Post-Helsinki*, Joint Economic Committee, Congress of the United States. See also Michael Gamarnikow, "A new economic approach," *Problems of Communism*, September-October 1972; and Alex Pravda, "Gierek's Poland: five years on," *The World Today*, July 1976.
2 By the end of 1976 Poland's total indebtedness to the West stood at 10.4 billion dollars, but since that time Warsaw has negotiated several new Western loans. In order to level off Poland's debts by the end of 1980 its exports to the West would have to be increased by over 10 per cent per annum, which is highly unlikely. Indeed, there is "... a significant probability that ... Poland ... will have to reschedule its hard-currency debts around 1980": Richard Portes, "East Europe's debt to the West: interdependence is a two-way street," *Foreign Affairs*, July 1977, pp. 757, 780.
3 For an interesting account of the developments in Poland in 1977 see Peter Osnos, "The Polish Road to Communism," *Foreign Affairs*, October 1977.
4 A concise exposition of the opposition strategy was presented by Adam Michnik on 16 December 1976 in *Le Monde*.
5 On 6 January 1978, on the occasion of his sixty-fifth birthday, Gierek received warm wishes from Brezhnev and was decorated by the Supreme Soviet with the Order of the October Revolution. It is worth while to remember, however, that when Gomulka reached the same age, on 6 February 1970, less than a year before he was ousted from power, he was similarly honoured by the Soviet Union.
6 For a penetrating analysis of State-Church relations in Poland, see Thomas E. Heneghan, "The Loyal Opposition: Party Programs and Church," RFE Research, 28 February 1978 (mimeographed).
7 Unfortunately, Cardinal Wyszynski's health is not good; in 1977 he twice underwent serious surgery. The Communist Government seems to be as much concerned about it as the rest of the country. When the Cardinal was hospitalized, official bulletins about his medical progress were issued regularly.

VII
The Opposition in Poland*

Poland has always occupied a special place among the Communist countries because of the scope of its internal freedom. For the more than 30 years that it has existed, the Communist government there has failed not only to establish its legitimacy in the eyes of many Poles but also to extinguish all traces of opposition. Indeed, when faced with workers' revolts in Poznan in 1956 and in Gdansk and Szczecin in 1970, the authorities retreated before popular pressure.

Again, in June 1976, when the workers in Ursus and Radom took to the streets in protest against food price increases, the Communist government hastily withdrew the objectionable measures. This time, however, popular ferment did not stop there. The "June events," as the Poles call them, produced a chain reaction which led to the emergence of a fundamentally new political situation in the country. Opposition, which in the past had been largely passive and scattered, has now become active—it has taken an organized, vocal, and increasingly influential political form.

A Shattered Modus Vivendi

Between 1956 and the mid-1970's, a subtle *modus vivendi* existed in relations between the Communist regime and various opposition groups. This was based on mutual acceptance of the country's difficult international position. Both sides, although for difference reasons, wanted to avoid direct Soviet intervention in Poland. For the Communists, such intervention would have meant even further curtailment of their domestic authority; and for opposition elements, it would likely have entailed drastic restriction of what modest freedoms they in fact enjoyed. The compact was never overtly spelled out, but its essential rules were well understood and generally respected by both sides. In exchange for the Communist authorities' excercise of a modicum of moderation, opposition groups abstained from challenging the regime outright. Indeed, the major confrontations during this period were entirely spontaneous and narrowly focused attacks on specific policies. The workers' outbursts stemmed from sheer desperation over their economic plight, and the peasants' stubborn and largely successful resistance again the collectivization of agriculture was instinctive.

The Catholic church also avoided unnecessary confrontations with the Communist government. Continued mass adherence of the population to the Catholic religion—rooted in long national tradition— made the church a powerful organized force in the country. However, it conceived its role as largely confined to spiritual, moral, and at most cultural spheres, and only rarely, usually at a time of major crisis, did it take a stand on political issues. Although the church steadfastly defended the principles of freedom of conscience and respect for human dignity, its position, as articulated by its venerable leader, Stefan Cardinal Wyszynski, was generally moderate. Indeed, in 1956 and again in 1970, when there was a danger that the escalation of domestic conflict might lead to Soviet intervention, Cardinal Wyszynski appealed to the Poles for calm and restraint.

During the period, the most articulate criticisms of Communist policies came from the intellectuals. The writers, scholars, and artists did not constitute an organized group, but through their frequent interactions, particularly in Warsaw, they formed a closely-knit milieu. As a matter both of principle and of fasion, in a sort of inverted snobbery, they strove to manifest their reservations about the Communist regime. These they punctuated by public protests against selected government measures. Generally, they denounced the restrictions on cultural freedom, but they also condemned some especially flagrant abuses of human rights. The intellectuals' proposals for reforms, however, stayed within the limits of the Communist system, for they were resigned to the fact that it could not be changed. Moreover, their criticisms were often constrained by their own pasts: most had been leftists, and many also had formerly been members of the ruling Polish United Workers' Party (PUWP). Of particular importance, the anticlericalism of many intellectuals prevented them from establishing solidarity with the Catholic church.[1]

In the mid-1970's the overall political situation in Poland changed dramatically as a result of a number of factors. To begin with, the opposition became emboldened by the improvement in East-West relations and by the example of Soviet dissidents' use of détente as a protective umbrella for their activities. In the eyes of many Poles, the Final Act of the 1975 Helsinki Conference on Security and Cooperation in Europe reduced the chances that the U.S.S.R. would intervene in their country as it had in Czechoslovakia in 1968. The Carter Administration's early pronouncements about human rights heartened them as well.

More important were the consequences of the coming-of-age of the postwar generation in Poland. Free of the defeatist memories of World War II, these younger people are impatient with their fathers' passive resistance to communism. They are no longer satisfied with the solution of "a little stabilization"—seeking refuge in private life and restricting one's interests to personal welfare—which was prevalent among the old generation the 1950's and into the 1960's. The ferment among the youth first became evident in 1968 during the widespread student riots, in Warsaw and some other university cities, against restrictions on cultural freedom. In 1970, a clandestine group of young people who smuggled political literature from the West through the Tatra Mountains (and were hence dubbed the "Alpinists") was discovered and tried. In 1971, there were several trials of members of another underground group called Ruch (The Movement), with most of the defendants being under 30 years old.

Finally, the Gierek regime itself, through its mistakes, helped the opposition consolidate its forces and come out into the open. Intoxicated with its relative successes in the early 1970's,[2] the PUWP in 1974 abandoned its generally moderate stance and launched an open "ideological offensive," intensifying pressures on both the Catholic church and the intellectuals. The next year, despite signs of rapidly deteriorating economic conditions, the party proposed amendments to the Polish Constitution that would bring the document closer to the Soviet model. These proposed changes were regarded by the opposition as a violation of the implicit compact between it and the government. The result was a deluge of formal protests, signed by some 40,000 people in all, including many prominent intellectuals.[3] The Catholic Episcopate and Cardinal Wyszynski personally threw their great authority behind the opposition. Under popular pressure, the party modified the most controversial constitutional amendments, but the harm to the Communist regime had already been done.[4] Its prestige was seriously undermined, and from then on opposition activities snowballed. In May 1976, a new clandestine group appeared, calling itself the Polish Coalition for Independence (PPN). Its manifesto, circulated in *samizdat* form, called for restoration of democracy in the country and for Poland's independence from the U.S.S.R.[5]

An open break between the opposition and the Communist regime soon ensued. When, following the Ursus and Radom demonstrations in June, the Communist authorities resorted to widespread persecutions of the workers involved, the intellectuals promptly rallied to the worker's defense. In July 1976, a prominent writer Jerzy Andrzejewski, praised the persecuted workers as "fighters for true socialist democracy" and pledged to persevere in efforts on their behalf.[6] To this end, on September 27, 1976, a Committee for Defense of the Workers (KOR) was established.

Committee for Defense of the Workers

The composition of KOR reflected the various layers of opposition in Poland. Among its members (fourteen originally and thirty-one as of this writing), there are several prominent prewar social democrats such as Professor Edward Lipinski, a respected economist, and Antoni Pajdak, one of the defendants in the trial of the Polish leaders in Moscow in 1945. They are all now in their 70's or even 80's. Another group is composed of well-known members of the wartime resistance movement. The youngest of these is a literary historian, Jan Jozef Lipski, who is now in his early 50's. But the largest, and also the most active, group in KOR consists of leaders of the 1968 student movement. Except for a former teacher, Jacek Kuron, who is in his 40's, these people are all in their early 30's or late 20's. The most widely known among them is a talented historian, Adam Michnik, who spent several months in Western Europe in 1976-77. Less known abroad, but no less influential, is another historian, Antoni Macierewicz, who, together with several of his friends and very much in the Polish tradition, joined the opposition ranks after having been active in the Boy Scouts movement in Warsaw.

A good many of KOR's supporters are student activists of 1968. Some of these have been members of Communist youth orginizations or come from families with Communist ties. They still consider themselves leftists, or even Marxists, but of a more Western, Eurocommunist, or even social democratic brand. Others, such as the former "Alpinists," simply regard themselves as democrats. A relatively large group of the young activists are devoted Catholics, who continue to participate in offical lay activities of the church. As a group,these young men and women, by now more mature and experienced than they were a decade ago and often hardened by years of imprisonment, are grimly determined to carry on their struggle for freedom.

KOR's initial aims were modest. Its first communiques, issued in *samizdat* form, reported on the persecutions of the imprisoned workers— with detailed accounts of police brutality—and announced a public campaign to raise funds for medical and legal aid. Gradually, however, the Committee's goals grew more ambitious. They came to include amnesty for all the imprisoned workers and their reinstatment in the same positions they had held before June 1976, plus punishment of those police officers guilty of abusing their powers. On January 16, 1977, KOR appealed to the Polish parliament (the *Sejm*) to appoint a special committee to investigate charges of beating and torturing of prisoners.[7] Eventually, KOR's activities broadened further and involved assistance to a variety of individuals persecuted by the authorities.

The Committee has developed quite ingenious methods for its activities. It has declared itself to be not a *political*, but merely a *social* body. To avoid submitting itself to public control by the Communist authorities, it has refrained from adopting a formal organizational structure. It has operated simply as a group of citizens spontaneously cooperating to promote common goals. All of the Committee's activities have been conducted openly, but, naturally, some of them, especially the publishing and distributing of the *samizdat* materials, have been carried on more discreetly then others.

KOR offers moral encouragement, legal advice, and financial aid to the politically persecuted. For this purpose, money has been collected all over the country. However, the major vehicles of KOR's influence have been the communiques, declarations, and appeals circulated throughout the country in *samizdat* form. It has regularly published its own paper, the *Biuletin informacyjny* (Information Bulletin), named, significantly, after an influential organ of the Polish wartime resistance.[8]

Around these activities, KOR has built an impressive popular following. By the summer of 1978, there were official Committee representatives in nine cities, and active KOR supporters in many other centers. The Committee's demand for the establishment of a parliamentary committee to investigate police abuses was supported by close to 2,000 people, among them many distinguished intellectuals.[9] Cardinald Wyszynski, in several sermons, threw his enormous prestige behind KOR. Although refraining from directly endorsing the Committee's politcal goals, he made it clear that he fully supported its activities on behalf of the persecuted workers.[10]

The government's initial reaction to KOR's activities was mixed. On the one hand, a systematic campaign of vilification of the Committee was mounted in the press. The members of KOR were characterized as enemies of the Socialist system in Poland and as collaborators of Western anticommunist centers. Several Committee members were dismissed from their jobs. Many others became objects of systematic police harassment and intimidation. At the same time, however, the arrested Ursus and Radom workers were being quietly released one by one. By the spring of 1977, only five of them still remained in prison.

This uneasy standoff broke down after May 7, 1977, when Stanislaw Pyjas, a Krakow student and an active KOR supporter, was found dead. His fellow students reacted swiftly to what they took to be a political assassination (although it is doubtful that his death was in fact a premeditated action). Solemn requiem masses were celebrated in all the university cities in Poland. On May 15, some 2,000 Krakow students staged a candlelight procession through the city. Tension was high, and it was feared that clashes between students and police might ensue, sparking an open revolt. At that moment, six key members of KOR, as well as four KOR supporters, were arrested and accused of cooperation with anticommunist centers in the West. The arrests produced a new wave of protests. At the end of May, eleven persons held a hunger strike in St. Martin's Church in Warsaw. An appeal for the release of the KOR members, characterizing them "not as criminals, but as dedicated social activists," was issued by seventeen prominent writers, scholars, and artists.[11] Under mounting popular pressure, the Communist government relented. On July 23, all of the prisoners—the KOR members and supporters, as well as the remaining five workers—were set free.

KOR has, since September 29, 1977, gone under the expanded name of Committee for Social Self-Defense—KOR (KSS-KOR), although its compoisition and its structure have remained basically unchanged. Now constituted as a permanent body, KSS-KOR has expanded its goals from the defense of persecuted workers to more general combating of violations of the law, fighting for institutional guarantees of civil rights, and assisting in all similar social initiatives.[12]

The achievements of KOR went beyond rallying a great number of people in defense of the persecuted workers and, through popular pressure, compelling the Communist government to abandon its reprisals. Perhaps even more important were the psychological consequences of this achievement. The Committee demonstrated that there is room in contemporary Poland for successful political action. By standing up to the

Communist authorities, KOR overcame the political inertia among various segments of Polish society, and its example led to a proliferation of similar activites in many other spheres of life.

Proliferation of Opposition Groups

On March 25, 1977, the founding of a new group, called the Movement for the Defense of Human and Civil Rights (ROPCiO) was announced. Its eighteen founding members were predominantly from Warsaw and Lodz. The most visible among them was Leszek Moczulski, a former journalist and historian of World War II, who is now in his mid-40's. For the most part, however, ROPCiO, like KOR, is composed of distinctly separate prewar and postwar generations. Among its older members are a prewar general, Mieczyslaw Boruta-Spiechowicz, and a leader of the former Christian Democratic party, Stefan Kaczorowski. The younger members are mostly former participants in the clandestine group Ruch. The best known of the latter is Andrzej Czuma, who in the spring of 1978 pushed Moczulski aside and emerged as the leading personality in ROPCiO.

In contrast to KSS-KOR, the Movement has no Marxist leanings; if anything, it has reverted to the political traditions of interwar Poland. It is more critical of the Communist system and is more far-reaching in its proposals for political change. The objectives of ROPCiO, as defined in its initial manifesto,[13] are to fight for respect for human and civil rights, to assist persons whose rights have been infringed upon, to publicize violations of the laws, and to strive for institutional safeguards of basic freedoms.

To promote these ends, the Movement has established offices in eleven Polish cities, where free advice is offered to citizens aggrieved by the Communist authorities. By the fall of 1977, they had a current docket of 43 such complaints. ROPCiO's organ is a *samizdat* monthly, *Opinia* (Opinion). In addition to publicizing the Movement's program and activities, the paper covers current domestic and international events quite extensively.[14] One June 5, 1977, ROPCiO sponsored the first reunion of former political prisoners, and on August 6 it organized a patriotic demonstration by the grave of prewar Polish Marshal Edward Rydz-Smigly. On December 30, an *Opinia* correspondent tried unsuccessfully to attend the Warsaw press conference of U.S. President Jimmy Carter.[15]

In addition to KSS-KOR and ROPCiO, various other groups and *samizdat* publications representing a wide diversity of opinion have appeared in Poland in the last year. About the same time that ROPCiO was set up, a Polish chapter of Amnesty International was founded, with some overlapping of key personalities. In the fall of 1977, the Polish Committee for the Defense of Life and Family was formed. It soon collected over 6,000 signatures on an appeal to parliament to abolish the existing, extremely liberal abortion laws.[16] In the spring of 1978, it came out with its own publication, *Samoobrona Polska* (The Polish Self-Defense), in which, in addition to continuing its antiabortion campaign, it openly reverted to the political tradition of prewar National Democracy. In the summer of 1978, Moczulski and some of his followers, after leaving ROPCiO, established a new monthly, *Droga* (The Road).

At the time of the demonstrations in Krakow in May 1977 the Students' Solidarity Committee (SKS) spontaneously came into existence. Its declared objective is to replace the Communist-dominated student organization with a body that truly represents the Polish students. SKS now has branches at virtually every university in the country and publishes two papers, *Bratniak* (Fraternity) and *Indeks* (Index). In the autumn of 1977, an independent journal of young Catholics, *Spotkania* (Encounters),[17] covering religious as well as social and political topics, was founded. In the autumn of 1977, the first issue of *Robotnik* (The Worker), a publication whose name was borrowed from the respected organ of the old Polish Socialist Party (PPS), appeared. It pledged to strive for replacement of the official trade unions with genuine workers' representation. This journal was soon followed by *Gospodarz* (The Farmer), addressed to the peasants and urging them to continue their opposition to collectivization of agriculture. Meanwhile, two literary *samizdat* periodicals, *Zapis* (The Record)[18] and *Puls* (Pulse), entered into circulation. Both were of exceptionally good quality, with the latter even including photographs and drawings. *Zapis* was issued by NOWA (Independent Publishing House), which at the same time accounced that it intended to undertake publication of books banned by censorship. By the spring of 1978, thirteen such volumes, six in belles-lettres and seven in the social sciences, had come out.

Side by side with these open opposition groups, various clandestine groups have continued to function or have started up in Poland in the last two years. For example, the Polish Coalition for Independence has continued to publish critical, often quite penetrating, analyses of various aspects of life in Poland, such as official discrimination against the Catholic church, lack of popular respect for the law, widespread corruption among the ruling elite, and apathy among the people. To oppose these negative phenomena, the PPN has prepared several practical guides to action which outline, for instance, how to cope with the security police and how to collect true information about the situation in the country.[19] In the fall of 1977, another clandestine group gave evidence of its existence with the first issue of a bimonthly, *Polska Walczaca* (Fighting Poland), whose name, significantly, was a cryptonym used for the Polish wartime underground. On October 20, 1977, a Declaration of the Democratic Movement, signed by 110 people, was published in still another *samizdat* paper, *Glos* (The Voice). The declaration observed with satisfaction that in the preceding two years Communist attempts to break the Movement had not only failed but had in fact made it even more popular, to the point that it now had "thousands" of adherents. The time had come, the declaration stated, for the Democratic Movement to undertake the struggle for Poland's democracy and sovereignty.[20]

The Opposition in Poland

Along with the flourishing of *samizdat* publications came a proliferation of discussion groups of all sorts, especially among the young people. Some of them have been sponsored by KSS-KOR, ROPCiO, or the SKS, while others have sprung up quite spontaneously. They have met in private homes and also, occasionally, on local church premises. In Warsaw and in some other major cities, veritable intellectual salons have emerged, where prominent writers read their works and well-known scholars give lectures.

The Flying University

In November 1977, at the initiative of the students' committees, an effort was made to transform some of these occasional lectures into systematic courses. The aim was to supplement the education offered at regular universities, especially in those fields where Communist ideology had placed political limitations on objective scholarship—i.e., in modern history, literature, philosophy, and the social sciences. This new venture has been designated the "Flying University" (UL), after a similar institution in Warsaw at the turn of the century that had played an important role in rekindling national consciousness among Polish students attending Russianized schools by giving secret training in native history and literature. Unlike its distinguished predecessor, the present Flying University is an open institution. It is sponsored by the Society for Educational Courses (TKN), which was founded on January 22, 1978, and is composed of 61 persons, including many prominent writers and scholars. To supervise the quality of courses offered at the UL, the Society established from among its members an Education Council.[21]

In the first trimester (or set of lectures), the Flying University offered five courses on an experimental basis, but by the third trimester, that number had risen to thirteen. These lectures took pace in Warsaw as well as in other major university cities. Although the UL offers no diplomas, its courses have proved to be quite popular. Attendance has averaged 30-40 students but has run as high as 100 for lectures such as Polish postwar history. As an aid to students, "flying libraries" of books banned from the regular university collections have been established. To cap things off, a Free Association of Research and Studies was founded in the spring of 1978. Composed of scholars who have been prevented from working at official institutions, it seeks to foster research free of political influence and to disseminate the results in the form of *samizdat* publications.

The Communist authorities have charged that the objectives of the Flying University are not educational but political, that its main aim is to spread opposition ideas among the young people. Consequently, the authorities have tried hard to restrict the scope of UL activities. Students participating in the courses have been warned by regular university officials about possible adverse consequences for them, and some SKS activists have been interrogated by the police. Several lectures, especially outside of

Warsaw, have actually been broken up. Moreover, a few younger lecturers have been arrested and detained long enough to prevent them from meeting their classes. Owners of apartments where lectures have been taking place have been fined for holding "illegal gatherings," and some have even been threatened with eviction from their dwellings.

Since late winter, as the activities of UL have expanded, the scope of official pressure has visibly intensified. Nevertheless, the lectures have continued, and in June 1978 the Flying University completed its first "academic year."

Debate Over the Opposition Program

Since the opposition has been divided into several groups, and since there have also been internal differences within each of them, no single political platform exists to which all adhere.[22] This does not appear to trouble many in the opposition. As Jacek Kuron has observed, they feel that the time is not as yet ripe for the adoption of a unified opposition program. Rather, what is needed at present is the open airing of various tentative proposals.[23] ROPCiO's monthly *Opinia* voiced a similar sentiment in a June 1977 editorial. While a single opposition movement would appear better suited to fight a one-party dictatorship, the article observed, a pluralistic society could only emerge from below, through the exercise of pluralism in the ranks of the opposition. The result of this situation has been a broad public discussion, with a veritable flood of articles and pamphlets on the country's external as well as domestic situation appearing in *samizdat* form in Poland or smuggled to the West for publication in the émigré press.[24] As one Polish writer commented, not since World War II "has there been a similar debate about the program of action and the vision of a future Republic."[25]

The debate as a whole has been characterized by a remarkable degree of sobriety. In a political treatise written at the end of 1976, an author using the *nom de plume* Marek Turbacz set the tone.[26] He observed that "thinking in clear political terms" had "been generally alien to the Polish intellectual tradition" and had not been encouraged by 30 years of totalitarian rule. Then he proceeded to put forward his own argument in a detached and precise, almost scientific fashion. His assessment of Poland's position vis-à-vis the U.S.S.R. was characterized by cold realism:

> *We are not able to free ourselves from the domination of Russia.... Poland, which is its most important satellite located on its road to Western Europe, cannot regain sovereignty as long as the Russian Empire exists. Neither will the Russian leaders permit Poland...to discard the Communist system. This would restrict their influence over us, and also set a dangerous example for the other satellites as well as for their own people.*
>
> *The restoration of Poland's sovereignty and a basic change of the present system would be possible only if preceded by a fundamental*

change in Russia itself, or a drastic shift in the constellation of forces in the world at large. For this we may have to wait as long as a quarter of a century.

Soviet domination of Poland, in Turbacz's opinion, determines the limits of viable change in the country. Moscow is likely to intervene should strong anti-Russion sentiments surface among the Polish people; should the PUWP be removed from power and a multiparty system be restored; or should a major reorientation in the country's foreign policy take place. Therefore, the opposition should not promote such developments.

At the same time, Turbacz maintained, the fact that Poland cannot free itself from the U.S.S.R.'s domination does not mean that the Poles should passively resign themselves to their fate and await changes in the internation sphere. "There is an essential difference," he pointed out, "between compromise and blind submission, as there is a distinction between a realist policy and collaboration." Within the existing framework, he argued, there still exists room for the Poles to try to improve their position. There are various domestic changes which the Polish Communist government could undertake without invoking the wrath of Moscow. It could carry ou substantial economic reform, expand the role of self-government, enhance the role of experts in the administration, improve the quality of information and broaden the scope of cultural freedom These measures would significantly reduce the gap between the Communist authorities and the Polish people, and in this way diminish the danger or repeated violent confrontations between them.

In Turbacz's judgment, however, the Gierek regime is not able to undertake such reforms; and the possibility that some other Communist leader will emerge in the near future who would be willing to do so is remote. Under such circumstances "changes must be extracted from the government through popular pressure." This pressure should not be exerted through sporadic outbursts, but should take the form of a long-term systematic campaign. The opposition, in the author's words, should not incite "revolutionary upheavals, but rather promote everyday demonstrations of civic courage."

Adam Michnik, during his stay in the West in late 1976, outlined an opposition strategy in terms similar to those of Turbacz. Among the changes in Poland which he proposed, and which, in his opinion, would not be incompatible with the Communist system, were: the establishment of independent trade unions; the easing, but not necessarily the complete abolition, of press censorship; the granting of freedom to youth orgainizations; and the ending of all religious discrimination. Michnik, too, felt quite strongly that popular pressure aimed at extracting reforms from the Communist government should be considerably intensified. He recognized that this might lead to Soviet intervention, but he dismissed the possibility as remote. Soviet military intervention, he argued, would be catastrophic for the present regime; consequently, the Polish Communists would try to avoid it at any cost. Moreover, since it would be highly detrimental to East-West détente, Moscow would be extremely reluctant to take such a step.[27]

Jacek Kuron, in a programmatic essay written toward the end of 1976, also disavowed any intentions on the part of the opposition to seek a confrontation with the government. He claimed that the opposition, on the contrary, is striving to promote peace in Poland. Soviet intervention, he argued, is more likely to be brought about by popular upheaval over some drastic government measures than by moderate reforms, which are the most effective way to pacity the Polish people.[28]

Not all of the statements in the *samizdat* publications, however, have been quite so reasonable as those just cited. Some have clearly gone beyond the limits which Turbacz warned the opposition not to transgress. Writing in the student paper *Bratniak*, Tomasz Mroz declared himself in favor of primacy of moral over political concepts. He rejected as naive the belief in the possibility of a compromise with despotic rulers and called for a struggle by the opposition conceived "as a moral necessity to fight against evil in political life." He argued, furthermore, that the acceptance of limited reforms would imply "the abandonment of maximum demands, and one must always keep in mind the ultimate goal ... a free and independent Poland."[29]

Similarly, *Opinia*, the organ of ROPCiO, has taken an increasingly militant stance. The editorial article in its March 1978 issue held that either one is in favor of the Communist system and Poland's subordination to the U.S.S.R., or one stands for democracy and independence. "A middle ground," the article concluded, "no longer exists."[30]

The Polish Coalition for Independence, in some of its statements, has also adopted fairly extreme positions. In the spring of 1977, it came out with an eloquent, but highly emotional, statement defending the anti-Russian insurrectionist tradition in Poland. "It is owing to the conspiracies, insurrections, and the resistance movements," it exclaimed, "that today we are a nation." Although the PPN declaration stopped short of actually calling on the Poles to rise to arms, it implored them to persist in the struggle for independence.[31]

The PPN's program was criticized by a writer using the pseudonym of Marek Brzost. He characterized it as noble but utopian, since it did not point to a practical way of regaining the country's independence. Resistance without the chance of winning would only result in unnecessary losses. Dictatorships "can be overcome, but it takes more than moral and intellectual forces to accomplish this." And in the present situation of Poland, Brzost concluded, "the time is not ripe to...resort to open resistance."[32]

The leaders of the main groups of the Polish opposition evidently agreed with Brzost, for at a meeting in the spring of 1978 they categorically repudiated conspiratorial and insurrection tactics and opted to continue open and peaceful activities. Their declaration on that occasion stated unequivocally that members of the democratic opposition "will not let themselves be driven into conspiracy, they will not be provoked and will never resort to acts of terror, which could be exploited to liquidate any authentic, spontaneously formed outlets of social initiatives."[33]

The New Opposition Tactics

As Adam Michnik has pointed out in a lecture delivered in Paris, the year 1976 represented a turning point in the tactics of the opposition in Poland. Until that time, and even during the confrontation over the constitutional amendments, opposition appeals has been primarily addressed to the Communist authorities. The opposition assumed that changes would come "from above." That is, the opposition "counted on the positive evolution of the [Communist] party due to the enlightened policies of its leaders, while it abstained from pushing them in this direction through organized and persistent social pressure." With the establishment of KOR, opposition tactics changed. Appeals were now directed at the people, with the aim of generating changes "from below."[34]

An example is the opposition's new role as "public ombudsman." KOR's campaign on behalf of the imprisoned workers from Radom and Ursus helped them regain their freedom. Since that time, both KSS-KOR and ROPCIO have been systematically collecting and publishing information about the police's abuse of power and about the courts' condoning of such practices. In the spring of 1978, KSS-KOR issued a White Paper describing in some detail 25 cases in which police officers had violated the law. The document emphasized that this evidence represented only the tip of the iceberg and that many more such instances were known to the Committee.[35]

Another role which the opposition groups have played is to exert pressure on various branches of the administration by publicly criticizing their practices. A special column in *Opinia* has regularly scrutinized the shortcomings of economic policies in a highly competent manner, and in the spring of 1978 KSS-KOR came out with a comprehensive pamphlet exposing the grave economic situation in the country.[36] *Gospodarz* has pointed out the inadequacies of the newly introduced pension plan for private farm owners; and *Robotnik* has reported on the waste and inefficiency prevailing in some factories.

All of the *samizdat* publications have mercilessly attacked the censorship of the official press. They were provided with a golden opportunity in the spring of 1977 by the defection to the West of Tomasz Strzyzewski, an employee of the censorship office in Krakow. Strzyzewski took with him substantial confidential evidence about the inner workings of censorship in Poland. These documents, which amount to a devastating criticism of the entire system, were also made available to KSS-KOR and have been systematically reprinted by the opposition press.[37]

Finally, the *samizdat* papers have increasingly taken direct issue with authors publishing in the official press, and have also come out with critiques, at times harsh, of specific plays, television shows, and films. In a fairly close-knit intellectual milieu such as exists in Poland, challenges of this kind tend to put strong pressure on the writers, scholars, and artists to improve their performances, if only to avoid public ridicule. Faced with such pressure, the intellectuals, in turn, are more likely to oppose interference with their works by the censorship authorities. The meeting of the Polish Writers' Union held in Katowice on April 7-8, 1978, affords a good illustration. Union members decisively repudiated crude Communist efforts to intervene in the union's affairs and, in fact, elected to the union's Executive several persons prominently linked with opposition activities.[38]

Although various *samizdat* papers reminded their readers on the occasion of the February 1978 local government elections that under Polish electoral law, they could abstain from voting or cross out names of candidates who do not merit their confidence, this was just a trial balloon. The opposition is clearly not prepared to test the Communist party in an electoral battle. For the present, as one of the editors of *Glos*, using the *nom de plume* Marek Tarniewski, argued, "for anybody outside of the [Communist] party to try to win power would be premature." For the time being, he wrote, the opposition should concentrate on rebuilding an "authentic" social life, "independent of the government."[33]

Turbacz, in the essay cited above, summarized the present, restricted, political goals of the Polish opposition as the creation of an unofficial national culture, and, above all, the development of Polish political thought free from the influence of communist ideology. This, he wrote, should lead to the rise of new cultural and political elites.[40] The existence in Poland of manifold *samizdat* publications, the ongoing debate in their pages about the opposition program, and the activities of various discussion groups and the Flying University suggest that these goals are well on the way to being realized.

An Uneasy Stalemate

Relations between the Communist government and the democratic opposition, as Antoni Macierewicz has observed, are currently stalemated. The opposition is unable to extract democratic reforms from the government, and the government is unable to prevent the opposition from trying to do so.[41] However, the fact that the activities of the various opposition groups are tolerated for the time being does not mean that their continued existence has been accepted by the Gierek regime. Short of a frontal attack, the Communist authorities are doing whatever they can to restrict, or at least to make as difficult as possible, opposition activities. The police keep close watch over all the groups. Between September 1976 and October 1977, there were at least 318 house searches, and about 1,000 people were arrested and interrogated.[42] Since early 1978, the intensity of police persecution, especially outside Warsaw, has, if anything, increased.

For the moment, the government can afford to tolerate opposition activities because they do not pose an imminent threat. The opposition has exerted influence basically among the intelligentsia, gaining only scattered support from the workers.[43] Two attempts to organize a free trade union movement—the first in Katowice in February 1978 and the second in Gdansk the following April—were confined to a handful of individuals and were both met with immediate and severe reprisals.[44]

Official propaganda tries to minimize the significance of the opposition groups still further by depicting them as a small bunch of extremists virtually isolated from the Polish people. In a statement for the foreign press, a government spokesman, Miroslaw Wojciechowski, estimated the strength of the opposition in Poland at some 100 hard-core members and about 1,000 sympathizers. The rest, he maintained, are people who will listen to the opposition arguments but who would not themselves get involved in its activities.[45]

Wojciechowski also catergorically rejected the possibility of the Communist authorities' entering into dialogue with the opposition. However, he did express the hope that at least some members of the opposition would perceive the unrealistic nature of their present course and avail themselves of the opportunities, which he claimed exist but are not fully utilized, to develop socialist democracy in the country. As to those people who would continue along their present road, Wojciechowski warned, there would be no need for wholesale repression, but selective reprisals against them would be used and might even be intensified in the future.

This official picture is all too sanguine. In reality, the strength of the opposition is considerably greater than Wojciechowski's estimate. There are at present in Poland at least 20 *samizdat* papers published regularly, with a total monthly circulation of no less than 20,000.[46] To write, edit, publish, and distribute them must take at least several hundred persons, with a protective network of sympathizers around them of several thousand people. Since each copy of a *samizdat* publication is usually passed around among several persons, it is probably no exaggeration to estimate that they reach some 100,000 readers, even if one takes into account the confiscation of some copies.[47] The scope of opposition activities, then is quite substantial, and to try to break the opposition would require a massive police action.

Resorting to mass terror would have disastrous political consequences for the Gierek regime. It would intensify the alienation of intellectuals from the Communist government and would lead to a new rupture in relations with the Catholic church. Furthermore, it would also adversely affect Poland's external relations, expecially its trade with the West. The disruption of this trade is something which the country, in its present precarious economic situation can ill afford, for any further deterioration of the standard of living could lead to what Gierek fears the most—namely, new unrest among the workers. Finally, use of mass terror would in all probability revive factional struggle within the PUWP itself.

It is very doubtful that Gierek could weather such a political storm. In this respect, the opposition's assumption that he will refrain from wholesale terror at all cost seems to be quite correct.

Thus, as long as the democratic opposition maintains its present course of abstaining from conspiratorial and revolutionary tactics, there is little danger that it will provoke wholesale Communist efforts to repress it. But persistent refusal on the part of the Communist regime to recognize the opposition's existence could aggravate the opposition's radical tendencies. In fact, the government has already contributed in one way to such a development. By firing more than a hundred young men and women from their jobs for political reasons, the Communist authorities have, in effect, created a full-time cadre of opposition activists.

Moreover, one important factor that has contributed to the moderate course of the Polish opposition—the close relationship of its younger leaders to the older intelligentsia in its ranks—may not continue to prevail forever. So far, more experienced hands have helped the younger oppositionists appreciate the harsh realities of Poland's international position. Yet the structure of both KSS-KOLR and ROPCiO is such that the initiative rests increasingly not with the older but with the younger members, who are often quite young indeed. In Polish history, there have been instances where such an imbalance ended in catastrophe. For example, the ill-fated anti-Russian insurrections of 1830 and 1863 were both started by young hotheads against the better advice of their elders.

The semiclandestine environment in which the opposition is compelled to operate and the subtle but unmistakable police persecution to which it is constantly exposed are also not helpful to its perseverance on a moderate course. Petty police harrassment, while totally ineffective in substance, adds to an atmosphere charged with emotion. Furthermore, being compelled to remain at the margin of open political life introduces an element of the unreal into the opposition's activities. Its leaders compensate by occasional outbursts of grandeur as when Moczulski claimed that it is the Communist party that finds itself in a state of seige,[48] or when Kuron declared that it is the opposition that tolerates the government and not vice versa (a statement that he later retracted).[43]

Last but not least, there is the danger that, in competing for popular support, the different opposition groups may seek to outbid one another by demonstrating their radicalism. Indeed, the increasingly militant tone of some samizdat publications indicates that this already may be beginning to happen. Yet, from the government's standpoint, intensified repressions would only enhance this tendency by pushing various opposition groups even deeper into the underground.

The Opposition in Poland

To sum up, then, the opposition appears to be pursuing a "calculated risk" strategy that rests on two assumptions. First, it anticipates that at some critical moment the Communist government would offer far-reaching concessions to the Polish people rather than risk Soviet military intervention. This assumption may well be valid with regard to the Gierek regime, which appears to understand that in the event of any political crisis of major proportions it would be swept from power. Yet there clearly are groups within the PUWP that would not be averse to, and might even welcome, direct Soviet involvement. As one Polish writer put it:

> ...there are people in the party who are looking forward to the confrontation—either because they believe that for a long time now the people have deserved a severe lesson in obedience, or because Moscow, the wiser for its experiences [of 1968] in Prague, may designate them as the leaders of the next, and this time carefully prepared in advance, new "government" of Poland.[50]

Radicalization of opposition programs, then, would only play into the hands of these Communist hardliners.

The second assumption underlying the opposition strategy is that in a climate of East-West détente the Soviet Union would be reluctant to intervene with force in Poland. This assumption is also probably accurate. The Soviet leaders seem to be well aware of the grave consequences such a step would produce for them in the international sphere. In the existing, strained state of East-West relations, it might well spell the end of détente. In order to avoid this risk, Moscow would probably accept substantial reforms in the present system in Poland as long as they were carried out in an orderly fashion under the aegis of the PUWP. Yet, as Turbacz rightly observed, there are limits to Soviet toleration. And not only has the gap between the political situation in Poland and that in the other countries of Eastern Eruope—not to mention the U.S.S.R. itself—become quite extensive, but it also seems to be widening.

Poland's present situation, then, rests on a delicate equilibrium among many competing forces. Failure on the part of any of these forces to exercise great caution could upset that equilibrium. For Gierek, or his successor, that will probably entail curbing the hardliners in the Communist ranks and offering tangible improvements to the Polish people. To produce such improvements, he may well have to expand the outside limits of Poland's freedom vis-vis the U.S.S.R., possibly even by standing up to the Russians. For the opposition, sufficient prudence not to push demands beyond the point of no return will obviously be indispensable. Kuron once commented that in Poland's position it is better to stop one step short than to go one step too far.[51] Will Poles manage to meet the challenge?

Footnotes

* Originally published in *The Problems of Communism*, September-October 1978.

1   For a critique of the leftist intellectuals' negative attitude toward the Catholic church in the 1960's, written by a young leftist leader of the opposition , see Adam Michnik, *Kosciol, lewica, dialog*, Paris, Institut Littéraire, 1977.

2   The situation in Poland in the early stages of the Gierek regime was reviewed in Adam Bromke and John W. Strong, Eds., *Gierek's Poland*, New York, N.Y., Praeger Publishers, 1973. On the activities of the opposition, see Peter Raina, *Political Opposititionin Poland, 1954-1977*, London, Poets and Painters Press, 1978.

3   Jacek Kuron, "Thoughts on the Program of Action," in *Ruch oporu*,Paris, Institut Littéraire, 1977, p. 198.

4   For the conflict over constitutional amendments see Alexandra Kwiatkowska and Georges H. Mond, "Strife to the East," *La Documentation française* (Paris), Sept. 9, 1977, pp. 8-11.

5   See "The Declaration of the Polish Coalition for Independence, in *Ruch oporu*, pp.187-93.

6   See *Aneks* (London), No. 12, 1976, pp. 43-44.

7   *Dissent in Poland 1976-77*, London, Association of Polish Students and Graduates in Exile, 1977, pp. 123-37.

8   For a comprehensive collection of KOR documents in English translation, see *Dissent in Poland 1976-77*.

9   Ibid., pp.123-37.

10   Ibid., pp. 149-64.

11   *Kultura* (Paris), June 1977, p. 142.

12   These were reported in *Kultura*, November 1977, pp. 144-45.

13   See *Dissent in Poland 1976-77*, pp. 182-85.

14   The first four issues of *Opinia* were republished in book form in the West: *Opinia, Pismo ruchu obrony praw czlowieka i obywatela, numery 1-4*, London, Polonia Book Fund, 1977.

15   See *Opinia* (Warsaw), No. 9, January 1978, and *The New York Times*, Jan. 2, 1978.

16   *Samoobrona Polska* (Warsaw), mimeographed, April 1978, p. 11.

17   The first two issues of this journal were published in book form: *Spotkania: niezalezne pismo modych katolikow* [Lubin, Nos. 1-2, October 1977-January 1978], Great Britain, n.p., n.d.

18   The first two volumes, *Zapis I*[May 1977] and *Zapis II* [October 1977], were republished by Index on Censorship, London.

19   For the initial program of PPN, see *Dissent in Poland 1976-77* pp. 165-70.

20   Reprinted in *Kultura*, December 1977, pp. 138-41.

21   Ibid., March 1978, pp. 86-87.

22   For a general, but cautious, review of the aims of the opposition by a close Polish observer see Andrzej Szczypiorski, "The Dissidents and Reality," *Europa Archiv* (Bonn), No. 6, 1978. Overlapping and differing objectives have not prevented opposition groups from cooperating with one another. Thus, in mid-1977, ROPCiO strongly protested against the arrests of KOR members; and in the autumn, KSS-KOR members denounced intensified regime harassment of ROPCiO supporters.

23   Jacek Kuron, "Thoughts on the Program of Action," loc. cit. p. 198.

24   This discussion had been heralded by several interesting programmatic statements written during the first part of the 1970's. Perhaps the most significant among them was that by Marian Kowalski, "The Need for a Program," *Kultura*, May 1975. Also in 1975 there appeared (largely unnoticed in the West) an excellent study of communism in Poland by Marek Tarniewski, *Ewolucja czy rewolucja*, Paris, Institut Littéraire, 1975.

25   Socjusz, "Political Activities and Programs," *Kultura*, September 1977, p. 31.

26   Marek Turbacz, "Possibilities for Opposition Activities in Poland," *Aneks*, No. 16-17, 1977, pp. 3-46

27   Adam Michnik, "Poland Lives," *Le Monde* (Paris), Dec. 16, 1976.

28   "Thoughts on the Program of Action," loc. cit., pp 208-09.

29   "Why Protest?" *Bratniak*, November 1977.

30   "The Problem of Democracy," *Opinia*, March 1978. p. 6.

31   "The Polish Homeland—The Independence Tradition and Its Enemies," *Tydzien Polski* (London), April 23, 1977.

32   "Some Remarks about the PPN Program," *Kultura*, November 1976, pp. 105-06.

33   Reported by Alexander Smolar in his article "Poland: 10 years After," *The Times*, (London), Apr. 17, 1978.

The Opposition in Poland

[34] Adam Michnik, "A Strategy for the Polish Opposition," in *La Pologne: une société en dissidence*, Paris, Maspero, 1978, p. 100. See also Jan Gross, "Political Opposition in Poland," *Aneks*, No. 15, 1977.

[35] *Dokumenty bezprawia*, Warsaw, NOWA, mimeographed, Apr. 7, 1978.

[36] *Uwagi o sytuacji gospodarczej kraju* Warsaw, NOWA, mimeographed, 1978.

[37] The first volume of the documents revealed by Strzyzewski has already been published in the West, and the second volume is soon to follow. See *Czarna ksiega cenzury PRL*, London, Aneks, 1977.

[38] *Trybuna ludu* (Warsaw), April 10, 1978, listed the members of the new Executive.

[39] Marek Tarniewski, *Dzialanie i przyszlosc*, London, Odnowa, 1977, pp. 26, 29.

[40] "Possibilities for Opposition Activities in Poland," loc. cit., pp. 22-23.

[41] Antoni Macierewicz, "Legality," *Glos*, March 1978, p. 5.

[42] Bogdan Borusewicz, "The Methods of Fighting the Opposition in Poland," *Spotkania,*, October 1977.

[43] Janusz Tapacz, "What Is It All About," ibid.

[44] A writer from Poland has compared the position of the working class in the stalemate between the opposition and the government to the role of nuclear weapons in East-West relations. Should either the principals reach for it, the other would respond with everything that is has. See Jan Kowal, "The Nature of the Ferment in the Country," *Trybuna* (London), No. 28, 1978.

[45] From an interview on West German television, reported in *Die Welt* (Hamburg), Mar. 11, 1978.

[46] It is estimated by opposition circles that by early 1978 close to 100,000 copies of *samizdat* papers and books have been issued. As of the spring of 1978, the circulation of *Robotnik* was 15,000; that of *Opinia*, 8,000; and that of *Glos*, 2,000. See Stefan Kawalec, "The Traditions of Political Action," *Glos*, March 1978.

[47] In a lecture given on Apr. 20, 1978, Teodor Palimaka, head of the Administration Division in the PUWP Secretariat, claimed that out of 20,000 copies of *samizdat* publications about one half are intercepted by the security police. *Zagadnienie z zakresu dalszego umacniania ladu, porzadku i dyscypliny spolecznj*, Warsaw, Ksiazka i Wiedza, May 1978, p. 18.

[48] Leszek Moczulski, "The Last Stand," *Opinia*, October 1977. Quoted from *Radio Free Europe Research* (Munich), RAD 255, Dec. 23, 1977.

[49] Jacek Kuron, "An Accord is Possible Between Polish Opinion and the USSR," *Le Monde*, Mar. 1, 1977.

[50] Leopolita, "Marginal Comments on the Program," in *Ruch oporu*, p. 238.

[51] Jacek Kuron, "Thoughts on the Program of Action," loc cit., p. 208.

VIII
Poland and Hungary in 1956*

The Hungarian Revolution of 1956 had a profound impact upon Poland. One reason for this was, of course, that the upheaval in Hungary coincided with Poland's "peaceful revolution" of the same year. The Poles watched the Hungarians' struggle with great interest and with immense sympathy. Probably nowhere else in the world did the Hungarian Revolution evoke at first so much spontaneous support, and, when it was all over, such genuine sorrow, as in Poland.

It was during a Hungarian demonstration of solidarity with the Poles on October 23, 1956—symbolically conducted in front of the statue of the Polish hero of the Hungarian Revolution of 1848-1849, General Jozef Bem—that the initial fighting in Budapest broke out. The Poles warmly reciprocated the Hungarian's sentiments and throughout the revolution repeatedly demonstrated their solidarity with the Hungarian "freedom fighters".

The press in Poland covered the events in Hungary extensively and faithfully. On October 28 the Polish communist party daily, *Trybuna ludu* [People's Tribune] declared that the source of the Hungarian tragedy "should not be sought in a simplified version of 'alien agencies', nor in looking for counterrevolution at every turn.... It should be sought primarily in the errors, distortions and even crimes of the former Stalinist period." On the same day the party's Central Committee issued an appeal addressed to "[our] Hungarian brothers" urging them to stop the shedding of fraternal blood Personal accounts of the battle in Budapest were published in the two popular weeklies, *Po prostu* [In Plain Words] and *Nowa kultura* [New Culture], and were widely read throughout the country.

Money, clothing and medical supplies were openly collected in Poland and it was from that country that the first plane carrying blood plasma arrived in Budapest. Youth rallies in sympathy with the Hungarians were held in various Polish cities. On November 2 a manifesto issued by the Central Committee of the Polish United Workers' Party accurately described the Polish attitude. "The Polish nation," it declared, "follows the course of events in Hungary with great emotion." Indeed, after the second Soviet intervention in Hungary, emotions in Poland were so intense that there was a distinct danger of a popular explosion. On November 7 Radio Warsaw reported that the situation in the country had "reached boiling point" and appealed for calm.

The Poles supported the Hungarians until the very bitter end. Even after the uprising was crushed, the Polish communist party clung to its own interpretation of the events in Hungary. It was over that issue that Poland took a step unprecedented for a member country of the Soviet bloc. On November 21, 1956, in the General Assembly vote on the admission of

United Nations' observers to Hungary, the Poles did not support the Societ Union but instead joined the Yugoslavs in abstention.

The suppression of Hungary was such a highly emotional issue in Poland that even in the spring of 1958, when the execution of Imre Nagy was announced, party First Secretary Wladyslaw Gomulka still displayed great caution. His comments on the subject were the last to be delivered by an East Central European communist leader and were couched in carefully measured terms. Speaking in Gdansk on June 28 Gomulka acknowledged the event but detached himself from it. "It is not up to us," he said, "to appraise the scope of the guilt and the justice of the punishment of the defendants in the Nagy trial. This is an internal Hungarian matter."

* * *

After the events of 1956 one question was often posed: why did the Soviet Union intervene in Hungary but refrain from similar action in Poland? The standard answer became that, in contrast to the Poles, the Hungarians had gone too far, particularly in striving to restore the multiparty system and to embrace nuetrality. The events in Czechoslovakia in 1968, however, confounded this explanation. The Czechs and the Slovaks attempted neither to overthrow communist party rule nor to withdraw from the Warsaw Pact, yet they suffered the same fate as the Hungarians.

The fact is that it is still not known what triggers Soviet intervention in the various East Central European countries. As a Polish writer, Marek Tarniewski, put it recently: "Russia's alarm reaction is difficult to anticipate; just now it is sporadic, but it always can happen and occasionally does happen, often over the most unlikely matters." The Eastern Europeans must always be conscious of Soviet presence. It is dangerous for a small country, the Polish author observes, whenever "a revolutionary situation occurs within its borders that does not coincide with the revolutionary situation outside. First the Hungarians, and then the Czechs and the Slovaks, had to learn this lesson."

Yet, Tarniewski adds, the reality of the Soviet presence in East Central Europe does not preclude all political change there. The mechanism of intervention is a delicate one and precisely what triggers it is probably not known even in Moscow. Rather, decisions are arrived at on the basis of the evidence available in each specific case. They are affected by the constellation of political forces in the U.S.S.R. and their perception of the situation in the international scene. The Soviet Union's alarm reaction, Tarniewski concludes, "can be adjusted; ... it depends on the specific circumstances existing in each country."[1]

The respective domestic situations in Hungary and Poland in 1956, as the Russians correctly perceived, were in many ways different. The Stalinist system in Hungary had been more repressive than in Poland and produced correspondingly stronger reaction. In Poland the alternative communist leadership under Gomulka had been permitted gradually to take over, while in Hungary First Secretary Matyas Rakosi's persistent efforts to stay in power had undermined Imre Nagy and produced a more explosive situation. In the final analysis, however, probably the major difference between the two nations was the differing perceptions of their respective situation in the international sphere in 1956.

For Hungary the experience of the Second World War was less traumatic than for Poland. On the one hand, the Hungarians did not play a major political and military role in it, trying instead to weather the storm as best they could. Their losses were less extensive than those of the Poles. They failed to win back their pre-1918 territory, but at least they retained that of 1938. On the other hand, though the Hungarians had historically experienced periods of accommodation with the Austrians and the Germans, dealing with the Russians was for them a novel experience. In short, the Hungarians were, relative to the Poles, internally stronger and they found Moscow's suzerainty over their country less tolerable.

In contrast, the Second World War marked a major watershed in Poland's history. From beginning to end the Polish question stood at the very center of wartime diplomacy and the Polish military contribution to the Allied side was considerable. The relative losses which Poland suffered during the war were second to none. The Poles thus were understandably embittered at the West for not helping them to preserve their independence from Moscow. They suffered sizable territorial losses in the east and the compensation they were given in the west aggravated tension with Germany. In these circumstances it was natural that the Poles embraced political realism and reverted to a stance they had already tried out in the nineteenth century, namely, seeking an accommodation with Russia.

* * *

It is within the context of the specific historical phase through which they were passing in 1956 that the Hungarian Revolution acquired a very special, one might say almost personal, significance for the Poles. There is no question that for a good many of them watching the battle in Budapest was a deep emotional experience—as if they themselves were taking part in it. There were several reasons why the Poles projected themselves in this fashion into the Hungarian scene.

First of all, the Poles and the Hungarians have been traditionally tied together by firm bonds of friendship. It is one of those rare situations in Europe where the two peoples genuinely like each other. Hungarian-Polish friendship has not been rooted in common interest—and perhaps for this reason it has been even stronger. In fact, on various occasions in the past— as, for instance, during the Second World War—the Poles and the Hungarians have found themselves in opposite camps, yet even then their mutual sympathy has been preserved and they have tried to help each other as best they could.

The friendship between the two nations goes back to their early history when several Hungarian kings occupied the Polish throne and Polish princes wore St. Stephen's crown. It was consolidated through the centuries of common struggle against the Turks. In more recent times, during the revolution of 1848-1849, many Poles fought on the Hungarian side against the Austrians and the Russians. It was while serving under General Jozef Bem that the great Hungarian poet Sandor Petofi, fell in battle. The close personal ties, especially among the aristocratic circles in the two countries, resulted in somewhat similar styles of life and, despite the major linguistic difference, a distinct cultural affinity still exists between the two peoples. No Pole feels quite alien in Budapest and probably no Hungarian is out of place in Krakow. Thus it is easy for each people to understand the emotions and to appreciate the actions, especially when directed against foreign power, of the other.

The battle of Budapest of 1956 appealed to the Poles' imagination even more because it reminded them so vividly of the Warsaw uprising of 1944. Indeed, there were strong similarities between these two historic episodes. In both cases a handful of freedom-fighters waged a desperate struggle against overwhelming odds and without any outside assistance. While watching the newsreels of the Hungarian uprising in 1956, many Poles must have relived their own—at that time still relatively recent—experience.

Yet it was precisely the traumatic shock of the defeat in Warsaw in 1944 which, more than anything else, made the Poles abandon their all-out struggle for freedom and embrace political realism. While watching the lonely Hungarian Revolution, then, the Poles' reaction must have been ambivalent and in some respects even contradictory. With their hearts they were with the Budapest freedom-fighters, but reason cautioned them against joining the "Hungarian brothers." In the end, though caution prevailed, it was certainly contrary to the Poles' own impulses and, in fact, it resulted in the Poles finding their own stance not to their liking. Their sentiments were articulated by Polish poet Adam Wazyk. who, writing in *Nowa kultura* on November 25, 1956, sadly observed: "We used to be the conscience of history but now our silence had become *raison d'état*."

When it was all over in Hungary, the Poles mourned, but the ambivalence of their feelings was nevertheless eased. They knew that, by joining the Hungarians in battle against the Russians, they would not have saved Budapest and they would have exposed Warsaw—once again—to a similar fate. They still admired the Hungarians for "acting like Poles," yet at the same time congratulated themselves for "acting like Czechs." In short, the outcome of the Hungarian Revolution was to convince the Polish people that their course of not counting on the assistance of the West and of striving for a *modus vivendi* with the Soviet Union was correct.

Paradoxically, it was the January 1957 issue of the communist theoretical monthly *Nowe drogi* [New Roads]—trying to make political capital for the then badly shaken Polish United Workers' Party—which accurately summed up the situation. "Let us remember," it declared, "that at the time of the Hungarian tragedy the foreign radio stations appealed to the Poles for reason and restraint. Those reactionary forces in Poland which would like to spread disorder ought to know that the Americans are extremely reluctant to shed their own blood."

The realist posture paid off for Poland. The "peaceful revolution" of 1956 brought about important changes in the country: the abandonment of the collectivization of agriculture, a marked improvement of the Roman Catholic church's position and the expansion of intellectual freedom. By the late 1950s Poland was by far the freest country in the communist bloc.

* * *

The defeat of the revolution in 1956, it seems, had a similar effect in Hungary to what the crushing of the Warsaw uprising in 1944 had in Poland. It resulted in the abandonment of an all-out struggle for freedom and the adoption of political realism. When in the early 1960s, after the initial period of repression, First Secretary Janos Kadar offered the Hungarians a possibility of acccommodation with the Soviet Union, they eagerly embraced it. Moscow's suzerainty was accepted in exchange for a modicum of domestic freedom. The compromise served the Hungarians well. In a few years the situation in the country improved markedly. In fact, it soon became better than that in Poland. Toward the end of the 1960s Hungary, in turn, was the freest and one of the most prosperous countries in the East Central Europe.

The *modus vivendi* with Moscow, however, also had its price. The communist system has become entrenched and the very man who betrayed the revolution of 1956, Janos Kadar, has stayed at the helm. In foreign policy Hungary has followed the Soviet Union at every turn. During the Czechoslovak crisis of 1968 the Hungarians acted even worse "than Czechs"; they helped the Russians—together with the Poles—to invade their neighbour, which was striving to free itself from Moscow's suzerainty.

There is no reason to believe that the Hungarians like their realistic posture any more now than the Poles liked theirs in 1956. Yet the memories of the defeat of their revolution are still strong enough to prevent them from moving away from it. The Hungarians' thorough-going realism was described by a participant in the 1956 uprising presently living in the West, Charles Fenyvesi: "The West will not life a finger and it is madness to think that we can bring a real change. Heroism is dead.... One makes a separate peace with the regime. The arrangement is comfortable, cozy. The trouble is that it stinks."[2]

It is ironic that, as the Hungarians embraced political realism, the Poles moved in the opposite direction, In the 1960s, as the defeatist memories of the Second World War faded, popular pressure steadily mounted in Poland. When Gomulka steered away from a program of reforms, he encountered strong opposition. Intellectual ferment once again gathered momentum and in 1968 the students took to the streets. In 1970 Gomulka, the hero of Poland's "peaceful revolution" of 1956, was overthrown by rioting workers and replaced by Edward Gierek. When in the mid-1970s Gierek in turn tried to move away from a program of reform, he found himself faced with the united opposition of the workers, the intellectuals and the Catholic church. The workers' riots in Radom and Ursus in June 1976 brought the country to the verge of a revolution and threw the communist party once again into a retreat.

In the 1970s Poland has thus caught up and in some respects even surpassed Hungary. In the economic sphere the Hungarians still remain ahead of the Poles; in the realm of intellectual freedom the Poles are more or less at par with the Hungarians, while the scope of religious freedom is greater by far in Poland than in Hungary. Both countries maintain broad contacts with the West, although the Poles are somewhat bolder in elevating them to the level of formal diplomatic relations.

Despite different approaches, there are considerable similarities between Hungary and Poland today. They occupy a unique position in the Soviet orbit. In the domestic sphere they are the two freest countries in Eastern Europe; in this regard they are by now ahead even of Yugoslavia. They are still subject to overall Soviet suzerainty and, given their geographic position, there is little prospect that this will change soon, but the communist systems in both countries have already been largely "domesticated." Evidently, the tactic of oscillating between idealism and realism, at times resorting to pressure and at times to compromise, has served the two nations well.

Footnotes

* Originally published in *East European Quarterly*, Boulder, 1978
[1] Marek Tarniewski. *Ewolucja czy rewolucja* [Evolution or Revolution] (Paris, 1974), pp. 69,272.
[2] "Hungary 20 Years Later," *The New York Times Magazine*, October 17, 1976.

IX

Poland and West Germany: Belated Detente*

Some twenty-five years after the end of the second world war, relations between Poland and Germany are still far from satisfactory. The German Federal Republic does not recognize Poland's western boundary; there are no diplomatic ties between the two countries; and until very recently the climate between Warsaw and Bonn was cool, if not openly antagonistic. The Polish-German dispute remains one of the major unresolved problems in Europe and, indeed, in East-West relations. In the past few months, however, there have been signs of a major thaw between Bonn and Warsaw. The Poles abandoned their polemical posture *vis-à-vis* West Germany and in May 1969 the Polish communist leader, Wladyslaw Gomulka, made an offer to the GFR to try to resolve the contentious issues between the two countries by direct negotiation. In November the new West German government, led by Chancellor Willy Brandt, responded favourably to Gomulka's appeal and by February 1970 the Polish-German talks were underway.

There is little doubt that the forthcoming Polish-West German negotiations are going to be difficult. Few countries approach the task of normalizing their relations with worse credentials than Poland and Germany. The tragic historical experiences and the existence of an unresolved territorial dispute, added to membership in two antagonistic alliances, breed distrust on both sides and stand in the way of reconciliation. Past attempts to overcome differences have been singularly unsuccessful. Since the mid-1950s—when the GFR assumed responsiblity for its own external affairs and Poland regained at least some freedom of manoeuver in international politics—the two countries have been conspicuously unable to attune their respective foreign-policy advances and retreats to the same cycle. Advances from one side have encountered a retreat from the other, with the result that German-Polish relations have neither contributed to, nor indeed have they been affected by, the partial détente which meanwhile has emerged in east-west relations.[1]

Past Failures

The first move to improve relations between the two countries came from the Polish side. Following the establishment of diplomatic ties between Bonn and Moscow, Polish Premier Jozef Cyrankiewicz called for friendship with the "whole of Germany."[2] After the political changes in 1956, the Polish government reiterated its willingness to enter into diplomatic relations with the GFR with no conditions attached. In West Germany the event's of the "Polish October" evoked considerable interest and sympathy, particularly among the intellectuals, and both the Social Democrats and the Free

Poland and Germany: A Belated Détente?

Democrats urged that diplomatic ties be established with Warsaw. The Adenauer government, however, rejected this option for fear of undermining its claim to be the only legitimate government of the entire German people, and lest such a step be domestically and internationally interpreted as a *de facto* recognition of the Oder-Neisse line. After 1958 the prospects for normalization of relations were further complicated by Gomulka's insertion of recognition of the existing Polish boundary as a condition, thereby mobilizing German domestic opposition to the establishment of diplomatic ties. Despite the immobility on the diplomatic front, some progress was made in the economic sphere. After 1956 annual trade agreements were concluded between the two governments and Bonn made available a yearly rotating credit to facilitate German exports to Poland.

In 1963 economic relations were placed on a somewhat broader footing by the conclusion of a long-term trade treaty and the establishment of a West German trade mission in Warsaw.[3] Outside the U.S.S.R., this was the first representation of its kind established by the Federal Republic in eastern Europe and it thus testified to the priority that Bonn assigned to relations with Poland. The establishment of formal trade relations signified a slight loosening in Bonn's eastern policy, a process which was accelerated under the Erhard government. The new government embarked on its new policy as a reluctant concession to the post-Cuban détente efforts of its western partners. Just as the Ulbricht government used its foreign-trade missions with broad competence in the economic, cultural, and political fields to overcome its international isolation, Foreign Minister Schroder adopted the same technique in the different eastern European capitals in order to outflank the rigidities of the self-imposed Hallstein Doctrine.[4] Under Schroder's more flexible eastern policy, the level of German-Polish trade rose gradually and reached an annual turnover of approximately one billion marks in 1966. But more spectacular projects, such as the construction of industrial plants in Poland with Polish labour and German capital and know-how, fell through. Also, German attempts to upgrade the role of its Warsaw trade mission by giving it consular and quasi-diplomatic functions were rebuffed by the Poles.

The immediate payoff from Schroder's "policy of movement" lay in the domestic debate that it stimulated in Germany rather than in any positive response from Warsaw. The government's more flexible approach acted as a catalyst which prompted many individuals and institutions to think about the unthinkable and to come to accept the finality of the Oder-Neisse frontier. In October 1965, a widely discussed memorandum of the Evangelical Church of Germany challenged the "right of homeland" thesis of German refugees, because it clashed with similar rights of the Polish residents who had been born in the disputed territory.[5] By the end of 1967, a public opinion survey revealed that 58 per cent of the West Germans were in favour of recognizing the Oder-Neisse frontier if this step would contribute to the improvement of East-West relations.[6] At the same time, the left wing of the SPD and certain CDU party officials began to challenge the government policy that upheld Germany's claims to the bondaries of 1937 until a peace settlement would determine the eastern frontiers of a reunited Germany.

In contrast to the earlier stand, the Polish communist government's response to the more accommodating foreign policy and the more realistic public opinion of the Federal Republic was entirely negative. At a time when there had been little public debate in Germany about the recognition of the Oder-Neisse line, Prime Minister Cyrankiewicz had officially acknowledged, even to an East German audience, that there existed in West Germany "deep currents favouring peaceful changes...which would choose the road of common sense, coexistence and peace."[7] But when wider segments of the German public had in fact moved in this direction, official Polish comments shifted ground and dismissed the newly emerging opinion in Germany as the voice of a small minority without any influence over policy. When in the spring of 1966 the German government sent a "peace note" proposing agreements to renounce the use of force in relations with its eastern European neighbours, the Poles denounced it as an empty gesture. Even more detrimental to the prospects of normalization was Warsaw's policy of escalating the conditions for improved relations. The price of establishing diplomatic ties, which had already been raised in 1958 when recognition of the Oder-Neisse frontier had been made a condition, was inflated still further in 1966 with Warsaw adding two more preconditions: a categorical renunciation of nuclear weapons and recognition by Bonn of the GDR. By deliberately linking the issue of a German-Polish detente to the unresolved question of German reunification in a manner that was clearly incompatible with the policy objectives of the Federal Republic, the Polish government postponed the prospects of reconciliation indefinitely.

Bonn's New Eastern Policy

Despite the negative response from Warsaw, the Great Coalition which took power in Bonn in November 1966 "left the trenches of the Cold War," to use Theo Sommer's phrase,[8] and committed itself to the process of building a detente in Europe. Its new *Ostpolitik* proceeded from the belief that the dilemma of German's division can be overcome neither by a policy of strength and confrontation, nor by a miraculous legal formula that would somehow turn the renunciation of her territorial claims beyond the Oder-Neisse into a reunification of the two Germanies. Instead, it is now accepted that the division could be overcome only as the result of a gradual reconciliatory process between eastern and western Europe, a process in which Germany would have to play a major part. While German's eastern policy under the Erhard government proceeded as a timid footnote to the conciliatory efforts of her western allies, it developed its own rationale and momentum under the Great Coalition. Moreover, if the preceding government consciously excluded East Germany in its policy of engagement in eastern Europe, the Great Coalition was careful to include the GDR in the emerging detente. Indeed, Bonn emphasized that it neither sought to isolate Pankow from its allies nor intended to "create or exploit differences between the Soviet Union and her allies."[9] In line with these proclaimed intentions, the Bonn government made numerous proposals for direct negotiations with the GDR and expanded the original "peace note" of March 1966 by expressing readiness to conclude agreement with East Germany on the renunciation of the use of force.

Both Chancellor Kiesinger and Foreign Minister Brandt have, on numerous occasions, singled out Poland for particularly warm and friendly comments. They have sympathized with Poland's desire "to live...within guaranteed borders, and not to be a 'state on wheels.' "[10] The decision to expand the renunciation-of-force-offer to include the GDR was in part at least, undertaken with the aim of accommodating Polish wishes. Also, with respect to the Oder-Neisse issue, attempts have been made to meet Polish demands on this sensitive issue, at least in a partial manner. The Christian Democrats have not deviated from their original position which reserved formal recognition for a final peace treaty, but they have emphasized that the 1966 "peace note" includes the pledge to respect the inviolability of Poland's present western boundary. At their 1967 party conference, the small opposition to the Great Coalition, the Free Democrats, openly debated and narrowly defeated the proposal for formal recognition of the Oder-Neisse frontier. In the spring of 1968, the Social Democrats settled for a compromise solution, the so-called Nurnberg formula, under which they are pledged to respect the Oder-Neisse line and to recognize it for the period for which the Federal Republic can commit itself, that is, until the signing of a peace treaty.

Initially at least, the German efforts to meet the Poles half way fell upon deaf ears in the official circles in Warsaw. The Polish communist leaders clung stubbornly to their preconditions for improving relations with West Germany while they ostentatiously demonstrated their support for the GDR. At the same time, the Polish mass media were conducting a systematic campaign vilifying the GFR. West German gestures towards reconciliation with the communist countries were minimized and right-wing opposition to this policy was blown up out of all proportion. Notably, at the time of the Czechoslovak crisis, the *Ostpolitik* was repeatedly denounced in the Polish press as a Machiavellian scheme to divide and overcome the communist states in eastern Europe one by one. In a speech on 8 September 1968, Gomulka openly posed the question as to whether the GFR harbours aggressive plans toward Poland. His answer was in the affirmative. "In the hierarchy of Bonn's goals," he argued, "the overthrow of Poland's frontier along the Oder, the Neisse and the Baltic occupies the second highest place. The first goal is a liquidation and absorption of the GDR. It need not be added, that these plans of West Germany are to be achieved through war."[11]

At the Fifth Congress of the Polish United Workers' Party in November 1968, still two more conditions were added for the normalization of relations with the GFR: Bonn's recognition of the Munich Agreement as invalid *ab initio* and renunciation of any claims to West Berlin. Poland's official attitude toward West Germany was now harder than ever.

Warsaw's Positive Response

In the spring of 1969, Warsaw's position was suddenly reversed. In an electoral address on 17 May, Gomulka took a surprisingly moderate stand *vis-à-vis* Bonn. Although he still qualified his statement at every turn, he now gave West Germany the benefit of the doubt. He acknowledged that "for some time there have developed in certain circles in the GFR tendencies which seem to indicate a somewhat different direction in Bonn's Eastern policy. It is difficult to judge whether this is a tactical manoeuver or whether it represents a genuine attempt to reappraise the present realities of Germany and Europe."[12] Moreover, the Polish Communist leader did not reiterate in his speech the five conditions for the normalization of Polish-German relations which he had stressed only six months before. The demands for the acceptance of the Munich Agreement as being invalid from the start and the renunciation of all claims to West Berlin were now conspicuously absent. Gomulka did reassert the demands for renunciation of nuclear weapons by the GFR and recognition of East Germany, but they were give little attention in comparison with his stress on the need to settle the territorial dispute between the two countries. Last, but not least, Gomulka singled out the SDP'S Nurnberg formula as a positive indication of growing reasonableness in West German politics. Even though he characterized this proposal as unsatisfactory because of its provisional nature, he called for the normalization of relations between the two countries. He explicitly invited the Bonn government to enter into negotiations to conclude a treaty similar to that which had been signed between Poland and East Germany in 1950 which would recognize the finality of the Oder-Neisse frontier.

With Gomulka's speech, the anti-German propaganda campaign in Poland came to an abrupt end. The Polish press and radio, of course, registered the negative responses to Gomulks's proposals in the GFR. The obdurate leaders of the expellees' organizations, including the Minister for Expellee Affairs, Heinrich Windelen, were singled out for criticism. The waivering in the ranks of the CDU, and on the part of Chancellor Kiesinger himself, was also noted. At the same time, however, positive reations to the Polish initiative were given considerable attention. The stand of the lay Catholic intellectuals, of the "Bensberger Kreis," was praised. The statements by the FDP and the SPD leaders, notably Foreign Minister Brandt, were covered objectively in the Polish papers. At the same time, the Polish communist leaders continued their conciliatory gestures towards the

Poland and Germany: A Belated Détente?

Federal Republic. Premier Cyrankiewicz in a speech in Cracow on 23 May, and Foreign Minister Jedrychowski in a speech in Szczecin on 26 May reasserted Gomulks's position. Klaus Arndt, State Secretary of the West German Economics Ministry, and Klause Schutz, Mayor of West Berlin, who visited Poland in June, were given friendly receptions. By early summer there was no doubt that a major shift in Poland's policy toward West Germany was under way.

What appeared to outside observers as a complete about-face in Polish foreign policy in reality was far less drastic. The change in Warsaw's attitude toward Bonn had been, in fact, in the offing for quite some time.[13] Throughout the 1960s Gomulka was under increasingly heavy pressure from various quarters to take cognizance of the changing political atmosphere in West Germany and to mitigate his hard stand *vis-à-vis* that country. The first open pressure came from the Polish Catholics. As early as 1962, the influential writers from the "Znak" group observed positive changes in the GFR. In 1965, the Polish Episcopate came out with a letter calling for a reconciliation between the two nations in a true Christian spirit. The positive response on the part of the German Catholics from the "Bensberger Kreis" was amicably acknowledged in the Polish Catholic weekly *Tygodnik Powszechny*.[14]

The opposition to Gomulka's stand on Germany, however, was not confined to the Catholics. There was also considerable dissatisfaction among the Polish communists. Many younger, better educated, and more open-minded members of the Polish United Workers' Party felt that Gomulka's policy was not only sterile, but was in fact detrimental to Poland's interest. Warsaw's purely negative posture toward Bonn discouraged the elements striving for a genuine reconciliation and played into the hands of the hard liners in the GFR. Moreover, Poland's uncompromising attitude toward West Germany stood in the way of improving its relations with other western countries and, as such, seriously restricted its scope of manoeuver in the international sphere. Finally, intense anti-German propaganda, at times bordering on hysteria, was obviously counter-productive in that it frequently hurt Poland's image more than that of the GFR. The dissatisfaction with Gomulka's policy was particularly strong among the foreign-policy specialists, who early on had advocated a return in relations with West Germany to the more rational and flexible policy of the 1950s.[15] By the late 1960s, with the nationalist sentiments generally on the rise among Polish communists, these views apparently gained acceptance in the upper echelons of the PUWP.

Foreign policy considerations also tended to push the Gomulka regime in the direction of gradual *rapprochement* with West Germany. Beyond the façade of solidarity and friendship, Warsaw's relations with Pankow were not without strain. The memories of bitter antagonism between the two Communist regimes from the late 1950s bred mutual distrust. The East Germans viewed with suspicion any Polish moves to improve relations with the west. At the same time, the Poles became increasingly aware that by tying their foreign policy to Ulbricht's creaking chariot they would remain on the side lines of international developments and would be unable to play any constructive role in advancing the East-West detente. The negative reactions of the GDR to the change in Poland's policy toward the GFR was openly confirmed in the speech given in Warsaw in July 1969 by the East German Premier Willi Stoph. Ignoring Gomulka's proposal to the Federal Republic to recognize Poland's western frontier, the East German leader insisted that the security of the Oder-Neisse border was inseparably linked with the maintenance of the Elbe-Werra line.[16] The different evaluation of their respective interests by Warsaw and East Berlin was now apparent.

With one eye to Pankow, Warsaw, of course, was not overlooking developments in Moscow. The Polish communists remembered very well Khruhchev's abortive plan to visit Bonn in 1965, which had signalled a possible shift in the Soviet attitude toward West Germany. The prospect of an accommodation between the U.S.S.R. and the GFR, reached over their heads, certainly did not appeal to them. Thus, the somewhat more relaxed atmosphere between Moscow and Bonn which emerged early in 1969 must have made the Poles apprehensive. Consequently, when in March the Warsaw Pact powers issued the Budapest Appeal for a European security conference, Poland exploited this opportunity to try to mend its fences with the GFR. The Warsaw move seemed to be well timed. By warmly endorsing the Budapest Appeal, Poland not only identified itself with Soviet long-term objectives, but also took this opportunity to advance its own initiatives in central Europe, showing a more distinct foreign-policy profile than had been the case since the late 1950s.

Last but not least, the economic motives, although clearly subordinate to political ones, favoured the improvement of relations between Warsaw and Bonn. Poland could clearly benefit from expanded economic contacts—trade, investment credits, and scientific assistance—with the GFR. Yet, since the mid-1960s there had been very little progress in economic co-operation between the two countries. West German visitors to the Poznan Fair in the summer of 1969 were therefore happily surprised when they encountered an entirely changed climate and met with an eager reception. State Secretary Arndt returned with the impression that the Poles were jealous of the close trading relations between East and West Germany and wished to establih similar relationships with Bonn, which, among other effects, would reduce Poland's economic dependence on the GDR.[17] Formal Polish-West German economic negotiations started early in the fall—the Poles seeking substantial long-term loans to expand their purchases in the GFR. Reportedly, the Germans expressed readiness to provide them with credits of approximately $500 million repayable in 10 years.[18]

All in all, by the end of the 1960s the Poles were also ripe for reconciliation with the entire German nation. A new mood, it seems, emerged in the country. It was significant that, when Gomulka proposed an international treaty with the GFR in his speech of 17 May, the audience, composed of people from the Praga district of Warsaw, responded with spontaneous applause.[19]

The Dialogue Continued

The initial German reaction to the Polish proposals revealed a split along the customary party lines. The leader of the CDU, Chancellor Kiesinger, was restrained in his comments. He merely registered willingness to discuss the border question with Gomulka and referred to Germany's standing offer for a renunciation of the use of force agreement.[20] The SDP leader, Foreign Minister Brandt, responded more warmly to Gomulka's speech. In a statement to the press on 26 May 1969, he styled a reconciliation with Poland a "moral and political duty" for Germany and called it a task of the same historical dimensions as Germany's reconciliation with France.[21] He reiterated the Nurnberg formula and added that it did not exclude other solutions from being worked out in bilateral discussions. The future of relations with Poland clearly became one of the divisive issues in the forthcoming West German elections.

Through the summer of 1969 the socialists pressed on with their programme of reconciliation with Poland. After his return from a visit to Poland in June, the Social Democratic Mayor of West Berlin, Schütz, declared himself firmly in favour of a broader agreement with Poland. He even went beyond the Nurnberg formula by stressing that the Polish people must be given an immediate assurance that their boundaries will not be changed.[22] On the thirtieth anniversary of the German invasion of Poland, the Socialist President, Gustav Heinemann, in a nationwide statement on radio and television, appealed for the overcoming of mutual distrust and the resolving of the dispute between the two countries. He urged them "to fill up the trenches so firmly that nothing can open them up again."[23]

Evidently the SDP position was judged satisfactory by Warsaw, for soon after the Party's electoral victory a new and encouraging gesture was made on the Polish side. On 16 October, Foreign Minister Jedrychowski granted an interview to the West German television network.[24] In his comments Jedrychowski underlined that even if the tragic experiences of the second world war are still remembered by them, the Poles are not anti-German. As evidence, he pointed to the strong interest existing in Poland in the various aspects of German culture. He also pointed out Poland's readiness to expand economic contacts with West Germany. As to improved political relations, the Polish Foreign Minister emphasized their importance to the progress of a detente in Europe. As he obviously awaited some new steps from the German side, he advanced no concrete proposals, but restricted himself to reiterating the Polish stand on the border issue and added that Poland took "no formal position" toward a normalization of relations with the GFR.[25]

The Poles did not have to wait long for the next step on the German side. In an address to the Bundestag on 28 October, presenting the programme of the Coalition government of the SDP and the FDP, Chancellor Brandt devoted considerable attention to the *Ostpolitik*. On several aspects, the new German eastern policy moved closer to the Polish position. Brandt announced Bonn's willingness to sign the nuclear non-proliferation treaty. He still refused to give formal recognition to the GDR under international law, but at the same time he expressed readiness to expand contacts with it on a *de facto* basis. The German leader also repeated the offer to renounce the use of force in relations with eastern European countries, and stressed that such agreements would "acknowledge the territorial integrity of the respective partners."[26] Finally, he expressed hope that direct talks with Poland would take place soon.

Less than a month later in an interview with the Warsaw daily, *Zycie Warszawy*, Chancellor Brandt reasserted his position *vis-à-vis* Poland, clearly implying that the guarantee of territorial integrity in a treaty renouncing the use of force in relations between the two countries would represent a *de facto* recognition of Poland's western boundary.[27] Brandt's proposals evoked various critical comments from the CDU leaders but, now in opposition, they were unable to block his initiative. Toward the end of November, the Bonn government made a formal offer to Warsaw to begin talks on "all questions of mutual interest."[28] Early in December Warsaw responded favourably.

The Difficulties Ahead

There is no question that in 1969 Poland and West Germany moved a long way from the cold war toward a détente. The atmosphere in relations between the two countries is at present better than it has ever been in the past. Still, their forthcoming negotiations, more likely than not, will be arduous. The favourable climate is important as a prerequisite to normalization, but in itself it is not a guarantee for an understanding. The two major obstacles to improved relations remain. These are (1) Polish support for the policies of the GDR in a manner which, to Bonn, must appear detrimental to the goal of reunification and (2) the contested territorial issue. The first obstacle would be mitigated if Warsaw dropped its demand for a *de facto* acceptance of the GDR by the Federal Republic. The territorial dilemma remains.

The Poles will not accept any solution short of recognition by West Germany of the finality of their boundary along the Oder and the Neisse. Indeed, a refusal to take this step by the GFR will probably make Warsaw adopt a tougher attitude on the issue of the recognition of the GDR as well. The Poles feel—and on this issue communists and non-communists are united—that the maintenance of the western territores is indispensable to their national survival. They consider that Poland, deprived of one-third of the country's industrial production would be crippled beyond repair. From the Polish point of view the matter is simply not negotiable.

In demanding formal recognition of their western frontier from all Germans, and not just from the GDR, the Poles seek not only assurance against an eventual revisionist revival, but also moral compensation for the suffering and injustice inflicted on them by the war. The maintenance of their boundary along the Oder and the Neisse is of immense emotional importance for the Poles. It symbolizes for them that Poland was on the victorious side in the second world war and that its tremendous losses were not in vain. Conversely, the refusal to recognize the existing frontier as final is viewed in Poland as a denial by the Germans of their own defeat and an attempt to turn history back to 1939. The Poles realize, of course, that the renunciation of one-fourth of their former territory is not easy for the Germans, but they feel that, after what happened during the second world war, a truly great sacrifice is necessary on the part of Germans to restore justice in relations between the two nations.

It is clear that the most unqualified formula for territorial recognition would have the greatest positive impact on Polish-German relations. Since it is unlikely, however, that the present German government will agree to a totally unqualified recognition, the corresponding improvement of Polish attitudes toward the GFR is bound to be limited. Distrust of Germany among the Poles will probably linger on and can be allayed only by repeated demonstrations of good faith on the part of the Germans. Yet, regardless of what legal formula is adopted to achieve this purpose, a settlement of the territorial dispute between the two countries would be of a great importance. Unless Bonn takes this first step, fear of Germany will continue indefinitely in Poland, and no true German-Polish reconciliation will be possible.

Towards a Détente

Recognition of the finality of the existing western boundary of Poland, which will clearly emerge as the main issue in the forthcoming German-Polish talks, would present any German government with a problem that might affect its very survival. A "Great Coalition" type of government, such as the one that was in power in 1966-9 and which received over four-fifths of the popular vote, might seem the best political constellation to make such a critical decision. But in the normal fashion of grand coalitions, the life of this grouping was purchased at the price of reduced political dynamism and decision-making capability. The minimum winning coalition that rules in Bonn today faces a dilemma at the opposite end of the spectrum, for its majority is so small that it might be disinclined to risk its life by tackling such a controversial issue.

There are several factors, however, that indicate that the present coalition may be inclined toward taking major initiatives on the Polish question as part of a wider European reconciliatory process. In the first place, it is led precisely by those elements of the SDP, notably Brandt himself, who over the past few years have committed themselves most firmly to a flexible and bynamic *Ostpolitik*. Secondly, the much decimated FDP will be inclined to continue its efforts on behalf of an active eastern policy in order to preserve an independent profile and to justify the inherent soundness of this policy in the face of some considerable voting backlash, which it seems to have suffered on account of its stand on eastern issues. Thirdly, the recent election setback of the NPD has reduced the threat of a massive shift toward the right in protest over a policy of accommodation toward the east, and the Small Coalition is thus provided with greater decision-making latitude in that area.

The government's conciliatory efforts, moreover, are assisted by a favourable emotional climate in German public opinion. The catastrophe of the last war seems to have had a cathartic effect in discharging much of the hostility and disdain about Poland and Polish culture that permeated virtually all segments of German life before the second world war. German news media project a generally sympathetic image of Poland's history, her culture, and her people, and in intellectual circles polonophile attitudes are *de rigueur*. Works by modern Polish composers are more frequently performed in German concert halls and opera houses than anywhere else in the west and the writings of both traditional and contemporary Polish authors are being translated into German.

Yet, the opposition to an explicit and formal renunciation of the territories east of Oder-Neisse is also formidable and it is entirely possible that even a combination of the dynamism of Brandt's government and a favourable public-opinion climate would not be strong enough to overcome it. As with the Poles, the resistance on the part of the Germans to recognition of the finality of the Oder-Neisse boundary is both emotional and political in nature. With the growing assertion of realistic calculations and under the compulsion of demographic developments, the number of Germans who are actively demanding the return of the regions lost to Poland is rapidly dwindling. Yet there remains the emotional resistance to a formal disassociation from cherished memories and a long historical tradition. To many people, an outright renunciation seems a denial of their personal identity. Much of this emotional reservation might be overcome if, in a final settlement, the Polish side were to express its regrets over the personal fate of those Germans who have been forced to leave their homeland to which they were bound by close personal ties and long tradition. Sentiments of this kind have already been expressed in the exchange of messages between the Polish and German Episcopate in 1965 and 1966.

As to the German political reservations, these can be summarized by two broad statements. First, at a future international peace conference, recognition of the Oder-Neisse frontier could serve as a *quid pro quo* to gain international support for German reunification. Second, by recognizing this particular frontier, Germany would confirm the *status quo* in Europe, and thus formalize her division. The first argument has lost much of its plausibility since it has become widely recognized that reunification cannot be achieved by legalistic acrobatics or a crude bargaining device but only as part of a gradual process of reconciliation in Europe. Regarding the argument that a unilateral recognition by Germany might pre-empt a final peace treaty and thus confirm the present division, German reservations might be overcome by a bilateral German-Polish agreement which would include the establishment of diplomatic relations, the renunciation of the use of force, and respect for territorial integrity by explicit affirmation of the Nurnberg formula, as well as an implicit assurance that Germany would not re-open the territorial issue at a future peace conference. Another form of agreement, and one preferable to Poland, would be one in which the Federal Republic, for its part, would recognize the finality of the Oder-Neisse line as Poland's western frontier, with both parties agreeing that this bilateral protocol would remain to be confirmed by an international peace settlement, thus preserving the option for such an international treaty.

At the same time, it must be realized that no international peace treaty is in sight and that an excessive preoccupation with legal formulae about frontier guarantees or, on the other side, frontier rectification procedures, might impede the process of detente between Poland and Germany. Normalization of relations between the two countries must be based on present realities, including Poland's present territorial status. Recognition must become part of, rather than a substitute for, a wider strategy of German-Polish co-operation that seeks to create a new political and security order in Europe.

The proposed European security conference could be one of the available avenues for moving toward the new order which would determine the status of nuclear weapons in Europe, the level of conventional forces, and the relationship between the two principal alliance systems, and which would also transform the character of existing boundaries to that they would lose their hitherto divisive character. Klaus Schutz aptly defined these sentiments in a message which he published after his recent visit to Poland: "It is not a question of altering boundaries and frontier markings, nor is it a matter of agreeing to a temporary truce on border questions—the question is one of transforming the very character of boundaries."[31]

Footnotes

* Originally published in *The Canadian Slavonic Papers*, Summer 1970. Co-author Harald von Riekhoft.

1   For a comprehensive review of Polish-German relations in the 1950s and the early 1960s see: Hansjakob Stehle, *The Independent Satellite* (New York, 1965), ch. 5; Karl Kaiser, German Foreign Policy in Transition (London, 1968), ch. 4: also A. Ross Johnson "A Survey of Poland's Relations with West Germany, 1956-1967" (RFE Research, 7 March 1968, mimeographed).

2   Stehle, p. 249.

3   For the analysis of the developments of 1963 see: Helmut Allard, "Deutschland und Polen," *Aussenpolitik* (May 1963); and Alexander Bregman "Polish-German Relations: A New Phase," East Europe (November 1963) pp.2-7.

4   The trade agreement was of particular significance to Germany because it included the so-called Berlin clause under which West Berlin was recognized as part of the D-mark zone, thus opening at least a minor breach in the hitherto concerted campaign to detach West Berlin from the Federal Republic.

5   Ludwig Raiser, "Deutsche Ostpolitik in Lichte der Denkschrift der evangelischen Kirche,"*Europa-Archiv* (March 1966), 195-208.

6   In public-opinion polls conducted by the Allensbach Institute in October 1967, 35 per cent of the respondents favoured, and 43 per cent opposed, resigning themselves to the Oder-Neisse frontier. But when asked whether the Oder-Neisse should be recognized "if recognition were to produce better relations with the East," 53 per cent favoured recognition and only 33 per cent opposed it (Allensbach, 7 November 1967, cited in Kaiser, p. 45).

7   *Trybuna ludu,* 4 July 1963.

8   Theo Sommer, "Bonn Changes Course," *Foreign Affairs* (April 1967), 488.

9   Willy Brandt, "German Policy Toward the East," *Foreign Affairs* (April 1968), 480.

10   *Ibid.,* 484.

11   Wladyslaw Gomulka, O *problemie niemieckim* (Warsaw, 1968), p. 492.

12   *Trybuna ludu,* May 1969.

13   An informed western specialist on Poland seems to believe that, had it not been for the events in Czechoslovakia, the shift in Polish policy toward West Germany would have probably take place earlier. A. Ross Johnson, "A New Phase in Polish West German Relations, Part III: A Preliminary Analysis" (RFE Research, 4 August 1969, mimeo-graphed), p. 6.

14   *Tygodnik Powszechny,* 17 March 1968.

15   In fact, the studies of alternative Polish policies *vis-à-vis* West Germany were undertaken by the specialists in Warsaw as early as 1964.

16   *Neues Deutschland,* 22 July 1969.

17   *Der Spiegel,* 16 June 1969, p. 31.

18   *The New York Times,* 9 December 1969.

19   Karol Malcuzynski, "Glos Polski w sprawach Europy," *Trybuna Ludu,* 21 May 1969.

20   *Die Welt,* 4 June 1969.

21   *Die Zeit,* 27 May 1969.

22   *Die Zeit,* 1 July 1969.

23   *The New York Times,* 2 September 1969.

24   The choice as an interviewer of Dr. Hansjakob Stehle, a noted journalist and author and a long-time advocate of *rapprochement* between Poland and the GFR, but a person who had been openly critical of various aspects of Gomulka's policies, in itself represented a conciliatory gesture on the Polish side.

25   "Polish View on Normalization of Relations between Poland and the German Federal Republic," *Polish News Items* (issued by the Polish Embassy in Ottawa, mimeographed).

26   *Die Welt,* 29 October 1969.

27   *Zycie Warszawy,* 23 November 1969.

28   *The Bulletin* (A weekly survey of German affairs issued by the Press and Information of the Government of the Federal Republic of Germany), 25 November 1969.

29   *Die Zeit,* 1 July 1969.

X
The West German — Polish Treaty*

The treaty with Poland signed on 7 December 1970 occupies a very special place in the West German *Ostpolitik* and in efforts to promote an East-West detente. Its significance goes beyond eliminating one more source of East-West tension and reaches into the more fundamental causes of the present situation in Europe. It is to be hoped the Warsaw treaty will end the international conflict which had preceded and, indeed, had played an important part in bringing about the present division of Europe. As such, the agreement, precisely because it contributes to long-term European stability, also represents a genuine achievement on the road towards improving East-West relations.

The treaty

As Chancellor Brandt indicated in his public address to the German people, the treaty itself offers no guarantee that a true reconciliation, such as had already taken place between the Federal Republic and its western neighbours, will follow between Poland and Germany.[1] But there should be no doubt that without an agreement which gives Poland secure possession of her present territory there can be no reconciliation. The present Government of the Federal Republic has shown both realism and courage in accepting this fact and in making it the basis for its foreign policy. And the communist Government of Poland, for its part, has revealed a good deal of flexibility and tact which has helped to make the agreement acceptable to West Germany.

An analysis of the treaty documents shows that in order to reach an accord both sides have modified their initial demands and made significant concessions. Warsaw has withdrawn its demand to include in the preamble an explicit reference to German war guilt for the second World War. The Bonn negotiators feared that such a reference to their past would create unnecessary emotional resistance in Germany, and therefore wished to give the preamble as futuristic a look as possible. In the final version, Poland is listed as the first victim of the war, but there is no specific mention of German war guilt. The general emphasis in the preamble is on the future; it refers to the younger generation and the need to secure a peaceful prospect for it.

Regarding the boundary question, the Polish position has basically prevailed. In the Warsaw treaty stipulations for the renunciation of force have been so completely fused with provisions for the acceptance of the territorial *status quo* that the end-product, in contrast to that of the Moscow treaty with the Soviet Union, is a border treaty with additional provisions for the renunciation of force, rather than the reverse. Both the Warsaw and Moscow treaties contain a *de facto* acceptance by Germany of Poland's western frontier since they specifically refer to the Oder-Niesse Line as being the western boundary of Poland. The Warsaw treaty, in addition, describes the course of the border and acknowledges that it was "laid down" by Chapter IX of the Potsdam agreements. And by offering the Poles even more explicit acceptance of the territorial *status quo* than they had extended to the Russians, the German negotiators respected Warsaw's desire to assert its independent stance in foreign affairs by obtaining an agreement that was not merely a carbon copy of the preceding Moscow treaty.

But even on the territorial question the Polish negotiators made some concessions in recognition of German sensibilities and their problems with regard to ratification. The text of the Warsaw treaty provides for the acceptance, but not for the recognition, of the territorial *status quo*. The German Government can point out that the treaty neither violates the rights of the Big Four nor pre-empts a final peace treaty with Germany,[2] and thus does not create any international legal obstacles to an eventual German reunification.

With respect to the German ethnic group, considerable concessions have also been made by the Poles to meet German demands. While this matter has not been formally included in the treaty clauses, as the Bonn negotiators had hoped, the Polish Government has nevertheless made an official declaration in which is promises to adopt a positive attitude in allowing "tens of thousands" of persons of indisputably German or mixed origin to emigrate from Poland in order to rejoin their families in Germany.

The ratification

A normalization of relations between Poland and the Federal Republic is still contingent on the ratification of the Warsaw treaty by the Bundestag. Domestic opposition in Germany is considerable. The Christian Democrats refused to send a representative to accompany Chancellor Brandt on his Warsaw mission. Indeed, their reaction to the Warsaw treaty was both more immediate and more hostile than the watchful waiting tactics which they had adopted after the Moscow agreement. The Association of Expellees has vowed that it will do everything within its constitutional democratic rights to bring about a revision of the boundary provision in the treaty. Rainer Barzel, Chairman of the CDU/CSU in the Budestag, called the Warsaw treaty a "very far-reaching, painful, and momentous decision" which had been made without the consent of those most immediately concerned.[3] The Opposition has drawn up its own version of a normalization agreement with Poland. It is on record as favouring improved relations, including diplomatic relations and economic and cultural contacts, but it desires a much more vaguely worded formula about the present status of the Oder-Niesse Line, together with an explicit statement that the Warsaw treaty does not pre-empt a final peace treaty with a reunited Germany.

Given the Government's slim majority in the Bundestag and some opposition from within its own ranks by refugee politicians, the possibility cannot be discounted that the treaty will fall short of the necessary majority, if the CDU/CSU maintains a solid opposition front. But in practice the Christian Democrats' effective opposition to the treaty may prove to be less adamant than the initial verbal hostility would indicate. Already, a group of younger CDU parliamentarians has emerged which is not fundamentally opposed to the treaty and might even vote for it. Industrial interests close to the CDU have great expectations regarding the potential Polish market and would view with disfavour any attempts to impede the process of normalization. Furthermore, by a veto of the treaty the Christian Democrats would incur the onus of having prevented the return of thousands of German families.

Other long-term calculations are also likely to soften the Opposition's negative stand. Last year's *Land* elections in Hesse and Bavaria underscored the viability of the FDP, and with it that of the Bonn coalition. The Christian Democrats are thus faced with the prospect of remaining in opposition for a long time. This realization is bound to produce some sober reflections. Protest movements can be upheld by small splinter parties. But the official Opposition in a Western democracy is ill-advised to isolate itself from the mainstream of domestic and international political developments.[4] The Christian Democrats may soon have to change their position regarding the Government's *Ostpolitik*.

A good many of the refugees, too, may come to modify their opposition to the acceptance of the Polish western boundary. The treaty imposes the heaviest burden on this particular group because it undermines their illusions. Yet, in concrete terms, it is precisely this group of refugees which stands to gain most from a normalization of relations with Poland. It is, after all, their relations and friends who will be able to rejoin them as the consequence of the treaty. Poland has promised to accord West Germans the same treatment regarding visas and foreign-currency regulations as now applies to other West Europeans. This will enable the German refugees to revisit their homeland. Rather than incite further bitterness, these sentimental journeys generally have a cathartic effect. Such visits remind the refugees how deeply they have become rooted in their new West German environment and give them a sense of affinity and understanding for those Poles who have rebuilt the war-ravaged lands and have made them their homes.

An early ratification of the Warsaw treaty by the Federal Republic, regardless of the future of the Moscow treaty, may even be expedient. For, despite the initial strong opposition, it would probably be easier and wiser for the Brandt Government to seek a separate parliamentary approval for the treaty with Poland than to insist on ratification of all treaties with the Communist countries at once—especially if such a package included a controversial agreement with the D.D.R. Moreover, it might be politic for Brandt to isolate the Warsaw treaty from the knotty issue of Berlin, the resolution of which Bonn has made a precondition for the ratification of the Moscow treaty. Should the negotiations over Berlin be delayed, the momentum of Brandt's Eastern policy could still be maintained by ratifying the accord with Poland. Indeed, should the *Ostpolitik* accomplish nothing else, laying the foundation for a reconciliation with Poland would give the German Chancellor an honourable place in history. Last but not least, a separate German ratification of the treaty with Poland, confirming its importance *per se*, would enhance even further Warsaw's independent foreign profile.

On the Polish side it is unlikely that ratification will run into any difficulties. The removal of Mr. Gomulka, less than two weeks after the treaty was signed, should make little difference. The new Communist leader, Edward Gierek, is anxious to achieve economic progress and must be well aware of the importance to Poland of expanding economic co-operation with West Germany. The more nationalistic elements in the new leadership, personified by General Mieczyslaw Moczar, should be pleased with those aspects of the treaty which enhance Poland's prestige in the international sphere. Furthermore, the present "collective Government" is more likely to pay greater attention to the wishes of the people. And the mood of the country is overwhelmingly in favour of the Polish-West German accord.[5] It is not only that the Poles welcome greater security on their western border, but to them the link with the Federal Republic is more important as another step in overcoming the division of Europe and bringing Poland closer to the West. It was significant that the Polish Episcopate, which had been the first to call for Polish-German reconciliation in 1965, warmly welcomed the signing of the Warsaw treaty.[6]

The Poles, moreover, are well aware of the obstacles which the Brandt-Scheel Government faces at home and they would not want to add to its difficulties. The West German Chancellor has won not only the trust, but also the sympathy, of the Polish people. The dignified but warm personality which he displayed during his visit to Warsaw greatly enhanced his already considerable popularity in Poland. The Poles certainly would not like to contribute to Brandt's political defeat. Their attitude was well expressed in an article written immediately after the signing of the Warsaw treaty. "We know that there exist in the GFR not inconsiderable forces opposed to the normalization of relations with the socialist countries... Nevertheless realism and reason seem to be in the ascendancy."[7] The Poles, then, are unlikely to become involved in the legal hair-splitting still fashionable in opposition circles in West Germany, and will probably overlook the semantic distinctions between 'recognition' and 'acceptance' of their boundary by the Federal Republic. They will view the treaty as a territorial 'recognition', but will not object if the Germans—largely to avoid the appearance of a preliminary peace treaty and the consequent requirement for a two-thirds majority in the Bundestag—place the accent on 'acceptance'.

The West German-Polish Treaty

In order to accelerate ratification, the Polish side will probably also do whatever it can to resolve satisfactorily the question of emigration of the German minority. Bonn having conceded that this is not a matter of international concern, there is no reason why Warsaw should not let these people go. Their departure will only further solidify Poland's hold over her western territories. The loss of population will not be a serious problem, as in the presently ailing Polish economy there is a surplus of labour anyway. Finally, the question of permitting a greater number of West German tourists to visit Poland should pose little difficulty. The Poles will proudly display to their visitors the progress which they have made in rebuilding the war-ravaged former German lands. They may even welcome the chance of establishing contact with the Germans revisiting their homeland, for there is a marked change in their attitude towards the German refugees. The Polish press has acknowledged that not all refugees stand for the revision of the boundary with Poland, and a popular Warsaw daily has admitted that acceptance of the existing realities must be particularly painful for the Germans born east of the Oder-Neisse.[8]

Towards the Future

Seen from a historical perspective, the Warsaw treaty represents a notable milestone in almost every respect. It is the first serious attempt after more than a generation to reach a real understanding. The rationale behind this effort at normalization does not conform with the classical "balance-of-power" concepts. This is not an agreement by which Germany opts for the East and turns her back on the West; nor does she seek to enlist the co-operation of Warsaw in order to conspire against Moscow. The agreement is not directed against a specific country but seeks to reduce tensions and to create a more secure and flexible political situation in Europe.

The treaty does not in itself normalize relations between the Federal Republic and Poland; it merely opens the way to such a process. It is thus extremely hazardous to speculate about its domestic and international political consequences. It will certainly not have the effect of taking either signatory out of its present alliance system. As a veteran German observer of the Polish scene, Immanuel Birnbaum aptly put it, in the *Suddeutsche Zeitung*: "... the great alliances remain the guarantee behind any continuation of the policy of relaxation which now is getting off to a cautious start."[9] The Bonn Government has gone out of its way to dispel even the shadow of a doubt that its *Ostpolitik* might evolve elements of disloyalty or disengagement from NATO and the EEC. Germany's activity in these organizations is thus more likely to grow than to diminish, all the more as her growing dialogue with the East European countries make her more central to NATO discussions about détente, balanced troop reductions, and the proposed security conference.

As for the other East European states, Germany's acceptance of the Oder-Neisse frontier has given credibility to her peaceful engagement in this field. The Warsaw agreement will in all probability have a catalytic effect in bringing the impending discussions with Czechoslovakia and Hungary to a successful conclusion. The growing web of agreements and contacts between the Federal Republic and the members of the Warsaw Pact cannot fail to affect inter-German relations as well. East Germany faces the risk of isolating herself from her allies and of being left behind the mainstream of political developments if she persists with her cold-war tactics. If the D.D.R. wishes to avoid the fate of becoming another Albania, she too will have to establish the modicum of a working relationship with her western neighbour.

It seems altogether possible that Chancellor Brandt will succeed where President de Gaulle—that master-mind in the art of extracting political leverage—failed, namely in augmenting his country's role in the Western alliance through its East European contacts. This simultaneous German expansion of relations with her neighbours West and East should contribute to the gradual overcoming of the division of Europe and, ultimately, to the growth of pan-European co-operation.

As for Poland, the immediate consequences of the normalization of relations with West Germany will be felt primarily in the economic sphere. There is likely to be a considerable readjustment of her trade from her Comecon partners to the Federal Republic and other EEC members. Her drive for economic modernization and improved managerial techniques will largely depend on increased imports of Western machinery and more access to Western technology. This, in turn, will depend on her ability to increase her exports to West Germany and the other Common Market members. The need for qualitative, as against mere quantitative, changes in the Polish economic system, then, is likely to be reinforced.

In the long run, normalization in Polish-German relations should also provide Warsaw with greater scope in its foreign policy. The Poles, no longer feeling threatened by Germany, should be in a better position to seek more freedom of manoeuvre in their relations with the Soviet Union. If the Communist Government fails to exploit these opportunities, attempts will be made to push it in that direction by the increasingly nationalistic sentiments in the ranks of the Polish communist party and by popular pressure in the country at large. What the Poles would like to achieve is not a replacement of one antagonism by another, but rather a normalization of relations with both their great neighbours. In a way, they consider friendship with the Soviet Union as a prerequisite for the improvement of relations with Germany. As Polish Catholic leader, Stanislaw Stomma, put it in a speech in the *Sejm*; "We have a paradoxical situation, as it were. Our alliance with the East may well lead to a stabilization and improvement of relations with our neighbour to the West."[10] Thus, in a new situation, a more assertive Polish foreign policy is likely to take the form of a gradual decline in emphasis on the formal alliance structure in central Europe, and its eventual replacement by an increase in multilateral co-operation among all the states in the region. Needless to add, such a development would bring Polish objectives closely into line with what appears to be Chancellor Brandt's ultimate design for Europe.

In the last instance, what the West Germans and the Poles have in common is that they both find the existing *status quo* in Europe unacceptable and hope gradually to change it. As long as the West Germans insisted that the change should include the revision of the boundary with Poland, the Poles had no choice but to oppose it. With the abandonment of the German claims, the stumbling-block preventing co-operation between the two nations has been removed. The unmistakable spontaneity which characterized the recent Polish-German *rapprochement* probably stemmed from instinctive realization of the future unity of their purposes. And perhaps this was the most important aspect of the encounters in Bonn and Warsaw. For it is human experience of this type, rather than the legal casuistries of an international treaty, which will form the real basis of a German-Polish reconciliation.

Footnotes

* Originally published in *The World Today*, March 1971. Co-author Harald von Riekhoff.
1 For a text of Chancellor Brandt's speech, see *Die Welt*, 21 November 1970.
2 Article IV stipulates that the Warsaw treaty does not affect previous international agreements by either signatory. In addition, the Polish Government took official note of an exchange of letters between the Federal Republic and the three Western allies in which they agree that allied rights and responsibilities on the German question remain unimpaired by the Warsaw treaty.
3 Cited in *Die Welt*, 21-22 November 1970. Dr. Barzel visited Poland from 20 to 23 January. He told a press conference in Warsaw on 22 January that difference of opinion on the assessment of the treaty "continue to exist." (*International Herald Tribune*, 23-24 January 1971). He said there were practical matters which could and should be considered before the ratification of the treaty—namely, the creation of a joint German-Polish chamber of trade and joint youth organizations, and travel arrangements between the two countries (*Neue Zurcher Zeitung*, 25 January 1971).
4 It may be recalled in this context that the SPD, when in opposition, initially objected to German entry into the European Coal and Steel Community and NATO, but subsequently has become a firm champion of European integration and the Atlantic Alliance.
5 It was characteristic that in his appeal to the populace for peace on 17 December 1970, Premier Cyrankiewicz singled out the treaty with West Germany as an achievement of the Communist Government.
6 Cited in *Krajowa Agencja Informacyjna*, 9 December 1970.
7 *Glos Pracy*, 8 December 1970.
8 *Zycie Warszawy*, 8 December 1970.
9 Quoted in *The Bulletin: A weekly survey of German affairs* (Press and Information Office, Bonn), 17 November 1970.
10 *Tygodnik Powszechny*, 13 July 1969.

XI
The CSCE and Eastern Europe*

1973 has been termed "the year of Europe." The three main East-West parleys at present under way all focus on Europe. The preparatory talks for a Conference on Security and Cooperation in Europe (CSCE) and the negotiations on Mutual and Balanced Force Reductions (MBFR) are both confined to European problems; the second round of the Strategic Arms Limitation Talks (SALT II), although conducted exclusively by the two nuclear superpowers, also affects in a major way the balance of power in Europe. Taken together these diplomatic activities amount to the most serious effort undertaken in the post-war years to arrive at a settlement of the European problem.

The negotiations paving the way for the CSCE have been going on for some time. Since the Communist countries revived their proposal in March 1969 at a meeting in Budapest to hold a European conference, several international accords substantially reducing East-West tensions in Europe have been concluded. The Berlin agreement, the treaty between the two German States, and the treaties signed by West Germany with the Soviet Union and Poland have made a major advance toward solving the hitherto insoluble German problem. The signing, during President Nixon's visit to Moscow, of the agreement on SALT I also greatly contributed to the growing climate of detente in Europe. Finally, the gradual narrowing of the divergent East-West views as to the format of the CSCE, and above all the acceptance by the Communist countries of the United States and Canada as fully fledged participants in the conferences, made it possible to start the multilateral preparatory talks in Helsinki at the end of 1972.

In the course of the early negotiations the Communist powers have displayed a good deal of moderation. Moscow's new course has been carefully presented as a continuation of the Leninist line of peaceful coexistence; yet there is little doubt that it has amounted to a major departure from the entire post-war pattern of Soviet foreign policy. On several issues the Soviet Union has met the West half-way; at times, and especially over the German problem, she even made significant concessions. In this way several apparently insurmountable obstacles to a European detente have been overcome.

In the West there are two schools of thought which explain the Communist persistence in promoting a European Conference. The first group of analysts look at the new Soviet policy with apprehension—they see it as a tactical manoeuvre to attain in a different way the same goal which the Russians failed to achieve through the cold war, namely the shifting of the global balance of power in their favour and to the detriment of the United States. Moscow's objective, according to this interpretation, is to reduce the American presence in Europe, to disrupt Nato, and ultimately, by dealing with individual countries, to achieve a 'Finlandization' of Western Europe. The second group of observers take a different view and attribute Soviet interest in the CSCE to difficulties at home and in the Communist bloc at large. Moscow's efforts to reduce political tensions with the West are seen as stemming primarily from economic motives. The Russians need expansion of international trade and access to Western technology to accelerate their industrial development and especially to provide more consumer goods at home. The conflict with China is often pointed to as another reason which has prompted the U.S.S.R. to reappraise her policies in Europe. Faced with the prospect of a protracted struggle in the East, the Russians may wish to stabilize their position in the West.

There is one point, however, on which the two schools agree. They both think that the paramount Soviet goal at the CSCE is to preserve the *status quo* in Eastern Europe. The advocates of the first school see it as a step toward spreading Soviet influence into Western Europe; while the exponents of the second school regard it as a goal *per se*. One way or another the East European question, although probably veiled behind some other issues, is likely to loom large at the CSCE. This should not be surprising—as the cold war started over Eastern Europe, it would be only fitting to put it to rest there.

Eastern Europe in the 1970s

There is, of course, no return in Eastern Europe to the situation which existed there in the late 1940s. Since then a profound transformation has taken place in that part of the world. The post-war generation, which knows no other system than the Communist one, has come of age. New ruling elites, which have risen to the top in the existing political structure and have vested interests in perpetuating it, have emerged in virtually all the East European countries. Various economic and social changes introduced by the Communists have been accepted by large segments of the population. The basically socialist system in Eastern Europe is there to stay.

In contrast to the immediate post-war period, the traditional anti-Russian sentiments of the Eastern Europeans have abated. The past wrongs inflicted by the Russians are certainly not forgotten, but they have been largely relegated to history. The younger generation is more preoccupied with contemporary problems. The difficulties which they encounter in expanding economic relations with the West (and which are likely to increase with the expansion of the EEC) force the East Europeans to recognize the benefits of their trading with the Soviet Union. The Poles, moreover, appreciate the Soviet support which has helped them to consolidate their western boundary with Germany.

Finally, in comparison with the situation in the late 1940s and the early 1950s, a drastic change has taken place in the attitude of the East Europeans toward the West. Its major attraction nowadays is less ideological and more economic. Few East Europeans today expect a "liberation" by the West. They are impressed by the rapid economic growth and the high living standards of the Western democracies, they would like to increase trade and to gain access to Western technology, and they are certainly interested in expanded travel to the West. The Western broadcasts are still listened to, especially at a time of crisis, but their impact has diminished. The emigre centres, except perhaps the most recent exiles from Czechoslovakia, no longer commmand support at home.

The Communists, then, when they call for continued vigilance against external enemies, are victims of their own ideological myths. The more militant Western broadcasts and the isolated attempts at conspiracy inspired from abroad represent more of a nuisance than a real threat to the existing political system. The best they can do is to exploit the difficulties which are produced by the system itself. Yet, the Communist leaders have valid reasons for concern. For Eastern Europe remains intrinsically unstable. The unrest, however, is not instigated from outside; it is inherent in the present stage of development of this region.

Paradoxically, much of the instability stems from the Communists' own achievements. The problems with which most of the East European countries are faced are typical of transitional societies. The traditional predominantly agricultural social structure has been uprooted by the industrialization and modernization imposed from above. These processes, however, have not as yet run their full course leading to the emergence of modern industrial societies, which again are characterized by greater stability. Meanwhile, the contrast between the uneven distribution of the economic benefits and the "rising expectations" of the masses produces social tensions, at times erupting into violence.

The Communist system, as it exists today in most of the East European countries, in several respects only intensifies the problems inherent in the process of modernization. It has been effective, if brutal, in pushing these societies through the threshold of industrialization; but it has been unable to maintain the same pace in transforming them into fully fledged industrial communities. Communism's autocratic political nature poses a serious obstacle toward the decentralization of decision-making which is essential to deal with the complex problems of modern society. At the same time, the egalitarian character of the Communist idealogy only aggravates the gap, as perceived by the people, between the promise and the reality.

Dangers of Soviet Interference

Social unrest is characteristic of all societies in transition. It is at present manifested in many different parts of the world. What is unique about social conflicts in Eastern Europe, however, is that they are externalized, Ferment in any Eastern European country is more likely than not to prejudice its relations with the Soviet Union. This is because Moscow insists that it has the right and a duty to protect socialism in that region. And the Russians do not mean *any* type of socialism., but the one basically similar to the system existing in the U.S.S.R. Although over a period of years they have become more tolerant of some minor divergences from this pattern in different East European countries, they insist that its hard core must be preserved. In the event of a major deviation from this norm, of which the Russians themselves are to be the judge, they are prepared to resort to sanctions including the threat, or even the actual use, of force. This was drastically demonstrated by the invasion of Czechoslovakia in 1968; it was subsequently reasserted in various Soviet enunciations, which were termed in the West, the Brezhnev doctrine.

Gearing the changes in Eastern Europe to the Soviet Union seriously restricts the ability of the East European regimes to cope with their social problems. The remedies available to them are placed in a foreign ideological straitjacket. As a result, in Eastern Europe, especially in its more advanced northern part, the scope of social reforms is often insufficient. Even when changes are introduced, they are carried out with one eye on Moscow. And the various half-measures instead of resolving social issues often only aggravate them.

The East Europeans resent Soviet interference in their domestic affairs. Contemporary nationalism in Eastern Europe is less oriented toward history and, therefore, a traditional anti-Russianism is not necessarily a part of it. Yet, if the Soviet Union continues to meddle in the internal matters of the different East European countries, stultifying the reforms necessary for their progress, it may well acquire a sharp anti-Russian edge. Moscow, it seems, has already brought about such a reaction in Czechoslovakia. The invasion of that country in 1968 has transformed the Czechoslovaks, who have traditionally been friendly toward Russia, into probably one of the most intensely anti-Soviet peoples in the region. Nationalism with some anti-Russian overtones has also been integrated into the official Communist ideology in Rumania; and in the late 1960s it was espoused by the "partisans" faction of the Polish Communist Party.

There is little reason to expect that for the rest of the 1970s the situation in East Europe will become stable. The internal dynamics of these societies will breed social unrest, and its repercussions on external relations will, unless Moscow drastically revises its policy, repeatedly push them into conflict with the Soviet Union. Russian intervention in the countries with a long tradition of armed resistance, such as Poland or Yugoslavia, might be particularly dangerous. The recent developments in Yugoslavia give ground for special concern. Social unrest coupled with the nationality conflict makes the situation there highly explosive. Should a succession crisis coincide with it, internal chaos may follow. At the same time, Soviet intervention in the domestic affairs of a Communist but neutral country, and one located on an area of special strategic significance for Nato, may have ominous international consequences.

So far Moscow has been able to deal with the various crises in the region one by one. The interdependence among the East European countries, however, has been growing. The example of the reforms in Hungary in the early 1960s contributed to the unrest in Czechoslovakia in the mid-1960s; and the changes in Czechoslovakia early in 1968 inspired the students' rebellion in Poland in that year. In the future, developments in these countries are likely to become increasingly interdependent. Personal contacts among the East Europeans, in contrast to those with the Soviet Union which still remain restricted, have been greatly facilitated. Tourism throughout the region has been expanded—visas for various countries have been abolished and in 1972 the boundary between Poland and the GDR was opened. Simultaneous crises in two or more East European countries might result in a conflagration of major proportions. There is little doubt, thus, that the perpetuation of Soviet influence in the region by force poses a serious hazard to peace and security in Europe.

Likely effects of CSCE

The externalization of social conflicts in Eastern Europe in turn provides a link between the developments in that area and the progress of détente in Europe. This relationship is a doubly dangerous one. For, on the one hand, the relaxation of international tensions is conducive to a continued ferment in Eastern Europe; while, on the other hand, unrest in that part of the world is detrimental, and may even prove to be fatal, to a European detente.

The relaxation of international tensions brings the East European countries closer to the West. In a favourable political climate trade, scientific and cultural exchanges, tourism, and other forms of human contacts tend to be expanded. Increased knowledge of the more advanced Western societies accentuates the "rising expectations" among the East Europeans and intensifies the pressure on their part for an improved standard of living. It was precisely the fear of the impact of the increased contacts with West Germany which made the Ulbricht regime resist the positive Soviet response to Chancellor Brandt's *Ostpolitik*. Ulbricht was ousted in May 1971, and Honecker, prodded by the Russians, approved the Berlin agreement and proceeded to conclude the treaty with the FRG. As a result of these accords human contact between the two parts of Germany have been considerably facilitated. Yet apprehension on the part of the East German regime has not been completely removed. In 1972 the concept of *Abgrenzung*, drawing a clear-cut demarcation between personal contacts and a continued ideological vigilance, was strongly emphasized by Honecker.

Another consequence of West Germany's *Ostpolitik* has been the elimination to a large extent of fear of that country, which in the 1950s and still in th 1960s pushed the Czechs and especially the Poles to seek protection from the Russians. In his address during the popular upheaval in Poland in

1956 Premier Cyrankiewicz strongly emphasized that German claims to the Polish western territories necessitated Poland's alliance with the U.S.S.R. Yet, in his speech during the Polish revolt in December 1970 this theme was absent. Two weeks after the visit of Chancellor Brandt to Warsaw to sign the Polish-West German treaty, which sanctioned Poland's present western boundary, it simply would not have been credible.

It is likely that some of the East European countries will try to exploit the European detente to win more elbow room from the Soviet Union. Assuming that in a relaxed international atmosphere the application of the Brezhnev doctrine is unlikely, they may hope to get away with more independent policies both at home and abroad. This may well be the reason for their interest in institutionalizing the CSCE and viewing the present negotiations as only the first of a series. The stand taken by Rumania in the early stages of the preparatory talks in Helsinki in December 1972, bluntly asserting the principle of the smaller states' independence, may be a harbinger of things to come. Substantial risks would be involved in such a development. The East Europeans may misjudge the extent to which the "spirit of Helsinki" would restrain the Soviet hand in that region. If the changes in Eastern Europe go too far and too fast, the U.S.S.R. may feel compelled to resort to the Brezhnev doctrine regardless of the international consequences.

However, in the mid-1970s, the chances of Soviet military intervention in Eastern Europe seem to have diminished, as compared with the situation even in the late 1960s. Since 1969 the U.S.S.R. has invested too much in the progress of European detente to contribute with her own hands to its ruin. There is reason to believe, moreover, that after their experience with Czechoslovakia the Russians have learned the high costs to them of invading any East European country with arms. The Soviet occupation not only patently failed to resolve the political crisis in Czechoslovakia; the international consquences of the invasion for the U.S.S.R. were no less harmful. The atmosphere in East-West relations cooled off markedly, delaying the start of SALT for one year, and being also largely responsible for the initial negative attitude on the part of several Western countries toward the CSCE. The visit of President Johnson to Moscow, planned for September 1968, was put off; and when President Nixon arrived there in May 1972, it was only after he had first visited China.

The revolt in Poland in December 1970 threatened even more serious international consequences. The opposition in the FRG tried to exploit the rebellion of the Polish workers for its own political ends, attempting to use it to prevent the ratification of the Polish-West German treaty. There is no doubt that if the situation in Poland had deteriorated any further, and particularly if the Russians had intervened militarily, the West German Christian Democrats would have succeeded in their objective. With the defeat of Chancellor Brandt's *Ostpolitik*, the progress of European detente, and especially the prospect of convening the CSCE, would have been delayed for a considerable period of time. Moscow was apparently aware of the high risks involved in the handling of the Polish crisis, for on that occasion it acted with remarkable circumspection.

The Russians, thus, are on the horns of a dilemma. On the one hand, if they continue the policy of detente with the West, this is likely to stimulate unrest in Eastern Europe. On the other hand, if they try to stamp out unrest there by force, this may well disrupt the European detente. And with ferment smouldering in the various parts of Eastern Europe, Moscow may soon be compelled to make a choice between these two alternatives.

Different East-West conceptions of security

The future of Eastern Europe will probably be one of the most divisive issues between the Soviet Union and the West at the CSCE. The two sides seem to share their concern over continued unrest in that part of the world. They also both view the externalization of East European conflicts, with its possible detrimental effects upon East-West detente, as undesirable. Yet, they differ sharply in their conceptions of the level at which this process should be contained.

The Russians see the CSCE as a way out of their dilemma. They would like to isolate social ferment in Eastern Europe, *and* their suppression of it by force, from the progress toward a European detente. To that end they would like to use the conference to extract from the Western powers their sanction of the present *status quo* in Eastern Europe. This, the Russians hope, not only would enable them to reap the benefits of a continued East-West detente, but would also enhance stability in Eastern Europe. The formal recognition by the West of Soviet domination in the region would make the Brezhnev doctrine more credible and the unrest in Eastern Europe would be effectively contained.

It is highly improbable that the Western powers will accept such Soviet proposals. It is not only that the West regards the aspirations of the East European nations to independence as perfectly legitimate and cannot repudiate them without undermining the very principles on which its policy rests. What is even more important is that the formal sanctioning by the Western powers of the existing *status quo* would not contribute to the emergence of a genuine security system in Europe.

The Russians are victims of their own ideological perceptions if they believe that the instability in Eastern Europe is instigated by the West. The removal of the remaining vestiges of Western interference in the domestic affairs of the East European countries, such as a moderation of the tone of the Western broadcasts directed at them, would probably make very little difference. The unrest in the region with its dangerous international implications would still continue. Furthermore, even if some Western government were willing to improve East-West relations at the price of accepting the Brezhnev doctrine, it cannot possibly guarantee that such a pledge would be effective. In pluralistic Western societies it is more likely than not that such a commitment would be used against the government by the opposition. Had President Johnson decided to disregard the Soviet invasion of Czechoslovakia and gone to Moscow in September 1968, this would undoubtedly have been used against the Democrats by the Republicans in the subsequent elections in the United States. Similarly Chancellor Brandt had no control over the way in which the Christian Democrats would politically exploit the popular reaction in West Germany to the 1970 Polish revolt.

The Western conception of European security is different from the Soviet one in that it strives to eliminate any externalization of social conflicts in Eastern Europe. The Western powers hope to create a framework within which the East European nations would be able to resolve their domestic problems in accordance with their own needs and without any outside interference. Needless to add, the Brezhnev doctrine would be incompatible with the evolution of such a system.

There are various means by which the West could advance its goals at the CSCE. The Western powers may agree to the Soviet proposal for renunciation of the use of force, but they should insist that this principle must have universal application. Relations between the U.S.S.R. and the Communist states in Eastern Europe should not be excluded from it. To ensure that the Brezhnev doctrine is not applied again, the Yugoslav and Rumanian proposals that no military manoeuvres should be held on foreign territory, or even close to the border of another European State, could be adopted. Observers could be exchanged to ensure that these rules are adhered to by both sides. At the same time MBFR could be used gradually to reduce Soviet garrisons in Eastern Europe.

In parallel, all-European cooperation should be developed. Bridging the gulf betweeen East and West should be designed in such a way as to assist the East Europeans in overcoming their domestic problems. Trade and other forms of economic cooperation, especially joint East-West ventures, should be expanded. Efforts could be made to reduce tariffs between the two parts of Europe. Scientific contacts may be intensified; joint research projects on various problems common to both parts of Europe, such as environmental protection, could be undertaken. Special attention should be given to cultural matters, opening the way for broad exchange of people and ideas. Gradually the division of Europe should be overlaid with a growth of common activities and, eventually, a network of international institutions.

Need for new concepts

In the era of negotiations a new approach is needed to deal with the East European problem. The area is too important to the overall progress of East-West relations to be ignored. The cold-war cliches of Eastern Europe should be discarded. Neither the notion of a "proletarian revolution" nor that of "the captive nations" fits the complex situation. New concepts that depict the existing reality more accurately should be found. As is the case with other East-West agreements, an effort must be made to search for novel solutions acceptable to both sides.

The philosophy underlying negotiations over Eastern Europe should be similar to that of SALT. The gap dividing the two sides is still too wide to rely on mere goodwill. The agreements should be arrived at, as Dr. Kissinger put it: "not on the basis of trust but on the basis of the enlightened self-interest of both sides."[1] The West must try to persuade the Soviet Union not to regard the CSCE as a zero-sum game where a gain for one side automatically amounts to a loss for the other. To prevent the unrest in Eastern Europe from spilling over into East-West relations is in the mutual interest of both parties.

The Western powers, and above all the U.S., should spare no effort to convince the Russians that they seek no influence of their own in Eastern Europe. Their goal is not to achieve "Finlandization" in reverse. Nor does the West seek the neutralization of the area. The concepts of "disengagement" current in the late 1950s no longer fit the situation of the 1970s. The West should emphasize that it is not opposed to continued cooperation between the U.S.S.R. and those East European states which deem it to be in their interest. Close bonds between the Soviet Union and the various countries located in the eastern part of the continent could be conducive to all—European cooperation. In this way Eastern Europe could perform the role for which it is fitted by its geographical position as well as by its historical heritage, namely, bridging the western part of the continent and Russia. It is, then, not a question of dissolving the existing bonds but rather of superimposing on them new forms of international cooperation.

There is little prospect that at the CSCE the Russians will readily agree to the Western counter-proposals concerning the future of Eastern Europe. Cooperation with the U.S. in obviating the danger of a nuclear war is ideologically less objectionable to them than the renunciation of their self-proclaimed right to intervene in the affairs of other Communist states. The Russians' sense of "territorial imperative" has always been very strong and they would probably be most reluctant to give up Eastern Europe as their exclusive sphere of influence. Yet, at this juncture in international politics it is unlikely that they would reject the Western design for Europe outright. They have invested too much in convening the CSCE to see it come to nothing. They are more likely, therefore, to engage in protracted negotiations with a view to wearing the West down and ultimately winning its approval of their own concept of a European system. They may hope that Western intellectual impatience with the remnants of the cold war would assist them in attaining their goal.

To counter the Soviet tactics the Western powers should adopt a three-pronged policy. First, they must accept the fact that the development of a new European system can proceed only in an evolutionary manner. The problems of Europe are too complex to be resolved all at once. Each step should be carefully prepared and be taken only when the time is ripe, but at the same time it should lead logically to the next one. Progress in security and cooperation—at the concurrent CSCE and MBFR parleys—ought to be especially carefully coordinated. Second, in order to advance on a broad front, a functional approach could be adopted. The building of a new European order should proceed at different levels at the same time. Endeavours to expand economic, scientific, and cultural cooperation between the two parts of Europe require a great variety of parleys. Some negotiations should be universal, while others should be confined to those states which have a direct interest in them. The preparatory work could be done in panels of various composition, depending on the subjects under discussion, some of them including one or both superpowers, with others being confined to the smaller countries—members of the two alliances as well as neutrals. It is through such a cumulative effort that the division of Europe may be most effectively overcome. Finally, the West should persevere in its efforts, not be discouraged by lack of response from the Soviet side, and patiently continue the talks. The road to achieving a true, not a spurious, system of European security and cooperation, based on mutuality of interests, will not be easy. Considerable progress has already been made, but many obstacles still remain. In the new round of negotiations Western diplomacy must persistently strive to overcome the ideological perceptions of the Russians, persuading them that the establishment of a peaceful and viable European order is in everybody's interest. An opportunity to arrive at a settlement in Europe, even if it is still elusive, is too important to be missed.

Footnote

* Originally published in *The World Today*, May 1973.
[1] Congressional Briefing by Dr. Henry A. Kissinger, *Congressional Record-Senate*, 19 June 1972, p. 9602.

XII

Czechoslovakia 1968 — Poland 1978
A Dilemma for Moscow*

No longer, when I hear the word 'Poland'
am I moved;
but I feel only a slight
embarrassment since that day I saw, aged 16
those columns of tanks advancing
to the south:
but yet, I do seem to begin to understand
patriotism
when I, in my hungry hands, hold,
clipped from a Western periodical,
a faded photograph of a student
from sunny Prague, whose name
was Jan Palach — the living torch of autumn ...

Antoni Pawlak, 'Beyond my Control'[1]

The Prague Spring and its suppression in August 1968 by the invading Warsaw pact troops had a direct, deep, and, in many respects, a lasting impact upon political developments in Poland. It contributed to the ferment among the Polish intellectuals and students in March 1968. It also affected, and to a large extent influenced, the outcome of the struggle for power which was under way at that time in the Polish United Workers' Party (PUWP). Last but not least, the invasion of Czechoslovakia, despite the participation of Polish troops, brought the two peoples closer together. Since 1968 there has been a growing realization among the Czechs, the Slovaks, and the Poles of the community of their fate.

Poland and Czechoslovakia are geographically juxtaposed—their common boundary, along the Beskidy and the Sudety mountain ranges, is one of the longest in Europe. They also maintain close economic bonds; each is the other's third most important foreign trading partner. The three western Slavic peoples, moreover, remain culturally related. There is a linguistic affinity among them—in his native tongue a Pole has little difficulty in communicating with a Czech, and even less with a Slovak.[2] The folk traditions are quite similar among the shepherds on the Polish and Slovak sides of the Tatra Mountains or among the peasants along the border betweeen Silesia and Moravia.

Yet since the two states re-emerged in their modern forms in 1918 they have rarely acted in unison. In the interwar period their relations were marred by a dispute over the Teshen district. The Czechs seized this area in 1919 when Poland was engaged in a war in the east, and the Poles took it back at the time of the Munich crisis in 1938. During World War II the territorial quarrel contributed to the collapse of plans, made by the two exiled governments in London, for close postwar co-operation.[3] The Teshen issue, however, was only the tip of the iceberg; it was a reflection of the very different conceptions of foreign policy held by the two countries.[4]

The Czechs, who, in modern history, have lingered on the verge of national extinction, were acutely aware of their smallness. When faced with a predominant power they tended to act in a circumspect and prudent fashion and generally preferred passive to active resistance.[5] Through this tactic they managed to contain their losses during World War II. In contrast, the Poles, whose memories of the greatness of their state are of more recent date, were more exuberant and daring. They had greater confidence in their own power, to the point of exaggerating it at times. During World War II they waged a continuous and fierce battle against Nazi Germany and, in the course of it, suffered tremendous losses. Needless to say, such different national traditions tended to crystallize on both sides into contemptuous stereotypes. The Poles were inclined to look down on the Czechs as a people devoid of self-respect, the cowardly "Szwejks"; and, in turn, the Czechs often regarded the Poles as the 'Kozietulskis,' the showy cavalrymen who, for no good reason, charge to their death.[6]

What was really at the root of the Czechoslovak-Polish animosity was the difference in their attitude toward Russia. For the Czechs the main enemy until 1918 was Austria-Hungary, and in the interwar years it was Germany. They had no quarrel with Russia. Indeed, in the nineteenth century, Russia's rivalry with Austria in the Balkans attracted many Czechs to the Slavophile programme. In the interwar period Masaryk and Benes had little sympathy with the Bolsheviks, but after Hitler's rise to power they felt that Czechoslovakia's alliance with France was not sufficient to protect its position, and in 1935 Prague entered into a defensive pact with Moscow.

Poland until 1914 was dismembered by Russia, Germany, and Austria, but the bulk of its territory belonged to the tsarist empire and many Poles believed that the Russians were their main enemies. They had no use for Slavophilism which they regarded as a tool of Russian imperialism. In the interwar period Pilsudski and his followers believed that the main threat to the Polish state came from the U.S.S.R. They certainly had no warm feelings towards Nazi Germany, but—having, like the Czechs, no great trust in their alliance with France—they tried to perform a balancing act between their two powerful neighbours, and in 1934 Warsaw concluded a non-aggression treaty with Berlin.

At the end of World War II the rivalry over Teshen came to an end. The dispute was settled in favour of Czechoslovakia and by now had faded into history. Yet, the differences between the two countries both in the style and in the substance of their foreign policies and, above all, in their attitudes towards the U.S.S.R. have remained. The Poles succumbed to communism after bitter resistance in the course of which they suffered additional heavy losses. It was only in 1947 that all opposition was crushed and the communist system became consolidated in Poland. Benes tried to salvage democracy in Czechoslovakia by maintaining friendly relations with the Soviet Union, but in 1948 when his efforts failed, he handed over the government to the communist leader, Klement Gottwald, rather than risk civil war.

For the next two decades the political cycles in Czechoslovakia and Poland were not in phase. When the Czech workers rioted in Pilzen in June 1953, Poland was still in the throes of Stalinism. Yet, in June 1956, when the Polish workers took to the streets in Poznan, and in October when Wladyslaw Gomulka was returned to power and introduced at least some popular reforms in Poland, the communist system was once again safely entrenched in Czechoslovakia. The dissatisfaction among the Czechoslovak youth and the writers was quickly extinguished. Thinly veiled attacks against the reforms in Poland were made in the Czech and Slovak party papers, and the Polish press was virtually banned south of the border.[7] By 1963, in turn, when political changes finally got under way in Czechoslovakia, the Gomulka regime was already in retreat form the "Polish October."[8] It was only in 1968 that popular dissatisfaction in the two countries coincided for the first time, although at that time the Czechs and the Slovaks were far ahead of the Poles.

I

In the mid-1960s, ferment among the intellectuals and students in Poland proceeded along lines parallel to those in Czechoslovakia. In March 1964 thirty-four prominent writers and scholars publicly protested against the restrictions on cultural freedom. In the fall of 1966, on the tenth anniversary of the Polish October, Professor Leszek Kolakowski delivered a lecture at the University of Warsaw in which he criticized the retrogressive policies of the Gomulka regime. Kolakowski was expelled from the Communist party, and subsequently also from his university chair, but his example served to embolden the opposition.

When the nineteenth-century Mickiewicz play, *Forefather's Eve*, which had some anti-Russian overtones, was banned from the stage of the National Theatre, the Warsaw branch of the Writers' Union came out with a vigorous protest on 29 February 1968, On 8 March clashes between the students at the University of Warsaw and the police ensued, and there were numerous arrests. Students in other cities joined in and for the next three weeks the sit-in strikes and demonstrations continued throughout Poland. The rebellion was crushed by force, with over a hundred students being given prison sentences of up to several years.[9]

"The March events," as the Poles call them, were clearly influenced by the developments in neighbouring Czechoslovakia. The Poles were greatly heartened by the ouster of Novotny and the evident progress of liberalization under Dubcek, and they openly manifested their solidarity with the Czechs and the Slovaks. The Warsaw writers sent fraternal greetings to their colleagues in Czechoslovakia, and the demonstrating students repeatedly praised the changes taking place in that country. The students' slogans called for "a Polish Dubcek" and for democratic reforms in Poland along lines similar to those south of the border. The Czech intellectuals and students warmly reciprocated the sympathy expressed by the Poles. The Philosophy Department at Prague University ostentatiously invited Kolakowski to continue his academic career there. And on 1 May 1968 the Czech students staged a demonstration in front of the Polish embassy protesting the repression of their Polish colleagues.

When the invasion of Czechoslovakia took place new statements of sympathy came from the Polish side. A well-known Polish writer, Jerzy Andrzejewski, sent a letter to the chairman of the Czechoslovakia Writers' Union, Eduard Goldstuecker, in which he expressed shame for the involvement of the Polish troops and declared his solidarity with the Czechoslovak intellectuals.[10] Although already decimated by arrests, the Polish students distributed leaflets in Warsaw protesting the invasion, and still more of them were thrown into prison. And one of the detained student leaders, Adam Michnik, even used the occasion of his trial to manifest his solidarity with Czechoslovakia. In his defence speech on 22 January 1969 he declared: "Since I was in jail at the time of the invasion I had no opportunity to oppose it; had I been free I would have undoubtedly done so, one way or another."[11] He was sentenced to three years' imprisonment.

The attitude of the Gomulka regime to the Prague Spring was proportionately inverse to that of the democratic opposition. The removal of Novotny from power in January 1968 was received with a noticeable lack of enthusiasm in Warsaw, and as the scope of democratic reforms in Czechoslovakia was expanded, the anxiety of the PUWP leaders became more and more evident. Gomulka was clearly worried about the impact this was going to have upon Poland, and the demonstration of the solidarity between the Czech and Polish intellectuals and students did little to dispel his apprehension.

Official Polish concern was articulated in speeches by Gomulka and some other party leaders as well as in thinly veiled attacks on the changes in Czechoslovakia in the Polish press and radio.[12] Some of the commentators even charged that the developments in Czechoslovakia were inspired by West Germany and that Poland's southern neighbour was about to abandon the Warsaw Pact. On 6 May 1968 Warsaw sent a stiffly worded official note to Prague, warning the Dubcek government that Poland would not allow the forces of a counter-revolution to prevail in Czechoslovakia. The meeting of the Warsaw pact leaders (excluding the Czechoslovak and Rumanian representatives), where the decision to proceed with the invasion plans was evidently reached, was held in Warsaw on 14 and 15 July. And the Polish forces, although relatively small in number and in a role subordinate to the Soviet one, took part in it.

In Poland, the "March events" coincided with an intense factional struggle in the ranks of the Polish United Workers' Party. Since the mid-1960s Gomulka had been increasingly challenged by a group composed of the wartime communist partisans and led by the Minister of Internal Affairs, General Mieczyslaw Moczar. The partisans had little sympathy with the programme of democratic reforms. Yet they were not adverse, if only for tactical reasons, to the activities of the democratic opposition and may even have used their control over the police to aggravate the students' rebellion. The resulting weakening of Gomulka clearly played into the partisans' hands; following the March unrest, in July 1968, Moczar was promoted to alternate member of the Politburo.

The partisans' attitude towards the changes in Czechoslovakia was ambivalent. Although they did not contemplate any democratic changes, they played up, with some success, the issue of Polish nationalism. The partisans' programme never took an overt anti-Russian form, but there was an implicit promise in it that after their coming to power they might seek Poland's greater independence from the U.S.S.R. The partisans then closely watched the efforts of the Czechs and Slovaks to win more elbow room from Moscow, When, at a meeting in Cierna at the end of July, it appeared that a satisfactory compromise had been reached between the Czechoslovak and Soviet leaders, Moczar considered this a defeat for Gomulka.[13] Conversely, the invasion of Czechoslovakia, which marked the reassertion of Soviet authority over Eastern Europe, represented a reverse for the partisans. From then on their influence waned steadily. At the 5th party congress, from 11 to 16 November 1968, Moczar failed to be elevated to full member of the Politburo and throughout its entire proceedings he remained silent.

Another challenge to Gomulka came from a faction led by a Politburo member and secretary of the Upper Silesian party or organization, Edward Gierek. In contrast to the cautious and increasingly conservative Gomulka, Gierek projected an image of dynamism and progress. His efficient management of Silesian industry had won him considerable prestige among the technocrats, and his appeals for rejuvenation of the party cadres had secured for him a sizable following in PUWP ranks. At the same time Gierek made it quite clear that he had no taste for either democracy or nationalism. In a hardline speech in Katowice on 14 March 1968 he denouced the student riots in Warsaw and declared that such activities would not be tolerated in Silesia. And in a speech, significantly delivered in the Polish part of Teshen, he stressed the need for "socialist unity" between Poland and Czechoslovakia.[14] Gierek's centrist course evidently paid off. At the party congress he was the first speaker after Gomulka, and he headed the nominating committee for the election of the new PUWP officials.

Throughout 1968 Gomulka continued to weather the political storm. At the party congress in November, with Brezhnev in attendance—and with both Communist leaders defending in their speeches the decision to invade Czechoslovakia—he was re-elected first secretary. Yet it was apparent that, as a result of the "March events," Gomulka's position was greatly weakened.

Czechoslovakia 1968-Poland 1978: A Dilemma for Moscow

He lingered on for another two years, but when a new political crisis broke out in December 1970—with the workers in the coastal cities taking to the streets in protest against the drastic food price increases—he was quickly ousted from power. Gierek took over as first secretary, while Moczar was promoted to full member of the Politburo. Moczar, however, soon went back into eclipse. In the spring of 1971 he was stripped of all his party functions and Gierek emerged as the undisputed leader of the PUWP.

II

In the early 1970s the Gierek regime did quite well. It adopted a vigorous expansionist economic policy, financed by a substantial influx of Western credits, and it showed considerable concern for improvement of the standard of living in the country. A new political style—demonstrating greater respect for the citizens' rights—was adopted by the communist authorities. Relations between the government and the Catholic Church improved markedly, and gestures of reconciliation were made towards the intellectual community. Several writers who had been banned from publishing in 1968 were now permitted to do so, and the students who had been arrested during the "March events" were quietly released from imprisonment. There was a new sense of direction and confidence in the country and Gierek's prestige soared.

By 1974 the situation in the country had once again begun to deteriorate. An over-ambitious programme of simultaneous wage increases and industrial investments, as well as a disappointing performance in foreign trade, resulted in a new economic slump. In June 1976 drastic food price increases were introduced, but when the workers in Ursus and Radom took to the streets the controversial measure was promptly withdrawn. Meanwhile, the Communist party made another serious error. At the end of 1975 amendments to the Polish constitution, which would bring it closer to the Soviet document, were proposed. This immediately evoked a storm of protest. The amendments were modified, but irreparable harm had been done to the Gierek regime.

Even though the government admitted its mistake by withdrawing the price increases, harsh sanctions were applied against the strikers from Radom and Ursus. Various opposition groups immediately rallied to their defence. On 27 September 1976 the Committee for Defence of the Workers (KOR) was formed. The committee launched a nationwide campaign demanding the end of persecutions and the immediate release of all the imprisoned workers. Despite public denunciations and police intimidations, culminating in the arrest of several KOR activists in May 1977, the committee persevered. Its activities received open support from many prominent intellectuals as well as from the Catholic Episcopate. Under mounting popular pressure the government relented and on 23 July the KOR people, as well as the remaining workers, were released.

The opposition's activities did not stop there, however. In September 1977 KOR transformed itself into a permanent Committee for Social Self-Defence, whose goals are combating violations of the law and fighting for institutional guarantees of civil rights. Meanwhile, another group, called the Movement for the Defence of Human and Civil Rights, came into existence. In the spring of 1977 the Students Solidarity Committee was founded in Cracow and it soon spread to virtually all the other university cities. In the fall, in co-operation with some well-known scholars, the students organized a "Flying University," in which lectures, held in private houses, are offered on a wide variety of subjects. At the same time the *samizdat* publications have proliferated. At present some twenty of them appear regularly, ranging from highly sophisticated literary journals to popular papers designed for distribution among the workers and peasants.

Thus, by 1978, there had emerged in Poland an open, vocal, and increasingly influential democratic opposition. At its core are the student activists from March 1968—at present in their late twenties and early thirties. These young men and women, by now more mature and often hardened by years of imprisonment, are grimly determined to carry on their struggle for freedom. In their demands for democratic reforms they have braod support form the intellectual community as well as from Catholic circles, and a growing sympathy among the people at large. The opposition displays a mood of self-assurance, perhaps over-confidence.

In contrast, the government conveys the impression of being disoriented and dispirited. The measures which it has adopted to cope with the economic crises have not brought any visible relief. Continued police harrassment of the opposition has failed to halt the spread of its activities. New cracks have opened up in Communist party ranks over the handling of the economic situation and the manner of dealing with the opposition.[15] The ability of its present leadership and, increasingly, of the first secretary himself to overcome the existing crisis has been brought more and more into question.

III

The rise of a democratic opposition in Poland coincided with the revival of open dissent in Czechoslovakia. In January 1977 Charter 77, denouncing the violations and calling for the restoration of basic civil liberties, was issued in Prague.[16] It was signed originaly by some 250 people; by June their number had risen to over 800. Three distinguished figures, headed by Jiri Hajek, who was foreign minister during the Dubcek era, became spokesmen for the Charter. They proceeded to issue communiques, circulated throughout the country in *samizdat* form, in which the violations of civil rights in Czechoslovakia are carefully catalogued. The Charter 77 movement did not profess any political aims, but it nevertheless had profound political significance. It dispelled the myth that the collaborationist Husak regime had won the passive acquiescence of the entire populace and demonstrated that the ideals of the Prague Spring are still alive in the country.

The Husak government responded to Charter 77 with stern reprisals. Its authors were attacked as traitors inspired by Western anti-communist centres, and many of its signatories were subjected to police intimidation. In March 1977 one of the three Charter spokesmen, a renowned philosopher, Jan Patocka, suffered a brain haemmorrhage and died after a prolonged police interrogation. Another spokesman, a prominent playwright, Vaclav Havel, was brought to trial in October and, as a warning, was given a suspended sentence of fourteen months. Three other defendants who were tried at the same time received various terms of imprisonment. Despite the persecutions, however, the Charter 77 movement has persisted. The funeral of Professor Patocka, attended by some one thousand people, turned into a demonstration of the dissenters' solidarity. And Charter 77 communiques have continued to appear.[17]

The ferments in Poland and Czechoslovakia in 1977 developed independently of one another, but they stemmed from basically the same roots. In both cases the opposition was emboldened by the improvement in East-West relations and encouraged by the example of the Soviet dissidents' use of detente as a protective umbrella for their activities. In the eyes of the Czechs and the Slovaks, the Helsinki Final Act amounted to a *post factum* condemnation of the Soviet invasion of their country; and, in the eyes of the Poles, the act reduced the chances of a Soviet invasion of Poland. The Carter administration's early pronouncement about human rights further heartened both peoples.

The two opposition movements not only developed along similar lines, but entered into contact with each other.[18] Soon after the appearance of Charter 77, expressions of solidarity and support were sent to Jiri Hajek by KOR. Since that time various Polish *samizdat* publications have been giving frequent attention to the activities of the dissidents in Czechoslovakia. The important document, Declaration of the Democratic Movement, issued in the fall of 1977, symbolically had as a subtitle, The Warsaw Charter 77.

On 31 October 1977, when news of the sentencing of the defendants in the Prague trial reached Warsaw, the Committee for Social Self-Defence issued 'A Letter to Our Friends the Czechs and the Slovaks.' It expressed shock at the brutality of the communist reprisals and characterized them as flagrant violations of the Helsinki Final Act. The document referred to the Prague Spring as an inspiration not only for Czechs and Slovaks, but for all nations in Eastern Europe, and asked for forgiveness for the participation of Polish troops in its suppression.[19] On 16 November the Czechoslovak dissidents sent a reply to their Polish friends. The letter stated that the Czechoslovak people were cognizant of the circumstances which led to the involvement of the Polish units in the invasion force in 1968 and pointed out that the reverse situation almost occurred in 1956.[20] Both documents stressed the solidarity of the two peoples in their striving for freedom and expressed hope for a firm and lasting friendship between them in the future.

In mid-summer 1978 representatives of KOR and the Charter 77 movement met in the Tatra Mountains near Zakopane, where they discussed their activities and ways of co-operation. They also issued a joint declaration commemorating the tenth anniversary of the invasion of Czechoslovakia. The documents praised the Prague Springs as "an attempt to establish a society based on true human values and to find an alternative to the totalitarian system." It pledged continued efforts by the two movements "to achieve truth, human rights, democracy, social justice and national independence—to be true to these ideals and to take further actions in this spirit."[21]

IV

In 1978, in contrast to 1968, the Poles are once again ahead of the Czechs and Slovaks. Yet the Polish ferment has not as yet reached the intensity of the Prague Spring. The present situation in Poland is, in fact, more comparable to that which prevaled in Czechoslovakia in the late stages of the Novotny regime.[22] Indeed, there are striking parallels between the two. In both cases the source of the political crisis lies in a profound failure of the economic system. In today's Poland, as in the Czechoslovakia of the mid-1960s, there is despondency, mixed with irritation, among the masses and a deep incredulity that the government can find a way out of the existing difficulties. Popular grievances are articulated by the intellectuals, with the young intelligentsia in the lead. Finally, the Gierek government, like the Novotny regime, reaffirms the impression of being immobilized. It does not seem to have any plan of action; instead it is responding to the various challenges with half-measures, hoping that the crisis will somehow go away.

Rien ne dure qu le provisoire. It took about five years for the Novotny government to collapse. The Gierek regime has already muddled through for over two years since June 1976, and it is conceivable that without doing very much it may still linger on for a while. Yet such a course is fraught with danger. It would neither dispose of nor appease the democratic opposition. As one of the latter's spokesmen, covering his identity under a pseudonymn of Marek Turbacz, puts it: "weak and sporadic reprisals only strengthen the opposition and in consequence deepen the political crisis."[23] In the end pent-up frustrations may result in an uncontrollable popular explosion which will sweep away the Gierek government. Under such circumstances it is doubtful whether communist rule in Poland could be restored without direct Soviet involvement.

The alternative course for the government would be to try to overcome existing problems by undertaking popular reforms. This would require devising an imaginative and energetic economic programme and, in order to secure the necessary support to implement it, the opening up of a genuine dialogue with the Polish people. There is a danger, of course, that once the programme of reforms got under way it would acquire its own momentum and might not be easy to stop. As Turbacz put it, yielding to the pressure for "evolutionary changes in the system might trigger an escalation of popular demands."[24] This is probably the main reason Gierek has been reluctant to initiate such a course of action. He is afraid that he might be caught in a situation like that faced by Dubcek, who was pushed by popular pressure beyond the point where the scope of the reforms would remain acceptable to the U.S.S.R.

No matter what course Gierek chooses, there are serious risks ahead. On balance, however, the second alternative seems to offer the only practical solution. This is because there are, in addition to many similarities, significant differences between the situation in Poland in 1978 and that of Czechoslovakia in 1968 which mitigate, although they do not eliminate, the threat of the Prague scenario being replayed in Warsaw.

First of all the leaders of the democratic opposition are themselves painfully aware of the limits of action imposed on them by Poland's juxtaposition to the Soviet Union. Marek Turbacz stressed this strongly in his essay: "We are unable to free ourselves from the Russian domination.... We have to act within the confines imposed by this fact.... It is feasible for Poland to expand the scope of democracy, and gradually to widen its sovereignty, yet these changes have to remain within the boundaries determined by Russian supremacy."[25]

Should the younger opposition leaders be carried away by their enthusiasm and try to go too far, however, there are various forces in Polish society which could effectively put brakes on them. The older intellectual community—who in the early stages of the Gomulka regime, and again after Gierek's coming to power, demonstrated a remarkable degree of sobriety—is one such force. The Catholic Church, which has consistently followed a thoroughly realistic policy vis-à-vis the Communist regime, is another. Both in 1956 and in 1970, when he felt that the domestic conflict might lead to a Soviet intervention, Stefan Cardinal Wyszynski appealed to the Polish people for calm and restraint. There is no doubt that should the situation threaten to get out of hand he would again use his immense prestige in the same fashion.

Another difference between the present situation in Poland and that in Czechoslovakia in 1968 is that the scope of the Polish reforms need not to be as sweeping as that of the Prague Spring programme. The Stalinist system lasted in Czechoslovakia, in effect, from the late 1940s until the early 1960s, and—despite or perhaps because of the country's democratic tradition—it was a particularly cruel one. When it was finally broken with the fall of Novotny, the pressure for radical changes was extremely strong, a natural reaction to many years of oppression, and Dubcek had difficulty controlling it. In contrast, Stalinism in Poland was less harsh and was terminated in 1956. Moreover, the process of democratization in Poland has been advanced in a piecemeal fashion. Even though Gomulka reversed many reforms which had been introduced during the "Polish October," some of them have been preserved. Similarly, despite Gierek's recent retrenchment, not all the innovations which he adopted in the early 1970s have been abandoned. Consequently, since the scope of domestic freedom in Poland is in many respects already considerable, its further expansion would not amount to a dramatic departure from the existing political system, but rather the next stage in its gradual evolution.

V

The present crisis in Poland is in many respects similar to that in Czechoslovakia in the mid-1960s, and unless it is defused in time, it may turn into another Prague Spring. Such a development would pose a serious dilemma for the Soviet Union. The Kremlin leaders would either have to come to terms with a situation which a decade ago they found intolerable, or once again resort to brutal force.

The costs to the U.S.S.R. of a military invasion of Poland would be substantially greater than those which it incurred in 1968 in Czechoslovakia. It is not only that Poland is a much larger country, both in terms of the territory and population, but that there is also a strong likelihood that the Poles, in line with their insurrectionist tradition, would resist the Soviet troops with arms. The intervention, then, could amount to a small-scale Russian-Polish war. The Poles, of course, would lose, but, depending on the intensity of the struggle, the damage to Moscow's international prestige would be proportionately magnified.

It must also be remembered that the invasion of Czechoslovakia took place in the pre-detente era. The solemn assurances of the U.S.S.R. to respect the principle of non-interference in the internal affairs of any country regardless of its social system, embodied in the Helsinki Final Act, amounted, in the eyes of the West, to a retraction of the so-called Brezhnev doctrine. The invasion of Poland would no doubt be viewed as a flagrant violation of this agreement, with the most serious consequences for East-West detente.

The Soviet leaders, it seems, are aware of the risks involved in trying to subdue Poland by force. They refrained from military intervention in that country in 1956, and again in 1970 (when it is reported that Gomulka pleaded for Brezhnev's assistance). Moscow's response to the present Polish crisis had been quite prudent. At least overtly the Soviet leaders have shown no signs of apprehension; they have continued to voice their full confidence in Gierek and have abstained from public attacks on the Polish opposition. It appears, then, that if the communist regime and the democratic opposition avoid an open collision, and domestic reforms in Poland continue to be implemented in a piecemeal and orderly fashion, there is a good possibility that these may be acceptable to Moscow.

There is, however, one danger. An important element in the Soviet decision to intervene in Czechoslovakia in 1968 was undoubtedly the fear of the spillover effects which the Dubcek reforms would have had in Poland. Ferment among the Polish students and intellectuals and the rise of nationalist sentiments in the PUWP only increased apprehension on the part of Moscow. Now, the Soviet leaders may be concerned about the possible impact of changes in Poland upon Czechoslovakia and, subsequently, upon other countries in east-central Europe. Should the programme of reforms advocated by the Polish democratic opposition be adopted, it might encourage the Charter 77 movement to make similar demands.

The possibility of a chain reaction between events in Poland and Czechoslovakia is real, and indeed, it might not remain confined to these two countries—it might continue into other countries in east-central Europe. Yet in the contemporary world a growing interdependence throughout the region, as well as closer bonds between it and the rest of Europe, are inevitable. The best chance for the U.S.S.R. to minimize the risks inherent in such a development is to use East-West detente as an umbrella beneath which changes would proceed in a gradual and peaceful fashion. Such evolution would permit the region to begin to function, as it is uniquely fitted to do by its geographical position and historical heritage, as a bridge between Western Europe and Russia. It is, then, not a question of dissolving existing international bonds but rather one of superimposing upon them new forms of all-European co-operation.

Conversely, should the Soviet Union refuse to adapt its policies to fit the aspirations of the peoples in east-central Europe, the international risks are going to be intensified. So far Moscow has been able to deal with the various crises in the region one by one. Simultaneous explosions in two or more countries might result in a confrontation of major proportions. This, in turn, would have profound consequences in the international sphere—it would certainly spell the end of East-West detente.

VI

The intervention in Czechoslovakia was a grave blunder on the part of the U.S.S.R. It occurred at a crucial juncture in Soviet-American relations, when President Johnson was just about to visit Moscow. The invasion of Czechoslovakia not only prevented Johnson from going to the Soviet Union, but it helped Nixon, for whom the Russians had little affection at that time, to be elected president of the United States. The Kremlin leaders, intoxicated with the progress of Soviet-American detente during the Nixon era, tend to forget that before coming to Moscow in 1972 the American President had previously visited Peking.[26] This master stroke of Kissinger's diplomacy is now being utilized by Brzezinski.

The invasion of Czechoslovakia also paved the way for China's growing influence among at least some countries in Eastern Europe. Since 1968 Peking's relations with Bucharest have been consolidated, and those with Belgrade have undergone marked improvement. Hua Kuo-feng's exchange of visits with Presidents Tito of Yugoslavia and Ceausescu of Roumania is the best evidence of this.[27] In the spring of 1969, after Soviet-Chinese clashes over the Ussuri River, the Prague students, in their anger and helplessness, shouted at the Russian soldiers: "The Chinese will teach you a lesson!"

The Russian invasion of Czechoslovakia alienated one of the peoples most warmly disposed towards them in the region. The intensity of the bitterness of the Czechs towards the U.S.S.R. can hardly be exaggerated.[28] There was no substance to the Soviet, or, for that matter, to the Polish, allegations that in 1968 Czechoslovakia was about to leave the Warsaw pact to re-align itself with West Germany. Yet, at present, especially since the issue of their boundary with Germany has been definitely settled, it would be natural for the Czechs to re-examine their traditional pro-Russian and anti-German stance.[29]

The Poles may have tried to balance Germany *vis-à-vis* Russia in the interwar period, but after World War II they had no use for the Germans. Not only the communists, but virtually all Poles, were in favour of Poland's alliance with Russia, especially since the U.S.S.R. was for a long time the sole guarantor of the Polish-German boundary.[30] There are signs, however, that this Polish attitude has also been undergoing some change. One of the contributing elements has been the settlement—although not quite final as yet—of Poland's territorial dispute with Germany. The other has been Russia's intransigence in insisting upon Poland's acceptance of a Soviet-style communist system.

Under these circumstances it is not surprising that one of the clandestine opposition groups, the Polish Coalition for Independence, addressed itself to the question of Polish-German relations. In the spring of 1978 it came out with a statement re-examining Poland's position between Russia and Germany. This document, written in a sober and restrained fashion, noted that the Polish-German territorial dispute is not as yet entirely settled. Yet it acknowledged the positive changes which have taken place since the end of World War II in West Germany and observed with satisfaction the growing integration of that country with the Western Europen community. Should this trend continue and, above all, should the Federal Republic of Germany unconditionally accept the present boundary with Poland, the most compelling reason for a Polish-Soviet alliance would disappear. This eventually could pave the way for the reunification of Germany and for Poland's freedom from Russia's domination.[31]

The frustration of the Poles with Moscow's repeated efforts to impose its ideological *Weltanschauung* upon Poland is well illustrated by the political evolution of one of the leading non-communist proponents of the Polish-Russian alliance, Professor Stanislaw Stomma. In 1957 Stomma entered the Polish parliament as a leader of the group of Catholic deputies, who in exchange for the democratic reforms offered their support to the Gomulka regime. In 1960 he published a book in which in a realist fashion —restricting himself strictly to geopolitical reasoning—he persuasively argued in favour of Poland's alliance with the U.S.S.R.[32]

Stomma remained in the parliament throughout the entire Gomulka era and into Gierek's early period. In the winter of 1976, however, he abstained in a vote approving the changes in the Polish constitution and did not enter the parliament elected the following spring. Soon afterwards he wrote an historical article, published significantly in the West, entitled "The Tragedies of Polish Realism." He reviewed in it various Polish attempts to find a *modus vivendi* with the Russians in the past and pointedly observed that virtually all of them ended in fiasco. There are limits, he concluded, beyond which the realists cannot go—when their repeated efforts at a compromise find no response from the other side, there is no other way but open resistance.[33]

Stomma's case is symptomatic of the changing attitudes of a great many Poles. They are utterly tired of Moscow's repeated, and clumsy, efforts at a sovietization of their country. With their religion derived from Rome and their culture strongly influenced by the Renaissance, the Western European democratic heritage is close to them, and they have no use for Russia's autocratic political tradition. The Poles well understand the potential danger posed to them by Germany, and they have little sympathy with China; indeed, they are even aware of the possibility of a collusion between these two powers. Yet, as Stomma pointed out, there are limits beyond which they are not prepared to be pushed. They would be willing to be an ally, but not a satellite, of the U.S.S.R.

The Soviet Union, of course, has it within its power to crush the Poles. This, however, would solve nothing. For over thirty years now Moscow has tried to impose its own brand of communism upon Poland, and its efforts have proved to be in vain. If anything, the younger Polish generation is even more strongly opposed to the communist system than the older one. There is no reason to believe that the Russians are going to be any more successful in the future. In the event of a Soviet invasion of Poland the democratic opposition would go even deeper underground and at the first opportunity would turn with vengeance against the communist regime. It remains to be seen whether the Soviet Union has learned from its error of 1968, or whether it would make the same blunder in Poland as it did in Czechoslovakia.

Footnotes

* Originally published in the *International Journal*, Autumn 1978.
[1]   Published, without the author's knowledge, in the Polish *samizdat* quarterly, *Puls*, October 1977.
[2]   One of the most interesting conversations that the author conducted in this fashion was his meeting on 4 June 1966, in Bratislava, with Dr. Gustav Husak, then a researcher at the Slovak Academy of Sciences.

3   The wartime episode is dealt with by Piotr S. Wandycz, *Czechoslovak-Polish Confederation and the Great Powers, 1941-1943* (Bloomington 1956).

4   For more extensive treatment of the impact of national traditions upon the respective foreign policies of the two countries, see my "Poland and Czechoslovakia: The Hesitant Alliance," *Central European Federalist* (June 1967); also Vaclaw Benes, "Psychology of Polish-Czechoslovak Relations," *ibid.*

5   The Czech and Polish postures in foreign policy have been characterized as "semi-arrested gesture and circumspect act" and "manifest gesture and act" respectively: W.J. Rose, "Czechs and Poles as Neighbors," *Journal of Central European Affairs,* XI (1951), 153.

6   The stereotypes of "Szwejk" and "Kozietulski" were frankly discussed at a meeting between the editors of *Kulturni Tvorba* and *Polityka* which took place in Prague late in 1963. *Polityka,* 2 May 1964.

7   For the impact of the Polish October upon Czechoslovakia see Otto Ulc, "How the Czechs Felt in 1956," *Central European Federalist* (July 1966).

8   The example of the Polish October, however, was not altogether wasted on the Czechs. The proposals for a reform of the Polish economic system, prepared by a team headed by Professor Oskar Lange in 1957 but not implemented, were well known and actually were used in the mid-1960s in devising the model of "market socialism" in Czechoslovakia.

9   The events in Poland in the spring of 1968 are presented in considerable detail in *Wydarzenia Marcowe, 1968* [The Events of March 1968] (Paris 1969), Lucjan Perzanowski and Antoni Kuczmierczyk, *Nie ma chleba bez wolnosci* [There is no Bread without Freedom](London 1971), and Marek Tarniewski, *Krotkie spiecie, Marzec 1968* [The Sudden Confrontation, March 1968] (Paris 1977).

10 *Le Monde,* 26 September 1968.

11 Quoted in Perzanowski and Kuczmierczyk, *Nie ma chleba bez wolnosci,* p. 215.

12 For a fully documented analysis of the attitude of the Gomulka regime to the changes in Czechoslovakia in 1968 see H. Gordon Skilling, *Czechoslovakia's Interrupted Revolution* (Princeton 1976) pp. 681-8; and Jan de Weydenthal, "The Dynamics of Leadership in the Polish United Workers' Party 1967-1968: A Case Study," unpublished doctoral dissertation, Notre Dame University, Notre Dame, Indiana, 1972, pp. 165-84.

13 Bernard Marguerite, *Le Monde,* 22 August 1968.

14 *Trybuna ludu,* 15 May 1968.

15 In the PUWP intra-party debate, there was recently a curious echo of the Prague Spring. In the fall of 1977 the editor of an influential party weekly, *Polityka,* Mieczyslaw Rakowski, proposed, as a remedy for the existing crisis, decentralization of the economic system. He was denounced by the hardline Warsaw daily, *Zycie Warszawy,* as a proponent of the discredited Czechoslovak "market socialism."

16 For the text of Charter 77 in English see *The Times,* 11 February 1977.

17 For a detailed analysis of the Charter 77 movement see H. Gordon Skilling, "Socialism and Human Rights: Charter 77 and the Prague Spring," *Canadian Slavonic Papers,* XX (June 1978); also Karel Klatovsky, "Czechoslowacja w roku 1977" *Kultura* (Paris) (January-February 1978).

18 Those contacts actually existed before; in some cases they went back as far as 1968. For instance, one of the defendants in the Charter 77 trial, Jiri Lederer, had published reports in the Czech papers about the brutal suppression of the Polish students in the spring of 1968.

19 For the text of the letter see *Kultura* (December 1977), pp. 144-5.

20 *Glos* (Warsaw), December 1977 (mimeographed).

21 "Czech and Polish Dissidents Forge Links," *The Times,* 18 August 1978.

22 For an interesting retrospective analysis of the gradual attrition of the Novotny regime see Frank L. Caplan, "Czechoslovakia's Experiment in Humanizing Socialism: An Examination of Ideological and Tactical Implications," *East European Quarterly,* XI, (Fall 1977).

23 Marek Turbacz, 'Mozliwosci dzialania opozycji w Polsce', *Aneks,* no 16/17 (1977), 8.

24 *Ibid.,* p. 36.

25 Turbacz, 'Mozliwosci dzialania opozycji,' pp. 15, 16.

26 For an evaluation of the consequences in the international sphere of the Soviet invasion of Czechoslovakia see my "Czechoslovakia and the World," *Canadian Slavonic Papers,* X (Winter 1968), and for the debate which ensued over it see Alastair Buchan, John C. Campbell, and Adam Bromke, *ibid,* XI (Spring 1969).

27 The growth of China's influence in Eastern Europe is discussed by Robin Remington in Charles Gati, ed., *The International Politics of Eastern Europe* (New York 1976); and my

"Polycentrism in Eastern Europe," in Adam Bromke and Teresa Rakowska-Harmstone, eds., *The Communist States in Disarray, 1965-1971* (Minneapolis 1972).

28 The Czechs' profound contempt for the Russians was well illustrated by a poster that this writer saw displayed in Prague in the fall of 1969. Under a photograph of Dubcek and Svoboda there was a quotation sarcastically selected from the writings of Karl Marx: "Only those nations are free, who do not deprive other nations of their freedom."

29 The Slovaks, it should be noted, never fully shared the anti-German sentiments of the Czechs. Their main grudge against the Austrians was that in the Habsburg empire they were left at the mercy of the Hungarians.

30 For an assessment of the Poles' anti-German and pro-Russian sentiments see my "Nationalism and Communism in Poland," *Foreign Affairs*, XL (July 1962).

31 Zespol Problemowy Polskiego Porozumienia Niepodleglosciwego, "Polska a Niemcy," *Tydzien Polski* (London), 10 June 1978.

32 Stanislaw Stomma, *Mysli o polityce i kulturze* (Krakow 1960). For a summary of Professor Stomma's ideas see my *Poland's Politics, Idealism v. Realism* (Cambridge, Mass. 1967), chap. 12.

33 Stanislav Stomma, "Tragedie Polskiego Realizmu," in *Ruch opozu*, (Paris 1977), pp. 229-35.

XIII
Restless Poles Fear
the End of Détente*

The Polish people, frustrated by economic failure and sporadic repression, are in a sullen, possibly dangerous mood, says Adam Bromke after a lengthy visit to Poland, his former homeland.

Spring was late in coming to Poland this year. May, usually a very beautiful month, was sunny but distinctly cold. Some Poles wondered out loud whether the chill from Afghanistan was responsible.

The Polish people are worried about the deteriorating climate in East-West relations, and they have good reasons. They suffered so much during World War II that they abhor the very thought of another conflict in Europe. They are also painfully aware that the breakdown of detente may lead to a closing of ranks in the Societ bloc and the isolation of Poland from the West. All this at a time when the domestic Polish scene is already fraught with considerable danger.

The Polish Communist government has reacted calmly to the worsening international situation. It had to side with the U.S.S.R. over Afghanistan, but it did so quite pointedly with as little enthusiasm as possible. If anything, the major thrust of Polish diplomacy has been to mitigate the adverse impact of the event in Southwest Asia upon East-West relations and, above all, to salvage detente in Europe.

At the Party Congress in February Afghanistan was barely mentioned, while the Party Secretary, Edward Gierek, offered Warsaw as a site for a European disarmament conference. In May the Poles played a moderating role at a meeting of the Warsaw Pact leaders in the Polish capital and soon afterwards Presidents Brezhnev and Giscard d'Estaing met in Warsaw as Gierek's guest.

A vital stake in keeping détente alive

There is a virtual consensus among Western diplomats in Warsaw that all these activities stem from Polish initiatives. The Poles' moves of course, are carefully coordinated with Moscow, but this makes Warsaw an even more interesting vantage point from which to observe East-West relations.

So far Poland's relations with the Western democracies have not been affected by the deteriorating international situation. Warsaw's contacts with Paris and Bonn have stayed as cordial as ever. There is a common bond in that all of them have good reason to protect détente in Europe.

Significantly, Poland has also preserved close relations with the United States. An American delegation, headed by the secretary of commerce, visited Warsaw in May to improve economic co-operation. In July a Polish-

American Roundtable Conference—to review bilateral relations as well as the broad trends in international politics—is to be held in the United States.

Yet in private the Poles are clearly concerned. Should the adverse international trends continue, they wonder how far they would be able to stay on their present course. They would undoubtedly find themselves under pressure from Moscow to support Communist unity.

The Polish government has a vital stake in protecting its cooperation with the West. Access to Western markets and credits is indispensable to the Polish economy. Poland's debts to Western countries are $18.5 billion. It is estimated, moreover, that this year Poland will need $5-6 billion in Western loans.

The Polish economy is in poor shape. There is a drastic shortage of many consumer goods. Long meat lines are a frequent sight. Inflation is accelerating rapidly— recently the prices of sugar, coffee and cigarettes went up sharply. A lot of construction in going on, but it is often shoddy and, apparently, still not enough. Young couples often have to wait 10 years before obtaining their own apartment.

Social scientists warn of popular explosion

People are tired and frustrated. They are resentful of the privileges accorded the ruling elite. One hears grumbling everywhere. "Its funny"—observed a taxi driver—"in the elections (last March) 99 percent of the people approved of the government, but all my customers are evidently from the remaining one per cent."

Last year a group of leading social scientists came out with a private report warning that unless the situation is soon improved it may lead to a popular explosion. They recommended that a broad programme of economic and social reforms be adopted. As a first step they urged the government to admit honestly to its economic fiasco.

At the Party Congress in February Premier Piotr Jaroszewicz was indeed submitted to harsh criticism and soon afterwards was dismissed from his post. He was replaced by Edward Babiuch, a man close to Gierek, who had hitherto been in charge of the Party organization. In his opening speech to parliament Babiuch admitted that there have been serious economic shortcomings and warned that the situation is not likely to improve for the next two or three years.

Babiuch has tried to convey the impression of more purposeful activity on the part of his government. A number of high officials have been dismissed and an austerity programme adopted. Some glaring privileges of the ruling elite have also been curtailed. A new clinic near Warsaw, which has been built exclusively for government dignitaries, was ostentatiously declared open as a public facility for cardiac patients.

The new government, however, does not intend to go beyond streamlining the present system. It has no plans to carry out major economic reforms. In fact, a group committed to such a course, headed by Politbureau member Stefan Olszowski, suffered a defeat at the last Congress. Babiuch's defence of his cautious approach is that it could be upsetting to introduce major changes into an economy as strained as Poland's is today.

Some long-range studies of economic reforms have been initiated, but whether they will ever come to fruition is a matter of conjecture. Many economists are cynical—they believe that once things do, eventually, improve, the government once again will see no need for changes. Others take a still more pessimistic view—they expect that the economic situation will continue deteriorating until new workers' riots, similar to those in 1970 and 1976, erupt. But they fear that a new explosion would be more serious than those in the past and might even lead to Soviet intervention in Poland.

Nevertheless, it seems that the removal of the highly unpopular Jaroszewicz and Babiuch's frank admission of the economic difficulties have been of some help. At least for the time being the tension in the country has been somewhat relaxed.

Gierek regime is walking a careful line

The Gierek regime is apparently well aware of the danger of a popular explosion for in its dealings with the opposition it walks a careful line. It must also realize that drastic repression against the dissidents would impair its image and, consequently, prejudice its chances of economic cooperation with the West. Detente then, serves as an effective protective umbrella over the human rights activists in Poland.

The Communist tactic is to contain and isolate the opposition rather than to suppress it outright. Police harassment is fairly widely used—apartments are searched, unofficial publications circulated in mimeographed form are confiscated and people are detained for interrogation. Only in exceptional cases, however, do the authorities resort to more drastic measures.

Towards the end of 1979 it appeared that repression was being stepped up. Several opposition activists were brought to trial either on outright political or, more often, trumped up criminal charges. In March the head of the unofficial publishing house, Miroslaw Chojecki, was arrested and charged with theft of government mimeographic equipment. There was apprehension, especially in view of the new international situation, that the Communist authorities had decided to lauch a frontal attack against the opposition.

Fortunately those fears proved to be unfounded. Protests against Chojecki's arrest came not only from the opposition, but from many other quarters. The Polish Writers' Union, upholding the principle of freedom of the printed word, strongly denounced his detention. On May 10, reportedly after personal intervention by Gierek. Chojecki was released.

Some people surmise that one of the reasons for the increased police surveillance of the dissidents is their new tactic of holding mass patriotic rallies. This practice was started in Warsaw in 1978, but has spread to other major cities.

Early in May a massive rally was organized in Gdansk—the scene of the bloody workers'riots in 1970. The demonstrations have often acquired not only overt anti-Communist, but also anti-Soviet overtones, and many Poles are dubious about the wisdom of provoking the Soviets this way.

Dissident groups are active all over Poland

The dissidents enjoy broad sympathy among various segments of the Polish society. They are popular among the younger people, especially the university students, and have the support of many intellectuals. They are active in virtually all major Polish cities and have some scattered following in the countryside.

The opposition groups, however, are divided and occasionally even antagonistic towards each other. They command only marginal influence among the workers. By themselves, although in fact only the most radical groups profess this goal, they would not be able to instigate a revolt. Yet in a highly-charged political atmosphere they may, even if only inadvertently contribute to starting one. In dealing with the opposition, then, the government has really little choice but to steer between the Scylla of tolerance and the Charybdis of repression.

The powerful moderating force in the country is the Catholic church led by venerable Primate of Poland Stefan Cardinal Wyszynski. The Primate, who will soon turn 79, is physically quite vigorous and mentally as alert as ever. He is well aware of his immense authority and of the great responsibility which goes with it.

The church wields a strong and disciplined organization and commands the support of the great majority of the Polish people. The triumphal visit of Pope John Paul II last year only confirmed the Poles in their strong attachment to Catholicism. The church also enjoys the respect, however grudging, of the Gierek regime.

Church and State are holding delicate negotiations

Recently the church has won several important concessions from the Communist government. Permission was given for 60,000 copies of the Polish edition of *L'Osservatore Romano* to be distributed in Poland. From now on priests will be eligible for social security benefits and are to be exempted from compulsory military service.

The Episcopate, however, is not prepared to stop there. Above all, it insists that the government must formally recognize the status of the church. It demands access to the media and educational institutions. It publicly condemns discrimination against Catholics holding public office. Delicate negotiations to resolve those issues are under way between the Episcopate and the authorities and between the Vatican and the Polish government. The church's attention is not confined to expanding religious freedom. It steadfastly upholds all human rights. The activities of the dissidents enjoy its sympathy and often its discreet protection. The Episcopate intervened, for example, and perhaps most effectively, on behalf of Chojecki. Yet the Primate maintains a statesmanlike distance from the activities of the various opposition groups. He also speaks with profound concern about the deterioration of the international situation.

Sober mood prevails despite the serious tensions

Under the surface of political uniformity and economic drabness Poland is a vibrant and exciting society. The Poles are remarkably well informed and highly opinionated about events in the world. Freedom of the spoken word is virtually complete.

In a broad spectrum of political views, however, a mood of sobriety prevails. Virtually all Poles are concerned about the decline of East-West détente and are aware that the present international problems must be resolved in a peaceful fashion. There is also a determination on their part to try to help, in whatever small way they can.

This is all to the good. For not only do the Poles need the continued relaxation of international tensions, but international détente needs a tranquil Poland. Should the situation in Poland get out of hand it could pose a serious threat to the future of East-West détente.

* Originally published in the *Toronto Sunday Star*, June 29, 1980.

XIV
POLAND: THE CLIFF'S EDGE*

The recent upheavals in Poland provide the West with an opportunity to rescue the sinking ship of détente in Europe. But they may also allow the Soviet Union to chose the dangerious alternative of sinking it beyond salvage. Western policy makers must consider whether Western policies can help avert destructive Soviet intervention and so speed the recovery of détente, and whether the United States and its European allies can help the Poles develop a political system more suitable for their own political culture, even while their country remains aligned with the Warsaw Pact.

The strikes during summer 1980 are the most recent in a series of labour disputes that have spurred political reform in Poland. In the absence of free elections, strikes have become the most democratic means available to the Polish people to push their government toward change. In 1956 the Poznan workers initiated a period of national agitation that ended the rule of the Stalinists and brought Wladyslaw Gomulka to power as the new first secretary of the Communist party. Gomulka himself was replaced by Edward Girek in 1970 following antigovernment protests among workers in the Baltic cities, including Gdansk. On those occasions, the communist government tried to suppress the workers by force before finally acceding to their demands. In 1980, however, violence was avoided. The workers did not take to the streets, but staged peaceful and orderly sit-down strikes, and the authorities did not use the police or the army to seize the factories.

In spite of their peaceful nature, the recent strikes have posed a more serious challenge to the communist system than did the unrest of 1956 and 1970. The establishment of the right to form free trade unions touches upon a particularly sensitive aspect of the official ideology. It undermines the legitimacy on which communist power rests, by refuting the claim of the Communist party to be the sole authentic representative of the working class. Moreover, allowing the workers the right to strike provides them with an effective instrument to defend their gains. Indeed, the workers have already demonstrated a capability to undertake a general strike.

As the workers lead the way toward a renewal of their entire political system, other segments of the Polish population are announcing demands of their own. There are signs of ferment among the private farmers, who have long felt neglected by the government. Students are groping for an organization independent of the Communist party. Intellectuals are insisting that censorship be curtailed drastically. The Catholic church will persist with its long-standing demand for official recognition as a legal entity, and lay Catholics will press for an end to the discrimination that prevents them from holding responsible administrative positions.

Overall, there is a remarkable congruence among these segments of Polish society. The workers, well aware that their strenth lies in concerted action, have symbolically labeled their new national union, Solidarity. The workers' demands were drawn largely from a report on the Polish economic crisis issued by some prominent Polish intellectuals, including both Catholics and communists, who are known as the Experience and Future group. The intellectuals also have strong bonds of cooperation with the students. Even the traditional gap dividing the liberal intellectuals and the Catholic church has been overcome. In its striving for greater freedom, the Polish nation is more united today than it has ever been in the postwar years.

In contrast, the Communist party is visibly divided and demoralized. The merry-go-round of personnel changes in top positions that began during the party's congress in February 1980 has revealed profound cleavages in the leadership. The new group in power, led by First Secretary Stanislaw Kania, subjected Gierek and his followers to harsh criticism, but by October 1980 it had failed to come out with any clear-cut program of it own. Instead, it has been reacting to popular pressures—accepting some demands for reforms and trying to ignore others. Its prestige has not been enhanced by revelations of widespread corruption in the party ranks, even though Kania pledged in early October to cleanse the Communist ranks of many offenders. The party's authority has not been so low since the de-Stalinization period of the mid-1950s.

At the time, Gomulka used his considerable prestige among the Polish people to revive the party. But Kania has no such popular standing, having spent his entire career in the party apparatus. He can restore the party's authority only by resolving the current economic crisis and improving the Polish people's standard of living. But his scope for economic manoeuver already has been severely restricted. In the 1970's Gierek also attempted to revive the government's legitimacy by raising the standard of living. In doing so, however, he has left Kania a legacy of a $20.5 billion hard-currency debt.

Moreover, the recent work stoppages did little to improve the economic situation in the country or to enhance Western bankers' confidence in the Polish economy. The stark reality is that Poland is faced with several years of rigid austerity. With little hope of an improvement for consumers, the government must meet at least some of the people's political demands in order to win their cooperation in an attempt at overall economic recovery.

Pantzerkommunismus

The crisis in Poland is by no means over. It is doubtful if Kania—even if he manages to stay at the top—will be able to consolidate his hold over the Communist party before the extraordinary congress planned for the first half of 1981. Meanwhile, the tug-of-war between the people and the Communists authorities will go on. Already, by the end of October 1980, the first test of will—this time over government efforts to alter key provisions of the founding charter of the independent union movement—had taken place. The Soviets summoned Kania to Moscow, and the threat of the use of force intensified.

Any attempt on the part of the government to reverse political changes by force, however, would most likely result in a general strike. Neither the Polish police nor the Polish army—even if the latter could be relied on to move against the people—could cope with such a situation. The only way to avoid a collapse of all Communist authority in the country, then, would be to call for Soviet intervention.

The Soviets are on the horns of a dilemma. On the one hand, they are unhappy over the concessions to the Polish workers. The establishment of trade unions independent of the Communist party strikes at the very heart of Marxist-Leninist doctrine and might also have important repercussions in some other countries in Eastern Europe. On the other hand to extinguish the Polish heresy with force will be extremely costly.

The Kremlin seems to realize that the Poles would not accept Soviet tanks entering Warsaw without a fight. The occupation of Poland would be a bloody and prolonged affair. Of course, in the end the Poles would lose, but this would resolve nothing. Under a *Pantzerkommunismus*, the Polish workers would not work any harder, and Moscow would have to assume responsibility for Poland's substantial debt to the West. Furthermore, such a development would have serious consequences for the U.S.S.R. in the international sphere.

The gap between Soviet communists and Eurocommunists would undoubtedly be widened by an invasion of Poland. Various Communist parties in Western Europe—notably the Italian and the Spanish—have already voiced their strong support for the Polish workers. Indeed, the Italian communist labor federation joined Italy's social-democratic and Catholic unions in a statement declaring that the Polish strikers' demands must be met without repression or outside intervention.

A forcible Soviet entry into Poland would bring to an end what little is left of East-West détente. It would alienate West Germany and France from the U.S.S.R. and effecively restore the unity of the Western alliance. It would wreck both the review of the Conference on Security and Cooperation in Europe, scheduled to open formally in Madrid on November 11, 1980, and the disarmament conference, proposed by the Soviet Union, to be held in Warsaw. The U.S. Senate would be even less likely than it is now to ratify balanced arms control agreements with the Soviets. East-West relations would regress to the frostiest days of the Cold War, and the risk of nuclear confrontation would be greatly increased.

The Poles do not want to provoke a Soviet invasion. Not only do they want to avoid spilling of any Polish blood, but they also believe that their deifferences with the Soviet Union can be resolved in a peaceful fashion. The report of the Experience and Future group strongly emphasized that the Poles have no intention either of leaving the Warsaw Pact or of abandoning socialism. The Gdansk strikers carefully abstained from any obviously anti-Soviet gestures and pledged that the new trade unions would not try to become political rivals of the Communist party.

The Catholic church also exerts a powerful moderating influence in the country. At the climax of the Gdansk strike, Stefan Cardinal Wyszynski, the Primate of Poland, appealed to the Poles for prudence and restrain, while Catholic intellectuals advised the workers on methods to resolve the dispute peacefully. The church will undoubtedly continue its conciliatory course, as the historic compromise betweeen the Catholics and the communists gradually becomes a reality.

A Useful Bridge

The Polish people do not want to bring about the demise of East-West détente. Détente has provided a protective umbrella for expanding relations with the West and for widening the scope of freedom at home. The signing of the Helsinki Final Act in 1975 constrained the Gierek regime from moving against unofficial opposition groups for fear that the flow of Western credits—so essential to the Polish economy— would be curtailed.

The Poles are well aware that their experiment could end in tragedy, as did the Prague spring. But Czechoslovakia in 1968, unlike Poland today, had had little experience with change. Stalinism had lingered in Czechoslovakia until the early 1960s, making the pressure for radical reforms extremely strong. Changes in Poland have been advanced over more than two decades. Consequently, the implementation of new changes should not be seen as a radical departure from the existing political system, but rather as the next stage in its gradual evolution.

But for a peaceful settlement to be advanced, the Soviet Union must also adopt a conciliatory,attitude. The developments in Poland are not the result—as *Pravda* claimed recently—of the activities of "anti-socialist" forces, but represent the aspirations of virtually the entire Polish nation. The Soviet model imposed upon Poland by force at the end of World War II has failed repeatedly, and by now the Poles are determined to adjust it to their own needs. The Kremlin leaders must realize that keeping 36 million people at bayonet point would only aggravate the Polish grievances against the U.S.S.R.

The Soviets abstained from intervening in Poland in 1965 and in 1970, opting for political solutions to both crises. Initial Soviet readiness to come to the rescue of Poland's battered economy suggest that once again the U.S.S.R. would prefer a peaceful solution. After the settlement in Gdansk, the U.S.S.R. extended $550 million in economic aid to Poland. Significantly, some of it was in the form of hard-currency loans aimed at bolstering Poland's credit worthiness in the West.

The Soviets' handling of the Polish crisis—their choice between military and political options—will reveal Moscow's intentions concerning East-West détente. It is a true test of whether the Kremlin leaders are ready to live up to their commitments—enshrined in the Helsinki accords—to respect the sovereignty of all and not interfere in the domestic affair of any European country.

Thus, the Polish question has again moved to the center of the international stage. The West has a vital stake in a peaceful resolution of the Polish crisis. It is not only that the aspiration of the Polish people toward greater freedom deserve the sympathy of the Western democracies; the destruction of East-West détente, which would inevitably follow a forcible subjugation of Poland by the U.S.S.R., would also be highly detremental to Western interests. The following suggestions would help Western policy makers prevent such an outcome.

Under no circumstances should the West convey the impression that in the event of Soviet intervention it would be able to render Poland any effective assistance. After Hungary in 1956 and Czechoslovakia in 1968, the Poles do not have great illusions on that score. Yet especially among young idealists there exists an affinity with the West and an undercurrent of hope that Poland will be treated differently. The rise to prominence in the United States of National Security Adviser Zbigniew Brzezinski and Secretary of State Edmund Muskie might have strengthened those sentiments. Therefore, while expressing sympathy for the legitimate aspirations of the Polish people. Western leaders should make sure that their statements are not misinterpreted. Utmost caution should be exercised by the Western stations broadcasting to Poland. The West should remember that in a highly charged political atmosphere too profuse an expression of sympathy could be taken as an encouragement to action.

As for the U.S.S.R., the Western objective should be not to condemn, but to prevent Soviet intervention in Poland. Western countries ought to make it clear that they regard the crisis in Poland as a strictly internal affair and that—in line with the Helsinki accords—they would expect the Soviet Union to take the same position.

This does not mean, however, that there is no room for diplomatic action. The West should not adopt a posture of studied indifference as it did regarding Czechoslovakia in 1968. Soviet leaders looking for excuses to intervene will find them in the volatile political conditions that inevitably will develop as Poland works out its new internal compromise. Therefore, the possibility of a disastrous Soviet intervention is not insignificant. As a precautionary move, the Western powers, and the United States in particular must communicate to the Soviets their deep concern over the possibility of Soviet interference in Polish internal affairs and the grave consequences such a step would inevitably have for East-West relations.

The West should strive to present the Polish problem within the broad context of détente in Europe. The Western powers should emphasize that they are not striving to detach Poland from the Warsaw Pact, but rather to develop new bonds of international cooperation. A Poland allied to the Soviet Union, but permitted to develop an internal system compatible with its own political culture, could serve as a useful bridge between the two parts of Europe. Gierek undertook to play this role with some success, and it is to be hoped that his successors will expand on it.

Such political development is not inconceivable in the case of Poland. The Soviets have overestimated the linguistic and cultural affinities that they share with the Poles. In fact, in terms of history and political culture, the Poles are westerners. The Soviet model of socialism has never fit Poland exactly and so had to be adapted to Polish circumstances in 1956 and 1970.

One way the West could directly alleviate Poland's crisis is by providing economic assistance. In the second half of 1980, West Germany and the United States each extended to Poland new loans of approximately $700 million. It is quite likely that Warsaw will ask for still more credits or even seek rescheduling of its debts. Such requests should be treated with sympathy by the Western governments.

In extending additional credits to Poland, Western banks will undoubtedly insist on monitoring the economic policies in that country. Such visible Western involvement in its economy might even be welcome to the Polish government as it could be useful in justifying the necessary austerity measures to the Polish workers. It could also benefit the reformers in the Polish Communist party, who are bent on rationalizing the Polish economic system. Thus, by joining hands with the U.S.S.R. in a rescue operation of the battered Polish economy, the West could transform a confrontation over that country into an area of East-West cooperation.

It is by no means coincidental that Poland should find itself once again at the center of East-West relations. After all, this ancient nation, the largest in Eastern Europe, has often played a prominent role in international affairs. It was over Poland that World War II started and largely over the Polish question that the Cold War began. It would be only fitting if, through East-West cooperation, the Cold War were put to rest there. It would be tragic if, through miscalculation on either side, Soviet intervention were to restore that war to its most dangerous phase.

* Originally published in *Foreign Policy*, Winter 1980-81.

XV
How Are We Seen?

A conversation with Henryk Zdanowski published in *Polityka*, March 14, 1981. (Translated from the Polish.)

HZ. Professor how are we seen in the West?

AB. With sympathy and respect. The Poles have impressed the world by their determination and courage in searching for and finding ways to improve their country's lot. And also by their composure and moderation.

HZ. But the world, and even the West itself, is by no means homogeneous. Have we been praised by everybody for everything?

AB. There is sympathy on both the right and the left, although for different reasons. The right is impressed with the libertarian and the left with the egalitarian aspects of the developments in Poland.

HZ. So we have been continually popular since last August?

AB. Since August there has been unprecedented interest in Poland. The subject seldom disappears from the newspapers' front pages. But lately there have also been some signs of apprehension and even of some criticism. Questions have been posed: how far can this go and how long can this last? Here and there one hears quoted that old derogatory phrase: "the *polnische Wirtschaft*". Of course one may remain curious about who really is responsible for Poland's state of affairs—the government or the strikers—but this does not change the fact that a certain fatigue is evident.

HZ. Professor, let's forget the press. After all, the situation in Poland has been dramatic enough to merit the front page articles and even to explain various journalistic attempts to make it still more sensational. But what do you think are the attitudes in the western political circles towards Poland?

AB. One can distinguish here two different tendencies or two distinct trends.

The first, to make it short, sees the developments in Poland primarily as a potential source of problems for the Soviet Union. This tendency, even if it may appear to be unreasonable, is only natural, especially in the United States where all international events—including those in Poland—are viewed in the context of global politics and particularly with reference to American-Soviet relations. For Washington, after all, developments in Cuba, Southwest Asia, the Middle east or even in Africa are of equal interest.

The second tendency is to see in the developments in Poland an opportunity to expand international cooperation. Let us not forget that Poland—regardless of whether one approves or not—is of special interest to the West as a potential bridge between the East and the West. This accounted for the interest in the Rapacki Plan and this was how the overall foreign policy of the Gierek administration was regarded.

This second tendency which assumes the continuation and even a further expansion of Polish foreign policy along the same lines, is particularly noticeable among the Western European countries. Foreign policy priorities of those countries are largely different from those of the United States; although, and this should be emphasized, the second tendency is also the dominant one in the United States.

HZ. You mentioned the Rapacki Plan and the Gierek foreign policy with its "opening to the West" as important elements of Poland's activism in the internation sphere. It seems to me, however, that today Poland is of greater international significance than ever. A lot depends in the world on our successes or failures in the political as well as economic and social spheres.

AB. That's correct. But one should remember that Poland has already enjoyed such an extraordinary importance once before. (I say "extraordinary" because the international position of, say, Britain or France is not affected by strikes or the activities of their trade unions!) That was in 1956. Although, mind you, at that time Poland's position was not entirely exceptional. The "Polish October" coincided with the de-Stalinization in the Soviet Union and was a part of the broader process of reforms which encompassed virtually the entire Communist movement. Now Poland stands alone in her experiment. And it is of interest only as long as it lasts and is successful.

Certainly, Poland has become a topic of international concern but there are hidden dangers we must allow for. Poland is a big, country with 36 million population, situated in the centre of Europe; this fact offers an opportunity but, at the same time, it implies a threat.

HZ. Professor, a danger, a threat—wat do you mean by that?

AB. Poland is a sovereign state—I disregard here the restrictions which are inherent in its participation in the bloc and the alliance. In any case, since last August, as a result of social agreements the scope for independent changes in the system has been considerably widened? The danger or the threat is what may result from going beyond a certain limit, from crossing some threshold.

HZ. And the West is also concerned that this should not happen?

AB. Certainly this is true of the second trend in the West, which has been supporting the policy of détente. It is well aware that there is a linkage between détente and the developments in Poland.

The progress of détente has been beneficial to Poland—to a large extent it has contributed to the recent changes. The Poles, then, should also be interested in a continuation of it. At the same time, however, the maintenance of peace in Poland is indispensable for the survival of international détente.

HZ. It is probably because of your interest in maintaining détente that last fall, writing in the Washington journal *Foreign Policy*, you made the following recommendation: "By joining hands with the U.S.S.R. in a rescue operation of the battered Polish economy, the West could transform a confrontation over that country into an area of East-West cooperation". What did you mean here by a confrontation?

AB. The belief that there are some subversive forces striving to detach Poland from the socialist bloc. In fact, even those who would like to see awkward problems for the Soviet Union in Poland, do not advocate a breakoff, but just problems. For everybody knows that dealignment is not possible, that it would ruin everything, and could even lead to a global conflict.

HZ. And yet, you have not always restricted the problem to just "problems". In an article of yours which appeared last February in the Canadian [Polish language] paper, *Zwiazkowiec*, you made the following statement: "Even the moderate leaders of the opposition in Poland, who advocate gradual changes, felt obliged to stress—thus tipping their hand—that their ultimate goal is an overthrow of Communism and the regaining of Poland's independence from the Soviet Union".

AB. All right, but I referred to it in the past tense, precisely as an illustration of a myth which has been dispelled. I believe that most Poles are well aware by now of the feedback which exists between their activities and détente. I should only add that very few people in the West would like to see the Poles go too far. For if the Polish experiment collapses not only will there be no progress of détente in the 1980's, but even the achievements of the 1970s will not be preserved.

HZ. You said that only a few people want the Poles to go too far. How would you define "too far" or "not far enough"?

AB. The limits are imprecise. For they depend not only on reality, but—and perhaps even foremost—on the perception of reality. Admissible boundaries may look different from the perspective of Gdansk, different from Warsaw, and still different from the allied countries. In other words it is not quite certain where the limits are. In such circumstances it is better to stop a step short than to go half a step too far.

HZ. And you think, Professor, that the Poles are sufficiently aware of this situation?

AB. In order to understand reality (and the differing perceptions are also a part of the reality) ideology is not indispensable. For the Communists reality is consistent with their doctrine, but for the Church, for instance, it exists objectively.

HZ. Thank you for this conversation.

XVI
Poland Lost Her Leader

With the death of Stefan Cardinal Wyszynski Poland has suffered a great loss. For over thirty years — since he became the Primate of the Polish Catholic church in 1948 — he was the country's spiritual as well as national leader.

Private audiences with Cardinal Wyszynski have been the highlights of my periodical returns to my native land. I saw him last on March 1. Intellectually he was as alert as ever, but he was visibly tired and drawn. I attributed this to the heavy toll which the crisis in Poland, under way since the previous summer, must have exacted on him. But he did not give me an opportunity to enquire about his health, immediately initiating a discussion of the dramatic events in the country.

During our conversations he always gave me an incisive account of the situation in Poland. Though he usually spoke in carefully measured terms, when he deemed it necessary he could be quite forceful too. In turn, he would ask my views about certain current international issues. He was an intent listener — only occasionally interrupting wih probing questions.

Cardinal Wyszynski was an extremely attractive person. Tall, and despite his advanced age, erect, he moved with both self-assurance and grace. He was a handsome man with distinct features, a friendly look and a radiant smile which made his guest instantly feel at ease. Yet, he was fully conscious of his immense authority and the awesome responsibility that went with it.

Stefan Cardinal Wyszynski was born on August 3, 1901, to a village teacher and a church organist. He was ordained a priest in 1924 and subsequently studied canon law and social sciences, winning his doctorate in 1929. After two years of further studies in Western Europe he became a teacher at a theological seminary. At the same time he was a prolific writer on social problems and was active in the Christian trade unions. During the war he worked among the academic youth and participated in the resistance movement.

In 1946 he was appointed Bishop of Lublin and two years later Archbishop of Gniezno and Warsaw — a position with which go the chairmanship of the Polish Episcopate and the title of Primate of Poland. In January 1953 he was elevated to Cardinal by Pius XII, but in September he was interned by the Communist authorities. In October 1956, after a popular upheaval in the country, he was released and triumphantly restored to his office.

As Primate of Poland Wyszynski transformed the challenge of the Communist government into an opportunity for the Catholic church. A conservative in matters of theology and morality, he was progressive over social issues. Well versed in political thought, he liked to joke about his encounters in the 1950s with the then First Secretary of the Communist party, Wladyslaw Gomulka, over some subtle points of Marxist doctrine.

Under his leadership the church went from strength to strength, attaining a position unprecedented in Poland's modern history. In a country ruled by the atheistic Communist party, some 90 per cent of the population stayed faithful to Catholicism. With the elevation in 1978 of Karol Cardinal Wojtyla to the Throne of St. Peter, the Polish church won international recognition.

Yet, Stefan Cardinal Wyszynski was more than just a religious leader. There is a tradition in the country dating back to the seventeenth and eighteenth centuries, when the Polish kings were elected, that when one monarch died and before another assumed the throne, the Primate of Poland ruled in the meantime. In the post-war years, since the Communist government has never attained popular legitimacy, Cardinal Wyszynski emerged as the true national leader in the eyes of the Poles.

Indeed, he was always concerned about the welfare not only of the church, but of the entire Polish nation. He often voiced interest in the well-being of the workers and the peasants and stood up in the defence of the Jews. His courageous upholding of religious freedom and human rights has gained him enormous prestige among the Polish people. He even won grudging respect from the Communists.

Cardinal Wyszynski was a great statesman. He never conceded, even at the risk of deprivation of his personal freedom, any matter of principle. But he was ready to negotiate and compromise with the Communist government over minor issues. He knew from a thousand years of its history that the church in Poland had lived through various social upheavals and that the time was on its side.

In foreign policy he was a realist. He steadfastly pressed for concessions from the Polish Communist government, but whenever the danger of Soviet intervention has arisen — as in 1956 and 1970 — he appealed to the Poles for calm and restraint. In the mid-1960s he paved the way for a reconciliation between Poland and West Germany, and in the 1970s he supported the progress of détente in Europe.

During the latest crisis Cardinal Wyszynski once again assumed a realist's stance. He vigorously advocated democratic reforms in the country; yet, in order not to provoke a Soviet intervention, he cautioned the restive workers not to move too far or too fast. At some critical junctures he used his authority in helping to resolve various industrial disputes.

In my last conversation with him he was pained by the criticism by some radical intellectuals of his moderate position. It was one of those rare occasions when he was quite forceful in articulating his views. He did not conceal his anxiety that the confrontationist tactics might bring about a national catastrophe.

The demise of Cardinal Wyszynski at a time when the crisis in the country is not yet over, and may be even approaching its climax, is a tremendous loss for Poland. His wise counsel will be sorely missed. His personal stature was so great that no one among the Polish Episcopate can immediately fill his role.

There is only one person who carries the same weight among the Poles and who shares Cardinal Wyszynski's notion of Poland's destiny. It is the Polish Pope, John Paul II. On his deathbed the Primate asked his people to pray, not for him, but for the wounded Pope. He must have been eased in his pain by the knowledge that John Paul II is making a good recovery.

There is another legacy that Cardinal Wyszynski has bestowed upon the Poles. He has made the Catholic church in Poland stronger than ever. He has shown to the Polish nation the road along which it can patiently, but most securely, improve its plight. He has also taught his compatriots the virtues of a commitment to humanistic values and charity towards their adversaries.

Stefan Cardinal Wyszynski was the greatest Pole of the post-war period. To those who were privileged to know him he was also a beautiful person.

* Originally published in the *Toronto Sunday Star*, May 31, 1981.

XVII
Poland's Upheaval
An Interim Report*

The upheaval in Poland has already lasted longer than the "Prague Spring" of 1968. And the Poles have gone further than the Czechs. Internally, there is a genuine popular revolution—although carried out without violence and in a gradual fashion—under way in Poland; and, externally, the ripple effects of the Polish workers' unrest have affected several crucial aspects of East-West relations.

The starting point for the Poles, of course, was more advantageous than that of the Czechs. In Czechoslavakia an oppressive Stalinist system continued virtually unchanged into the 1960s. In Poland the Stalinists were removed from power after a popular upheaval in 1956 and various reforms were adopted. Some were subsequently withdraw, but some have stayed. Collectivization of agriculture was for all intents and purposes abandoned and the Catholic church went from strength to strength, a process culminating in 1979 in the triumphal visit of John Paul II to his native country.

Likewise, when the increasingly unpopular Gomulka regime was toppled by the workers' revolt in 1970, some additional reforms were instituted. The Communist government began showing greater concern for the people's standard of living and Poland's contacts with the West were considerably expanded. Since the mid-1970's the activities of an unoficial democratic opposition have also been tolerated. Thus, when in 1980 in the face of a new workers unrest the Gierek regime collapsed, it was generally anticipated that some new reforms would again be carried out.

Challenge to the system

The latest changes in Poland, however, have exceeded all expectations. Never before in any Communist state has the working class issued such a massive challenge to the rulers; and never before has a Communist government gone so far to appease a restive people. The emergence of free trade unions touches upon a particularly sensitive aspect of Marxism-Leninism. By refuting the claim of the Communist party to be the sole authentic spokesman for the working class it undermines the very legitimacy upon which Communist power rests. The workers, moreover, have made good use of their newly won right to strike. The industrial labourers' trade union, "Solidarity", some ten million strong, has secured a virtual power of veto over government's decisions and, so far, has won all the major confrontations with the Communist authorities hands down.

With the workers leading the way towards changes, various other segments of the Polish society have come out with demands of their own.

Private farmers have won recognition for their own organization, similar to "Solidarity". The church has also obtained some new concessions. A regular broadcast of a Sunday mass has been introduced on the Polish national radio network and a Catholic member of parliament has been appointed a Deputy Premier. The writers and journalists insist that censorship be drastically curtailed and have elected as presidents of their professional associations men who have been closely identified with the reform movement. The students have secured the abolition of compulsory courses in Marxism-Leninism and the professors have been quietly restoring the universities' traditional autonomy.

If permitted to continue, the process of "renewal"—as the Poles have labelled it—will lead to a major transformation of the entire system. The façade of Communism would be preserved, but its substance would be radically changed. Already there are plans for a comprehensive overhaul of the national economy including the restoration of a market mechanism, the granting of autonomy to individual enterprises and provisions for worker participation in management. There is also a strong egalitarian aspect to the current Polish upheaval. The workers are adamant in pressing for the abolition of the privileges of the Communist elite and for a genuine improvement of the living conditions of the poorest strata of the Polish society.

The parliament has largely resumed its role in redressing popular grievances and in scrutinizing government measures. Cabinet appointments are no longer routinely approved and various ministers are submitted to some sharp questioning. The post of chairman of a special parliamentary committee to implement agreements with the workers has gone to a non-party member of parliament, a highly respected sociologist, Professor Jan Szczepanski. It is also expected that a new Chairman of the State Council—formally the highest office in the country—will also be a non-party deputy. The Democratic Party, hitherto a pliable tool in the Communists' hands, has reasserted its separate identity. Various lay Catholic political groups have been given opportunity to expand their activities. When the present parliament terminates there will be, no doubt, pressure to revise the electoral system with a view to achieving a more genuinely popular representation.

The Polish people are grimly determined to press on with their demands. Having been repeatedly deceived by the Communists in the past they will no longer be satisfied by mere promises—this time they strive for institutional guarantees that the reforms are there to stay. They are also in a defiantly nationalistic mood. The strength of Polish nationalism clearly surfaced last summer. Striking factories were draped with national banners and often displayed portraits of John Paul II. The striking workers—most of whom were born and raised in People's Poland—wore red and white armbands reminiscent of those of the wartime resistance. Clearly a new mood of confidence, if not of buoyance, has emerged in Poland.

In this respect there is a remarkable congruence among various segments of the Polish society. It was dramatically demonstrated during the unveiling of the monument commemorating the workers felled by police bullets in December 1970, which took place on the tenth anniversary of that event in Gdansk. In attendance were the leaders of "Solidarity" and church dignitaries, while smartly dressed marines placed a wreath from the Polish government. A popular poem has captured the present mood of the Poles: "Should someone try to set our house on fire we should be prepared, for it is better to die standing than to live on one's knees."

Repeated confrontations

The agreement between the government and the workers concluded in Gdansk on August 30, 1980 was a compromise, and a vague one at that.[1] In exchange for the right to establish independent trade unions the workers pledged to respect the existing political system and the leading role which the Communist party plays in it. In the subsequent months many more such accords—over 600 of them altogether—have been concluded. They have dealt mostly with local issues, but they have all adhered to the same general political formula.

In a Communist system, where all the major economic decisions are made by the government, to draw a clear distinction between a pure trade unionism and a political action group is by no means easy. Even with best intentions on both sides, then, implementing the Gdansk compact would have been a complex undertaking; but mutual trust has not always been there. The Communist government has proved reluctant to carry out the agreements in practice. The authorities have adopted a narrow, restrictive interpretation of various provisions or have simply stalled on their implementation. They have often given in only when faced with the threat of new strikes—thereby losing the workers' confidence even more. There have also been numerous attempts at intimidation, and even the use of physical violence, against the trade unionists, which have poisoned the atmosphere still further.

As a whole "Solidarity" under the leadership of Lech Walesa, has steered a moderate course. It has carefully refrained from issuing any outright challenge to the existing political system. Yet, at least among some segments of "Solidarity", there have been tendencies to reach beyond economic issues into a political sphere. In fact some provisions of such nature, for instance, a demand for the release of all political prisoners, were already included in the Gdansk accord. As time went on the attempts at politicization of the free trade unions were intensified.

It is only natural that in an organization so new and so untested as "Solidarity" some leaders have emerged who have had little preparation for the roles which they have assumed.[2] Some of them are very young and inexperienced, and they have been overimpressed with their successes to date. They have seemed to believe that the best way to deal with the

Communist government is to keep it constantly off balance and, consequently, they have tended to abuse the strike weapon to win not only national, but also some local issues. This attitude has also been encouraged by the young hotheads from the democratic opposition who here and there have assumed advisory roles to the unions. Indeed, the mood of some "Solidarity" branches has been buoyant. Early in March, for instance, the Szczecin branch requested the parliament to admonish the First Secretary of the Communist party, Stanislaw Kania, for the submissive nature of his address to the Soviet party Congress in Moscow.

As a result an endless series of disputes between the government and the workers has ensued. It was virtually uninterrupted throughout the fall and the winter. To cope with this situation a new government headed by the Minister of National Defence, General Wojciech Jaruzelski, was appointed early in February. The choice of a military figure as a new Premier was clearly a warning to the restless workers—only one step short of introducing martial law in the country. At the same time, however, the appointment of Mieczyslaw Rakowski—formerly an editor of a popular weekly *Polityka* and a man long identified with the programme of reforms—as a Deputy Premier in charge of relations with the unions, indicated that the door has not been closed to compromise. In order to bring the rapidly deteriorating economic situation under control the new government requested that the unions abstain from strikes for 90 days. Indeed, at least some lingering industrial disputes were soon settled.

On March 19, however, a new and grave confrontation between the government and the unions erupted. Riot police were used in the city of Bydgoszcz to break up a union peaceful demonstration and in the process some paarticipants were beaten so severely that they required hospital-ization. "Solidarity" responded by threat of a general strike unless there was a full investigation of the incident and the responsible officials punished. The new confrontation coincided with the begining of Warsaw Pact military maneouvres called "Soyuz 81", conducted on Polish territory. The atmosphere in the country became extremely tense. To resolve the crisis intense negotiations between the government and "Solidarity" were undertaken and at the last moment a compromise, averting the general strike, was reached.

In search of a compromise

During the latest crisis an important moderating role has been played by the Catholic church. The Episcopate, of course, has been fully supportive of the process of "renewal" and has often used its considerable influence with the government to obtain concessions for various segments of the Polish society. It has steadfastly upheld civil rights activists and more recently it has been largely instrumental in winning official recognition for the private farmers- union. At the same time the church has been critical of the confrontationist tactics of the radical elements in "Solidarity" which, it fears, might carry the country over the brink.

Stefan Cardinal Wyszynski, thus, has repeatedly cautioned the workers not to step beyond purely economic demands and John Paul II in various messages to his compatriots has also urged prudence. Behind the scenes, and at some critical junctures even openly, the bishops have acted as mediators in various industrial disputes. Lay Catholic intellectuals, who have been placed in key advisory positions to "Solidarity", have provided an effective link between the unions and the Episcopate. Walesa, himself a devout Catholic, has kept closely in touch with Cardinal Wyszynski and in January travelled to Rome to pay him homage to the Pope.

The Bydgoszcz incident evidently served as a sobering influence upon both sides. The officials responsible for the police abuses were dismissed; at the same time Walesa removed from the "Solidarity" leadership some individuals who had pressed for continued confrontation. Early in April, Premier Jaruzelski won from the parliament a 60-day moratorium on strikes. Simultaneously new talks were undertaken between Rakowski and Walesa to resolve the outstanding issues in a calmer atmosphere. Various working groups of government and "Solidarity" experts are preparing legislative measures to regulate the activities of the free unions within the existing political system.

Peaceful resolution of the latest conflict was apparently received with relief by the country at large. The Poles are by now weary of the persistence of the political crisis—the constant ups and downs in the confrontation between the government and the unions with the danger, at each stage, that the situation could get out of hand. Many have gnawing doubts that the reforms have already gone too far and fear that the entire experiment will be crushed by a Soviet intervention.[3] Public opinion seems to be shifting against the radicals in the "Solidarity" ranks.

The Poles are also painfully aware of their country's desperate economic plight. Since last summer the economy has continued to decline—there have been increasing shortages of consumer goods, and particularly of food, an accelerated inflation, and Poland's hard currency debt has risen to some $27 billion. There are fears that the food situation may reach a critical situation by late spring. The Polish people, thus, appear to be willing to accept the austerity measures proposed by the Jaruzelski government: the rationing of some essential products and even the introduction of drastic food price increases—the step that sparked the strikes in the first place.

Most of the Poles wish General Jaruzelski well. As a professional soldier who in the past has shied away from politics, and because of his modest demeanor, the new Premier enjoys widespread popularity. Many Poles also believe that his regime may be the last chance for the country. It is possible, then, that, given time, the Jaruzelski government will succeed in calming down emotions and will gradually lead Poland out of the present crisis. Yet, the truce between the Communist government and "Solidarity" is a precarious one and any false step on either side may throw the country once more into a vicious descending spiral of repeated confrontations.

Disarray in the Communist party

The situation in Poland is further complicated by a profound crisis in the ruling Polish United Workers' Party. The revelations of incompetence of its leadership and widespread corruption in its ranks have badly shattered the party's prestige. Gierek and most of his supporters on the Politbureau have by now been purged and some have also been charged with criminal offences, but this has helped little. There are no signs as yet that the PUWP has regained even a semblance of credibility among the populace. Meanwhile, the rank and file of party members—over 3 million strong—have become demoralized and divided. The party is at present split three ways into hard liners, reformists and centrists.

On one side the present party leaders are opposed by the hard-liners, who, ostensibly for ideological, but more often for purely opportunistic reasons, resist the process of "renewal". They are afraid of losing their power and privileges and are desperately trying to stop the changes in the country. The hard-liners are still well entrenched in many positions in the party, particularly at the provincial level, and often use their influence to sabotage cooperation with the unions. The police attack against the unionists in Bydgoszcz was apparently one more such a provocation on their part.

From the other direction the current leadership is challenged by the reformists. This wing of the party is relatively weak at the top, but it enjoys broad support at the grass roots. It is estimated that almost 40 percent of the party members, especially in the major industrial centres, have joined "Solidarity". Like the rest of their fellow trade unionists, they advocate a comprehensive overhaul of the entire system, economic as well as political. Indeed, they also stand for democratization of the internal structure of the party.

The reformists in effect repudiate still another Leninist tenet, namely, democratic centralism. They argue that, so far, the PUWP has been run entirely from the centre—hence its errors—and demand that this situation be rectified. The changes which they propose include democratic elections to all party posts and a restricted term for its top officials. To advance their programs a so-called "horizontal linkage" movement has been formed within the PUWP. In mid-April it held its first conference in Torun with some 750 delegates from all over the country. The revolt at the grass roots, in fact, has been so formidable that it has led to the postponement of the party Congress, originally scheduled for March, until July.

The centrist group led by First Secretary Stanislaw Kania, does not have any special commitment to reforms, but for reasons of practical politics is willing to go along with them. Even if some members of that group may resent the existence of "Solidarity", they realize that they could not possibly suppress it, at least not without throwing the country into utter turmoil. The centrists also seem to understand that they need cooperation from the unions to maintain order in the country. Without "Solidarity" channeling the workers' sentiments into peaceful purposes the strikes could deteriorate into anarchy. The centrist group, thus, accepts the existence of independent trade unions, but would like to restrict them basically to economic activities.

The present leadership, however, is by no means monolithic. It was assembled haphazardly, and has undergone many changes. In fact, from the full-members of the Politbureau elected at the last Congress in February 1980, now only Kania himself and three other persons survive in office. Among the replacements there are, significantly two of Gierek former rivals: Stefan Olszowski, who was ousted from the Politbureau in February 1980, and Mieczyslaw Moczar, who was removed as early as 1971. The rest are relatively little-known men promoted either from the second echelon of the Gierek group or from the provincial party apparatus.

Within the generally centrist orientation of the present leadership, thus, there are differences over the desirable limits of cooperation with the unions and the degree of forbearance to be shown to the rebellious groups in the party, as well as over the assessment of the threshold beyond which the U.S.S.R. might not be willing to tolerate changes in Poland. In recent months a conservative group in the Politbureau has crystallized around Olszowski (even though in the late Gierek years he was known as an ardent proponent of reforms), posing a potential challenge to Kania.

The differences within the PUWP leadership probably will not be resolved until its Congress meets in July. Should, however, some new crisis erupt in the meantime it may widen the present divisions and lead to a bitter factional struggle in the Politbureau. And, in turn, a paralysis at the centre of the PUWP would enhance the prospect of Soviet intervention.

Poland and the U.S.S.R.

Poland's position vis-à-vis the Soviet Union is much stronger than that of Czechoslovakia in 1968.[4] Moscow's suppression by force of the "Prague Spring" took place in the closing days of the cold war era. It was followed, however, by a decade of East-West détente when the standards of Soviet behaviour on the international scene were considerably raised. The Helsinki Accords of 1975 repudiated the Brezhnev doctrine by prohibiting an invasion of any European country regardless of its social system. Paradoxically, the weakening of détente in recent years may have helped Poland too. The invasion of Afghanistan has put the western powers on alert against the Soviets' continued readiness to use force in promoting their international objectives. The western leaders, therefore, have sternly warned the Kremlin not to intervene in Poland.

Ignoring the western advice would ultimately ruin Brezhnev's policy of peaceful coexistence. Whatever small chance the Kremlin leaders might have at present to enter into a dialogue with the Reagan adminstration would be abruptly terminated. Western European countries would be also alienated from the U.S.S.R. and the cohesion of NATO would be effectively restored. The Madrid Conference would be wrecked and the entire CSCE process would come to an end. Various arms control negotiations would be postponed, if not altogether abandoned. Thus, East-West relations would return to the coldest days of the cold war.

Yet, there is a distinct danger that, all the international consequences notwithstanding, the U.S.S.R. might invade Poland. To the Soviet leaders the developments in Poland must look ominously like those of the "Prague Spring", and Brezhnev explicitly drew the parallel at the recent Czechoslovak party Congress. They are well aware of the challenge which the existence of free trade unions and the disarray in the PUWP pose to Marxism-Leninism and are worried about the possible impact of the Polish example upon some other Communist states. The Kremlin might also interpret the unwillingness, or rather the inability, of the Polish Communist leadership to reverse the reforms as evidence of their abandonment of proletarian internationalism.

The Soviet Union, thus, has conducted a systematic war of nerves against Poland. The Soviet press has denounced "Solidarity" for its alleged "counter revolutionary" activities and has branded the "horizontal linkage" movement in the PUWP as "revisionism". The Kremlin leaders have repeatedly admonished the Polish Communists to stop the process of "renewal." Since late last fall Soviet forces have massed around Poland, and especially after early spring "Soyuz 81" maneouvres on Polish territory, they remain in position to strike at short notice. In the event of a new crisis in Poland the odds are that they will move in.

The Poles do not want to provoke a Soviet invasion. They certainly have no desire to spill any Polish blood. They are well aware that a return to the cold war would be detrimental to them for it would separate them once again from the West. The Polish people, however, do not feel that they threaten the U.S.S.R. in any way by reforming their own political system. They have no intention of withdrawing from the Warsaw Pact for they share the Soviet apprehension about the security of its western border. They also have no designs to overthrow the Communist system. At the same time the Poles are determined to put their own house in order and will not rest until this is accomplished.

When in 1944-45 the Soviets imposed Communism upon Poland that country, devastated by war, was extremely weak. By now the Polish nation has recovered from its war wounds. Subjugating 36 million modern and proud people by force in 1981 would require massive and sustained efforts. In the end the Soviets would prevail, but this would resolve nothing. Even under a *Pantzerkommunismus* an organization as formidable as "Solidarity" would not disappear. Some its segments would go underground and with the long Polish tradition in this regard they would be capable of inflicting considerable damage on a quisling Communist regime. The only way resistance could be crushed would be by a return to brutal, Stalinist-like repressions.

Yet, it is doubtful whether neo-Stalinism could be restricted to Poland alone. Most likely it would spill over into other Eastern European countries and into the U.S.S.R. itself. The justification for a brutal suppression of Poland would require a refurbishing of the hard-line Communist ideology and an erosion of the essentially bureaucratic rationality of the present Soviet regime. The military and the security apparatus would gain in influence, while the position of the technocrats would be further weakened by the cutoff of economic bonds with the West. On the eve of a new struggle for succession in Moscow such developments could have far-reaching repercussions. The revival of the cold war in the international sphere could be accompanied by a return to Stalinism throughout the Soviet orbit.

There is no easy way out of the Polish situation. It is precisely because its domestic and external aspects are so inexorably meshed that their sorting out will take time. And only the Poles themselves can do it. An outside attempt to end Poland's crisis would only bring about an even more serious juncture in the international sphere.

Footnotes

* Originally published in *The World Today*, June 1981
[1] For a comprehensive account of the summer strikes and the Gdansk accord see: Jan B. de Weydenthal, "Workers and Party in Poland", *Problems of Communism*, November-December 1980.
[2] An excellent analysis of the "Solidarity" movement is presented in Z.A. Pelczynski, "Stalemate and after in Poland", *New Society*, 5 February 1981.
[3] Early signs of political fatigue in Poland were, in fact, already noticeable in the fall of 1980. See John Darnton, "60 Days that Shook Poland", *The New York Times Magazine*, 9 November 1980.
[4] For a penetrating analysis of Polish-Soviet relations see Philip Windsor, "Can Poland strike a balance?", *The World Today*, October 1980; and Seweryn Bialer, "Poland and the Soviet Imperium," *America and the World, Foreign Affairs*, 1980.